THE 10 BIGGEST LEGAL MISTAKES WOMEN CAN AVOID

How to Protect Yourself, Your Children, and Your Assets

MARILYN BARRETT

CAPITAL
BOOKS, INC.

STERLING, VIRGINIA

Capital Books, Inc.
P.O. Box 605
Herndon, Virginia 20172-0605

Disclaimer: This publication is designed to provide accurate and authoritative information in regard to the subject matter covered. The legal consequences of any specific situation vary with the particular facts at issue, and this book should not be construed as the rendering of legal services to any specific individual. This book is sold with the understanding that the publisher is not engaged in rendering legal, accounting, or other professional services, and that the author is not rendering legal services. If legal advice is required, the reader should seek the services of a competent legal advisor.

ISBN 1-89213-29-0 (alk. paper)

Library of Congress Cataloging-in-Publication Data
Barrett, Marilyn, 1952-
   The 10 biggest legal mistakes women can avoid: how to protect yourself, your children, and your assets / by Marilyn Barrett.
   p. cm.
   ISBN I-892123-29-0 (alk. paper)
   1. Law--United States--Popular works. 2. Women--Legal status, laws, etc.--United States--Popular works. I. Title: The ten biggest legal mistakes women can avoid. II. Title.

KF390.W6 B367 2000
349.73'082--dc21

                                                   00-059906

Printed in Canada on acid-free paper that meets the American National Standards Institute Z39-48 Standard.

First Edition

10 9 8 7 6 5 4 3 2 1

To my mother and the women of her generation, who sacrificed many of their own dreams so that we daughters might pursue ours

Contents

Preface

The anguish and humiliation was palpable the second she walked into the door. She smiled weakly and nervously sat down in the chair that I waved her to. She was at least six feet from me, yet the pain and grief that reverberated from her felt like a twenty-foot wave crashing over me. I immediately knew her story; I had heard it so many times.

I asked her if she wanted coffee, and she said no, looking down at the floor as she grasped and wrung her handbag and tried to muster up the courage to tell me what happened. I gave her the most reassuring smile I could summon and asked her what was going on, what could I do for her. She slowly and reluctantly began to tell me her story as the blush of shame crept over her and her eyes alternated between darting glances at me and long, studious inspections of the floor.

Her name was Beverly. She had been happily married, or so she thought, to Bill for twenty-two years. They had three kids. Everything was going so well. They had a nice home, the kids did well in school, and, although the passion she and Bill felt toward each other when they first married had faded, they had a warm, contented marriage. Bill worked hard and took good financial care of them.

But her life had turned upside down a few months ago when Bill suddenly announced that he was leaving their marriage, his business was failing, and they owed tons of money to creditors and to the IRS. Bill had disappeared, and Beverly was besieged with persistent demands from their creditors. At the same time, she discovered that the documents she innocently signed when asked to by Bill were in fact mortgages against the only property she and Bill owned and now the money and their equity in the property were all gone.

Beverly and her kids faced total financial ruin, and they were on their own. How did this happen, she asked herself? Why had she relied solely on Bill to make sure their finances were sound? Why hadn't she done more to protect herself and her kids? How were they going to make ends meet?

This story, or one like it, happens to women far too often, and that is why I wrote this book. I have represented too many women who suffered such harm, and I want to help you avoid the same type of financial and emotional trauma that can befall you if you do not take care of your legal affairs.

Your greatest protection from legal and financial harm is awareness of your legal risks and your legal responsibilities, and your willingness to take responsibility for your legal affairs. This book will tell you how to do it.

—Marilyn Barrett, Attorney-at-Law

Acknowledgments

By the time any author makes that last revision, she or he knows the journey would not have been possible without the support and contributions of many. So many people supported me in this effort that I hesitate to name names out of fear that I will fail to name someone I should. If I do, please attribute the omission to short-term memory loss that seems to come with advancing age and not as an intentional omission.

My family is a constant resource of encouragement and friendly advice. My mother, Marge Barrett, has always supported me in whatever I pursued and she offered her usual patience, warm support and enthusiasm to this endeavor. My sister, Gini, and her husband, Richard, invariably offered me solace and support when I needed it most. Gini also reviewed a late draft and provided critical contributions to the book's final form. My sister M.J. took time from her too busy schedule to read an early draft of the manuscript and gave invaluable pointers. I am also grateful to Pat, Lucinda, Linda, Steve, John and Shelley, who offered frequent and much needed strokes of reassurance.

I am privileged to have many close and supportive friends who encourage me in all of my efforts but were of particular comfort as I spent hours toiling away on the manuscript without any certainty that it would even be published. I first proposed the topic to my friend and fellow writer Jennie Blackton who instantly saw the potential and encouraged me to proceed. Other friends providing support and encouragement were Nettie

Pena, Terres Unsoeld, Sue Frauens, Ann Jacobus Irmas, Craig Morris, Sunny Miller, John Hyde, and Kate Morris Hyde. My friend Terry Cuff was particularly generous with his effusive and fortifying support and encouragement. I have the good fortune to have some excellent lawyers among my friends who provided invaluable editorial suggestions and legal review. I am extremely grateful for the legal expertise and contributions of Stacy Phillips, Suzanne Harris, Faith Dornbrand, Victor Marmon, Kathy Davidson, and Teri Hyde. My law partners and colleagues at Alschuler, Grossman, Stein & Kahan, LLP were remarkably supportive and tolerant of my divided attentions while finalizing this book. Kim Hampton undertook the arduous task of providing editorial comment to an early draft of the book and pointed out the many sections that lacked clarity and coherence, and Leslie Behr proofread and made much needed editorial revisions to the final draft. Kathleen Hughes, publisher of Capital Books, fortunately shared my desire to help women, and Julie Kuzneski, my editor at Capital Books, expertly marshaled the book through its production. Rani Stoler taught me much about how to write books that people might actually want to read. And without Laurie Harper, my agent, this book would remain only a file on my computer hard drive and an unfulfilled dream.

Introduction

*"Learn from the mistakes of others. You can't live
long enough to make them all yourself."*
Martin Vanbee

Ivana Trump probably thought she had found both true love and a lifetime of financial security when she married Donald Trump, one of the most successful real estate developers around. Marla Maples probably thought so too when she married Trump soon after he and Ivana divorced. However, they both signed prenuptial agreements because Trump insisted they do so as a condition of marriage. And they both paid a high price for doing so.

Donald Trump was married to Ivana, a vivacious, smart, and beautiful blond who successfully assumed serious positions in his businesses for twelve years. Not only did she sign a prenuptial agreement, but after their marriage, she signed three additional antenuptial agreements. Eventually, "The Donald" became involved with Marla Maples — also known as the "Georgia Peach." After a widely reported stormy encounter between Ivana and Marla on the Aspen slopes, the divorce began. By this time, Trump's wealth was enormous. Ivana tried to get out of her last antenuptial agreement, but the court held her to it. Despite the fact that Trump's wealth was estimated to be in excess of $1 billion and despite Ivana's contributions to the success of his business, Ivana walked away with only $26 to $40 million.

The Georgia Peach fared much worse. She too signed a prenuptial agreement but claims she did not read it when Trump gave it to her just two days before their wedding. When she and Trump divorced, Marla got a lump sum payment of only $2 to $2.5 million. Although the settlements Ivana and Marla both received were more than most women ever dream of, they were a mere pittance of Trump's wealth.

Doris Day, America's sweetheart, was financially devastated when she relied on her husband, Marty Melcher, to manage their finances and gave him a power of attorney to do so. Marty hooked up with a lawyer and the two of them began investing Doris's money in more and more speculative ventures — oil wells, cattle, and big hotels. Marty constantly brought home new investment papers for Doris to sign. Doris became concerned about these investments because she believed they were too risky. When Marty demanded that she trust him, she decided to do so and continued to act in films while Marty continued to handle their finances. When Marty died and Doris's son was appointed executor of his estate, Doris found out the sad truth. Marty had wasted away her estimated $20 million in earnings and, even worse, she was flat broke and in debt.

Alice wanted to start a retail business. Her lawyer advised her to set up a corporation, which, with filing and legal fees, would cost about $1,500 to $2,000. Alice decided, however, that she did not want to spend that much money just to form a corporation. She thought the money would be better spent if she bought more inventory to display at her store. So, Alice leased space in a retail shopping center and set up shop as a sole proprietorship. She used a combination of her savings and trade credit to buy inventory, furniture, and office equipment, and to pay the initial salaries of employees. After a year of struggling to make the store a success, Alice finally had to close it. Although Alice was able to pay her employees the wages she owed them, she was not able to pay her trade creditors, and they began calling and demanding payment. By this time, her liabilities exceeded $100,000. Alice was personally responsible for these debts, even though she had closed the business, and she had to consider filing for bankruptcy.

Jessica and Daryl started their own accounting business. One day, one of their employees who had been suffering from depression and was taking antidepressants went off her medication and angrily threw a book at Jessica. Luckily, Jessica ducked in time to avoid injury. Jessica and Daryl felt bad for their employee because they knew she was troubled, and they did not immediately fire her. Instead, they suggested she take several weeks off from work. When the employee returned, she was still belligerent and troublesome. Jessica and Daryl decided they no longer felt safe working with this employee and wanted to terminate her employment. However, they received a letter from a lawyer threatening litigation if they did so. Jessica and Daryl found out that, because they had become aware of the employee's disability, under the Americans with Disabilities Act they could be sued if they fired her now.

Martha, a schoolteacher, was married to an attorney, Jeff. After more than twenty years of marriage, Martha learned that Jeff had embezzled funds he held on behalf of several of his clients. Jeff pled guilty to several felony counts of theft and tax fraud. Martha had no knowledge of his embezzlement, because Jeff maintained all his law practice records at an outside office and the money he stole was used to try to start a new business that Martha didn't know about. Jeff and Martha divorced and Martha was left with only their modest home and wages from her own job. Unfortunately, Martha had signed joint federal income tax returns for the years during which Jeff embezzled the money, but he did not report it on their tax returns. The IRS assessed taxes, interest, and penalties against Martha for the income Jeff embezzled and failed to report on their tax returns, even though the IRS acknowledged that she did not participate in the embezzlement, did not know about the embezzlement, and did not personally benefit from the stolen money.

Do you know women who have gone through experiences like the women in these stories? Could one of these stories ever be your story? Perhaps you signed some documents at your husband's request without reading them. Perhaps you filed a joint income tax return with your husband but did not make sure the taxes were actually paid. Perhaps you delegate all your family's financial affairs to your husband and don't have a clue about what you own and what you owe. These stories are like hundreds of stories I have heard — stories in which a woman was suddenly faced with financial disaster, she was betrayed by her husband or someone else she trusted, she feared she would not be able to take care of herself and her children, she lost her business and seriously harmed her family's finances, or she was otherwise placed in financial or legal peril because she did not vigilantly watch over her own legal affairs.

Are you ready to take control of your legal life and protect yourself and your children from legal calamity? *The 10 Biggest Legal Mistakes Women Can Avoid* will help you do just that. Although this book by no means deals with all the legal mistakes a woman can make, it deals with the ten most common ones. These mistakes can be avoided by simply following the recommendations in this book. This book will help you protect yourself, your children, and your assets and will help you to affirmatively take charge of your legal affairs. It teaches you about prenuptial agreements and what signing one will mean to you. It guides you on how to protect yourself during marriage and, if your marriage ends in divorce, how to protect yourself and your children when you and your husband divide your property. Because more and more women are starting their own businesses, the book also discusses ways to avoid making legal mistakes when starting and running a business. It also talks about taxes, possibly the most burdensome debt you can ever incur, and how to make sure your property is handled the way you wish after you die. Finally, the book talks about how important it is that you read and understand the legal documents you sign and how to deal with lawyers, whom you will need to help you review these documents and to otherwise protect you from legal mistakes.

Are women more likely than men to make legal mistakes? It is certainly true that men do make legal mistakes and incur substantial debts they might have avoided if they had taken steps to protect themselves legally. However, women seem particularly prone to legal missteps. A woman may lack the knowledge or experience needed to handle her legal affairs, she may find legal affairs boring, she may be too busy, or she may trust someone who later proves untrustworthy. She may harbor an idealistic belief that life should and will be fair (as she perceives *fair*), and that if she is not treated fairly, it is not her fault and she won't be held accountable. Or she may believe that her own good intentions will entreat the people she deals with to behave fairly and reciprocate with similar good intentions. Unfortunately, the law makes few exceptions for lack of knowledge or experience, boredom, neglect, trust, or naivete. We are expected to read, understand, and appreciate the consequences of the legal documents we sign. We are expected to find out what laws and regulations we are subject to and to comply with them.

Today, women have more career opportunities, greater marital property and child support rights, and greater educational opportunities than ever before. However, new opportunities bring new responsibilities; new benefits bring new burdens. Legal responsibility is one of them. In the eyes of the law, women generally are equal to men and are held to the same legal standards. By handling your legal responsibilities appropriately, you will exert much greater control over your own legal destiny. Knowledge of the potential legal dangers will enable you to avoid, or at least minimize, the financial and other legal damage that can result from blindly trusting others to make your legal decisions. After twenty-three years of practicing law, I have found that it is not enough to provide information about what to do after the harm has occurred. By that time, all that can be done is to attempt to minimize the damage. And even if you are reasonably successful at accomplishing this, you probably will have incurred extensive legal costs and suffered months or even years of anguish and uncertainty. To protect yourself from ruinous legal fees and despair, you must know the legal risks you face *before* you enter into a legal commitment and do what you can at that time to eliminate or reduce these risks.

This book is not intended to be an exercise in male bashing, although many of the stories involve situations in which a man takes advantage of a woman's trust or naivete. Men who are too trusting or naive in legal matters can and do suffer terrible legal consequences, just as women do. This book, however, is written for women and is about women. The stories I use are intended to illustrate the devastation women experience as a result of unanticipated legal consequences. The stories are based on actual incidents, but, except for publicly reported cases, the names and identifying characteristics of the people involved have been changed. Some of the stories I have used involve men, because they are the best stories I found to illustrate the problems that can befall both women and men when they don't protect their legal affairs.

You may find this book a little bit frightening because it

highlights legal dangers that can ruin you financially — legal dangers you may not know even exist. However, your greatest protection from legal and financial harm is *awareness* of your legal risks and your legal responsibilities, and your *willingness* to take responsibility for your legal affairs. You can protect yourself, your family, and your assets. You can make sure you get your fair share of marital property when you sign a prenuptial agreement or when you divorce. You can save yourself and your children from financial disaster by making sure that your family finances are handled properly while you are married and that your own separate property remains your own. You can start a business and run it successfully without running afoul of legal requirements. You can face up to your tax obligations and reduce the possibility of future, ruinous tax bills. You can make sure your property goes to the people you love when you die. And you can do all these things and more by making sure that you read and understand all the legal documents you sign and that you have the right lawyer to advise you when you do so. The following chapters will start you on the road to your legal empowerment as a woman.

LEGAL MISTAKE #1:

FAILING TO PROTECT YOURSELF IN A PRENUPTIAL AGREEMENT

*"Before getting married, find out if you're really
in love — Ask yourself, 'Would I mind getting
financially destroyed by this person?'"*

Johnny Carson

Jennie was extremely busy these days. Between work and finalizing wedding arrangements, she barely had time to see her fiancé, Jim. With his typical good humor, he had accepted her jitters and absorption with making sure the wedding went "just so." He was bemused by her concerns; he knew their family and friends would be there to celebrate with them and would have a great time even if the flowers were not perfect, and even if the dinner was served a few minutes late. But Jennie just couldn't calm down and worried incessantly that an important detail might be overlooked. Today, Jim's tone was different; there was a sense of urgency that was not like Jim. He had to see her for dinner. Was he getting cold feet? Was he going to break up with her? Jennie drove to their favorite restaurant barely able to breathe. Jim was there waiting for her, a look of guilt and apprehension on his face. Jennie thought she might faint as she slowly crept toward him and somehow managed to slump into the booth. Shakily, she asked, "What's up?" "I want you to sign a prenuptial agreement. Dad took me to his lawyer's office today and they don't think I should marry you unless you agree to sign one," Jim said, as he pushed the agreement across the table toward her. Jennie didn't know what to do or say. She and Jim had never talked much about money. She knew that his dad was wealthy and that Jim, who worked in his father's business, would eventually take over the company. But she thought their love was so strong, their trust in each other so complete, and the possibility of divorce so remote that she never thought about what would happen if their marriage didn't work. Suddenly she felt cheap. Did Jim's father think she was marrying Jim just for his money? Did Jim not trust her or believe in their love as deeply as she? Confused, bewildered, betrayed, she began to look through the agreement with teary eyes.

Prenuptial agreements are becoming more and more common today. The higher divorce rate, second marriages, and the greater number of women in the workforce today all contribute to their greater popularity. What would you do if you were presented with a prenuptial agreement shortly before your wedding day? Would you be devastated that your fiancé could even question the purity of your love? Would you be mortified by his doubt about the permanence of your commitment? Would you be repulsed at such a tawdry mention of money? Marriage is about love, trust, and lifelong commitment. It's about staying together through thick and thin, in sickness and in health, until death do you part. It's about raising children together, working together, growing old together. Or, do you think having a prenuptial agreement is a smart thing to do? A mature thing to do? A realistic thing to do? After all, marriage is much more than passion that fades over time, blind trust that leads to misunderstandings or deception, or putting up with each other at all cost. Look at the 50 percent divorce rate, you say. Marriage is a financial arrangement, a pooling of assets, an economic partnership. Financial problems and misunderstandings can lead to fights, misconceptions, and disappointments, the risk of which might be reduced by a well-written, understood prenuptial agreement.

Do you even know what a prenuptial agreement is? Do you know what it would do? How it would affect your life? If you give up your career to raise children, do you want to make sure you and your children will be taken care of? What if you are the one with the money and the well-paying job. Do you want to prevent your spouse-to-be from getting a big chunk of it if your marriage goes sour? Do you want to make sure you don't pay big bucks for a bad marriage? This chapter teaches you what a prenuptial agreement is and what you should do to make sure you understand why it is good or bad for you.

What Is a Prenuptial Agreement?

In basic terms, a prenuptial agreement is one entered into by a couple planning to get married, in which they agree how their property will be divided if they divorce or one of them dies. In other words, it changes the division of marital property from what state law would otherwise provide for.

You should always check the specific laws of your state. Most states employ either community property laws or equitable distribution laws to determine each spouse's legal ownership of marital property. Only one state, Mississippi, is a common-law state. The law of the state in which you reside may contain special rules about how married couples can hold property.

Under common law, when a couple divorces, the spouse who holds legal title to the property is awarded that property. Even income earned by one of the spouses during the marriage is awarded to the spouse earning the income. Only property that is jointly owned by both spouses can be divided by a court. The obvious inequity in this system (and to women in particular, because most property is still owned by men) explains why forty-nine states have now rejected it.

In community property states, all earnings during marriage and all property acquired with those earnings are community property, and are deemed to be owned one-half by each spouse, regardless of which spouse earns the income. In a few community property states, if a spouse committed adultery or engaged in other improper conduct and is deemed at fault in the divorce, such spouse may be awarded less than 50 percent of the community property. Most community property states are no-fault divorce states, and a spouse's misconduct does not alter the division of property. Currently, nine states are community property states: Arizona, California, Idaho, Louisiana, Nevada, New Mexico, Texas, Washington, and Wisconsin.[1]

In equitable distribution states, assets and property accumulated during marriage are divided equitably at divorce. Equitably does not necessarily mean one-half, and sometimes the more wealthy spouse may well be awarded as much as two-thirds or more of the assets and the less wealthy only one-third, or even less. This is often seen in high net worth cases in which the less wealthy spouse receives a considerable amount of property, although less than 50 percent. Forty states are equitable distribution states. The factors that the courts examine to determine an equitable distribution vary from state to state, but most equitable distribution states use the following criteria:

- Duration of the marriage
- Age and physical and emotional health of the parties
- Income or property brought to the marriage by each party
- Standard of living established during the marriage
- Any written agreement made by the parties dealing with division of their assets
- Income and earning capacity of each party

- Contribution of each party to the education, training, or earning power of the other

- Contribution of each party to the value of the marital property as well as the contribution of a party as a homemaker

- Tax consequences to each party of the proposed distribution

- Present value of the marital property

- Need of a parent who has physical custody of children to use the home and household furnishings

- Debts of the parties

- Need to provide for foreseeable education and medical costs of the children or one of the parties.[2]

Under both community property and equitable distribution systems, some property is considered to be separate property and is not owned by both spouses, but only by the spouse who acquired the property. The definition of *separate property* varies from state to state. Generally, separate property includes property owned prior to marriage, property acquired during marriage with the proceeds from the sale of separate property, personal injury damages, property that the spouse acquires by inheritance or gift, and property acquired after the parties are separated. On divorce, the separate property is not divided, but remains the property of the spouse who owns it. Under most state laws, if separate property is commingled with marital property, it loses its status as separate property and becomes community property (if you live in a community property state) or joint tenancy property (if you live in an equitable distribution state). This can easily happen with bank accounts. Commingling is discussed in more detail in the next chapter entitled "Failing to Protect Yourself and Your Children in Marriage."

A prenuptial agreement most often deals with how marital property will be divided on divorce and can cover many things. For example, a prenuptial agreement might provide that the spouse who owned the marital house prior to marriage gets to keep the house if the couple divorce. The agreement might provide that, in the event of divorce, a nonworking spouse will get a property settlement of a specified number of dollars, a specified living allowance each year, or certain assets, or some combination thereof, and no more. In community property states, prenuptial agreements often specify what property the couple owns will be treated as community property, jointly owned, or separate property owned by only one spouse. The prenuptial agreement can specify the character of property that is owned by the couple at the commencement of their marriage, or that is acquired after they marry. Property characterization as community or separate is important because, on divorce, only community property is divided between the spouses. Separate property of one spouse remains the property of that spouse.

Other matters that are commonly included in prenuptial agreements are as follows:

- The right of each party to mortgage, sell or otherwise dispose of, and/or manage and control specific property

- An agreement that each party will make a will or trust agreement that carries out the intent of the prenuptial agreement

- An agreement that each party will waive certain rights he or she is granted by law to his or her spouse's property should the spouse die

- An agreement about who owns the death benefits of a life insurance policy and how such death benefits will be disposed of

- Any other rights, including personal rights and obligations (that is, who will take out the garbage, who will put the kids to bed, and the like), as long as these provisions don't violate public policy

Some states also allow spousal support or alimony to be modified or waived in a prenuptial agreement. Other states do not because they believe such agreements violate public policy. No state permits waiver or modification of child support obligations. Appendix C provides a sample of a simple prenuptial agreement.

Historically, prenuptial agreements (also referred to as premarital agreements) have been tools utilized by an extremely rich spouse to keep his or her less well-heeled future spouse from claiming entitlement to a bounty of wealth, in the event of divorce or death. Today, prenuptial agreements have become more and more common and are no longer vehicles used only by the wealthy. They are now used by couples in all economic strata to accomplish a variety of objectives.

For instance, prenuptial agreements are often used when one member of the couple to be married has an interest in a business owned and operated by that individual's family. That family wants assurance that in the event of divorce or death, the ex-spouse won't be able to interfere in business operations or retain any ownership interest in the family's business. Even though in both community property and equitable distribution states, property owned prior to marriage, such as stock in a family-owned business, is generally treated as separate property and not subject to division on divorce, an ex-spouse can still claim rights to the property. Appreciation on such property can be subject to division, particularly when the ex-spouse worked in the family business and the couple largely relied on the earnings for support during their marriage. Moreover, whether property is separate property can become muddled over the years if the property's separate identification is not clearly established at the outset of the marriage and is not clearly maintained during the marriage. A prenuptial agreement can clarify and confirm that a spouse's interest in a family-owned business will remain his or her separate property and that the other spouse will not be entitled to any portion of the increased value of the business that accrues during their marriage.

Prenuptial agreements have become more frequently used by people who have children from previous marriages. Currently, in about 40 percent of marriages in the United States, one or both parties have already been married at least twice.[3] Unfortunately, an estimated 60 percent of these marriages will also end in divorce.[4] Before entering into a new marriage, people often wish to make sure that on their death or divorce, their separate assets remain their own, or that on their death, these assets are transferred to their children from the previous marriages, and not to the new spouse and/or his or her children.

Prenuptial agreements can also help shield one spouse from the bad credit rating of the other. By entering into a prenuptial agreement and pledging to keep assets and debts separate and by actually keeping their separate property separate and not commingling (discussed in more detail in chapter 2 "Failing to Protect Yourself And Your Children In Marriage"), a spouse with an unblemished credit record may avoid the taint of the bad credit rating accrued by his or her spouse before or after marriage. It is crucial that all new creditors be informed of this financial arrangement to maintain the separateness of the spouses' credit rating.

Prenuptial agreements can also be used to ensure that if one spouse sacrifices his or her career in order to put the other through school or to pursue career goals, the spouse who made the sacrifice will be appropriately compensated in the event of divorce. In the past, the man contemplating marriage was usually the party seeking to enter into a prenuptial agreement, because he generally had greater wealth and earning potential. However, as women climb higher and higher within the economic structure, they are more frequently the party that may have to pay a lot of money in property settlement should they divorce their husbands. Kim Basinger reportedly paid more than $60,000 and deeded a $700,000 house to her first husband, Joan Collins paid $1 million to one of her husbands, Jane Fonda paid at least $10 million to Tom Hayden on their divorce, Joan Lunden pays $18,000 in monthly alimony to her former husband, and Jane Seymour pays $10,000 per month.[5] Roseanne Barr certainly wished she had a prenuptial agreement when she divorced Tom Arnold and reportedly sued her attorney for not advising her to obtain one.[6] She claims "there will be prenuptial agreements up the ying-yang from henceforth."[7]

In one of the more infamous alimony/property settlement cases in recent years, Ivan Boesky settled for $20 million in cash, $15,000 per month in living expenses, and an expensive Malibu, California, home, when he divorced his wealthy wife, Seema. Boesky, once a high-flying securities trader, pled guilty to illegal stock trading in 1986 and as a result incurred fines of $100 million. His lawyer had argued in court that Boesky deserved one-half of Seema's fortune, or about $100 million, because he had made Seema "rich beyond her imagination" through his legal and illegal business activities. Seema's lawyer countered that Boesky would not have amounted to anything without the backing of her wealthy family, and that Boesky injured the family far more than he helped them

because of the massive fines levied against him and the resulting damage to their reputation. In any case, it appeared that
much of Boesky's divorce award would be used to pay off his
many creditors.[8]

Prenuptial agreements will generally be enforced by the
courts if certain conditions are met. State laws vary from one
state to the next, but the usual conditions that must be satisfied
for a prenuptial agreement to be upheld are as follows:

- Both parties must provide full and accurate
  disclosure of all their assets and liabilities

- Both parties must have been represented by
  independent legal counsel or have had the
  opportunity to be represented by independent
  legal counsel.

- The prenuptial agreement must have been entered
  into by both parties voluntarily and free of duress,
  fraud, coercion, or mistake of fact.

"If you don't have a prenuptial agreement, don't see a lawyer.
See a psychiatrist."
Raoul Felder (Donald Trump's lawyer)[9]

Donald Trump, also known as The Donald, doesn't need
a psychiatrist (at least for this purpose). He has a lawyer and is
a veritable champion of prenuptial agreements. By anyone's
standard, Trump has led a colorful life. A billionaire real estate
developer, he owns office buildings and casinos, and recently
considered a serious run for president of the United States.
Trump's penchant for beautiful women is so public that it
inspired a Doonesbury lampoon in which Duke decided to run
for president and, needing a beautiful blond by his side to do
so just like Trump, hired Boopsie as a stand-in wife. Trump is
widely reputed to be audacious, arrogant, and clever. Among his

most audacious and clever business deals are his prenuptial agreements. He was married to Ivana for twelve years, a vivacious, smart, and beautiful blond who successfully assumed serious positions in his businesses and, since their divorce, has flourished and become a celebrity and force to be reckoned with in her own right. According to Trump, he and Ivana "represented a look, an age, a style, a certain success everyone seemed to be attracted to."[10]

Before Trump married Ivana, he persuaded her to sign a prenuptial agreement. Although he acknowledges that some women who love their future husband may refuse to sign such an agreement on principle, he believes that "the man should take a pass anyway and find someone else."[11] During their twelve-year marriage, The Donald continued to refine his property agreement with Ivana and persuaded her to sign three more successive marital property agreements.[12] Donald and Ivana's marriage eventually started to sour. Trump claims his big mistake with Ivana was "taking her out of the role of wife and allowing her to run one of [his] casinos in Atlantic City." Apparently, Ivana only wanted to talk about work after that.[13] Donald eventually fired Ivana as president of the casino and found solace in the arms of the "Georgia Peach," Marla Maples. After a widely reported stormy encounter between Ivana and Marla on the Aspen slopes, the divorce began.

By this time, The Donald's wealth was enormous. Ivana believed that she had helped him build that wealth; after all, she ran one of the casinos and played other important roles in his businesses. Ivana thought she was entitled to more of Trump's property than was stated in the last agreement she had signed. She told the court she had signed the agreement under duress and asked the court to set it aside. To her chagrin, the court refused and Ivana learned that prenuptial and marital agreements are generally enforced if both parties were represented by lawyers, all assets owned by each spouse are fully disclosed to the other, and neither signed under duress.[14] Under this agreement, Ivana walked away with a settlement reputed to be from $26 to $40 million.[15,16] In view of Trump's vast wealth, then estimated to be well in excess of $1 billion, and Ivana's contributions to the success of his businesses, many thought that her settlement was far short of what it should have been, even though it was substantial by the standards of most ordinary people.

The Georgia Peach fared much, much worse. Marla Maples moved to New York from a small Geogia town with dreams of becoming a famous actress. A striking beauty, she soon attracted the attentions of Donald Trump and fell into the glitzy life of the other woman of a media-crazed businessman. Marla reportedly claims that she did not read the prenuptial agreement given to her by Trump just two days before their wedding. In fact, she claims that she did not read the document until after they separated. Had she read the prenuptial agreement, Marla claims she would not have signed it and probably would not have married Trump.[17] Under their prenuptial agreement, Marla was entitled only to a lump sum payment of $2 million to $2.5 million,[18] an extraordinarily low amount given Trump's vast wealth. Reportedly, their prenuptial agreement provided that she would get this payment and child support (if applicable) if they separated prior to the fifth anniversary of their marriage. If they did not separate until after their fifth anniversary, Marla would be entitled to substantially more. Shrewd businessperson that he is, Trump had read their prenuptial agreement closely and was well aware of the five-year term; he initiated divorce shortly before their fifth wedding anniversary.

While Donald Trump and his wives livened up New York society, Jack Kent Cooke, former owner of the Washington

Redskins, and his Bolivian-born wife, Marlene Ramallo Cooke, livened up the Beltway. Their acrimonious marriage and Jack's will-writing ways keep many a newspaper reporter in business. Amid scandalous accusations, including a felony drug charge against Marlene and the possibility of her deportation back to Bolivia, Marlene's arrest following a Georgetown cruise with a man clinging to the hood of her Jaguar, and claims by Marlene that Jack secretly taped their telephone conversations, Jack amended his will as many as eight times during the last few years of his life. She was in, she was out, she was in, she was out. In his seventh amendment, Jack left Marlene $5 million cash, a $10 million trust, and $150,000 per year. Unfortunately for Marlene, shortly before his death he executed one last amendment. She was out.

Marlene hired lawyers and they claimed that, as his widow, she was nevertheless entitled to one-third of Jack's estate. She had, however, signed a prenuptial agreement the day before their second marriage in 1995. (They had married a second time when they discovered that Marlene's prior marriage may not have been legally dissolved at the time of their first marriage, thereby possibly making their first marriage invalid.) The prenuptial agreement permitted Jack to totally cut Marlene out of his estate if she was not living with him full-time at the time of his death. Marlene's attorneys, which included Brenden Sullivan, the famed lawyer who defended Oliver North in the Iran-Contra scandal, claimed that she was forced to sign a prenuptial agreement the day before their second wedding, that she did not sign the prenuptial agreement voluntarily, and that "she signed it only as a result of coercion and undue influence."[19]

Under Virginia law, the state in which the Cookes resided, a wife is automatically entitled to one-third of her husband's estate, no matter what his will states. However, this law does not apply if the wife waives her right to this share in a prenuptial agreement, and Jack's lawyers said she did just that. The ensuing legal battle provided much fodder for local reporters and speculation by legal experts. Legal experts opined that Marlene should argue that the prenuptial agreement was not valid because she had signed under duress and Jack had failed to properly disclose to her the vastness of his estate. Other legal experts doubted the likelihood that a Virginia court would not enforce the prenuptial agreement and questioned whether Marlene had married Jack primarily to avoid deportation and hence was not under duress, at least not duress caused by Jack, when she did so. Amid indication that the Virginia courts would enforce the prenuptial agreement, the parties eventually settled the dispute for a reported $20 million. The bulk of the remainder of Jack's reported $500 to $825 million estate went to charity.[20]

Few of us face the question — Should I sign away marital rights to such riches? However, many will have to face the question, Should I sign a prenuptial agreement if my fiancé asks or should I ask my fiancé to sign one to protect my own property and income? Is it wise to have a prenuptial agreement? Many experts say yes, but no matter what, if you do agree to sign a prenuptial agreement, it is imperative that you read and understand its terms. As Marla Maples found out, waiting to read the agreement at the time of the divorce is too little, too late.

If you sign a prenuptial agreement and you later regret it, you may not be able to get out of it. Certainly, there are some situations in which you may be able to challenge the legality of the prenuptial agreement. You may be able to prove duress; you may be able to prove that your spouse completely misled you about his assets or income. In all cases, however, it may cost you a small fortune in legal fees to do so. In addition, a legal battle often requires that a lot of dirty laundry be aired in public, which can be very ugly and embarrassing. Moreover, the judge may not agree with you and may hold you to the terms of the prenuptial agreement. The laws of each state vary and judges vary significantly in their willingness to consider claims of coercion or duress, or other defenses, even when the prenuptial agreement is presented immediately before the wedding. You may be stuck with what you signed no matter how unfair you think it is. That's why it is important that you're aware of your legal rights and responsibilities before you sign away your future rights to marital property. Had Marla Maples read the prenuptial agreement before she and Donald married, she might have been able to renegotiate it. In that case, Donald would not have had such a great incentive to divorce her before their fifth anniversary.

Read and Understand the Prenuptial Agreement

Throughout this book, I discuss your legal responsibility when signing legal documents, beginning here with prenuptial agreements. A prenuptial agreement can dictate your financial security currently and many years down the road. It is one of the most consequential documents you will ever sign, and it is absolutely imperative that you understand the terms of a prenuptial agreement before you sign it. Some courts, in ruling a prenuptial agreement valid and binding, have held that if a party to a prenuptial agreement fails to hire his or her own attorney and signs a prenuptial agreement he or she does not understand, it is that party's tough luck and he or she must suffer the legal consequences. Some courts have reached this conclusion, even when the prenuptial agreement was given to the person only a few days before the wedding. Other courts have been more sympathetic and have ruled some prenuptial agreements to be unenforceable, particularly when they found that the prenuptial agreement contained provisions that are promotive of divorce. The courts find such provisions to violate public policy.

This bears repeating. If you sign a prenuptial agreement you don't understand, or don't agree with, you run the risk of being bound to the provisions contained in the prenuptial agreement. Although you may be able to challenge the legality of the prenuptial agreement, a court challenge will require that you hire an attorney, potentially causing you to incur appreciable legal costs. Legal battles over the enforceability of prenuptial agreements are not only public but can be very ugly. Moreover, there is no assurance that the prenuptial agreement will be set aside by the court. You can never presume that a court will rule in your favor. What you can presume is that it will cost you massive legal fees to fight a prenuptial agreement that you have signed.

What if you are the one who wants a prenuptial agreement and wants to make sure it's enforceable? Perhaps you identify with Joan Collins, whose fourth husband demanded $80,000 per month in alimony despite their brief thirteen-month marriage and reportedly picketed Collins's home with a sign reading: "Joan, you have our $2.5 M 13,000 sq. ft. home which we bought for CASH during our marriage. I am now homeless. HELP!"[21] After winning a four-day trial, Joan declared that "I have been ripped off by my three husbands. I would never have married [her fourth husband] without a prenuptial agreement. I don't want to lose all that money again."[22]

Get Lawyers for Both Spouses

A prenuptial agreement may not be enforced if the less wealthy spouse can prove that he or she was coerced into signing the agreement, signed under duress, or didn't really understand what it meant. The likelihood that a prenuptial agreement will be overturned by a court can be radically reduced if each party, particularly the less wealthy one, has his or her own lawyer to advise what the prenuptial agreement means and how it will affect him or her in the event of divorce or death. If both parties have their own lawyers, the odds are greater that they will both truly understand what the prenuptial agreement means, and will enter into the marriage with full knowledge of their respective rights and obligations. This should reduce the possibility of serious misunderstandings and disharmony down the road.

The laws of some states require that both parties be represented by separate and independent counsel before certain provisions that might be included in a prenuptial agreement will be enforced. For example, a provision to waive your inheritance right to your spouse's property if he or she dies may not be valid in some states, if you were not independently represented by legal counsel. If you are less wealthy, or if you plan to end your career and take care of the house and family after you marry, you definitely need to know what your rights will be in the event of divorce or the death of your spouse. Otherwise, you could end up penniless after years of marriage and devotion to the family and home of your spouse.

Most lawyers who represent the wealthier spouse insist that the less wealthy spouse hire his or her own lawyer to review the prenuptial agreement. These lawyers further insist that the less wealthy spouse be entitled to employ a lawyer of his or her own choosing, rather than try to insist that he or she employ a "friendly" lawyer. Typically, each lawyer certifies in writing that he or she has fully explained the provisions in the prenuptial agreement to their respective clients and has fully responded to all of their questions. These precautions, of course, don't absolutely ensure that the less wealthy spouse understands the prenuptial agreement and has voluntarily signed it with a full appreciation of how it would affect him or her; however, the precautions do at least demonstrate that the less wealthy spouse had the opportunity to be fully informed. Because some people are reluctant to hire their own lawyer because of the legal cost, many lawyers advise the wealthier client to offer to pay the legal expenses incurred by the other spouse to employ an independent lawyer, and to pay such costs with no strings attached.

There have been a number of cases in which the less wealthy spouse was not separately represented, did not understand the terms of the prenuptial agreement (or at least asserted that he or she did not understand the terms), and nevertheless was held bound to the prenuptial agreement. In other cases, the judge did not uniformly enforce a prenuptial agreement when the less wealthy spouse was not separately represented by counsel, particularly when the terms of the prenuptial agreement were grossly unfair. It is never possible to predict what a specific judge will rule in the future. However, it is predictable that it will cost you an arm and a leg in legal fees to find out.

Negotiate the Prenuptial Agreement Well in Advance of the Wedding

Some courts have ruled that the less wealthy spouse was bound to the terms of a prenuptial agreement even when the agreement was presented to him or her on the eve of the wedding, and the other party threatened to cancel the wedding if the less wealthy spouse did not sign. Stories abound about weddings being delayed when the groom or bride is handed a prenuptial agreement at the last minute, while guests await the ceremony. Some courts have opined that a threat on the eve of a wedding may be "unkind, but cannot be deemed illegal," and that, in the absence of fraud or other misconduct, the parties are bound by their execution of the prenuptial agreement.[23] Other courts have been more sympathetic to the less wealthy spouse, and have concluded that such circumstances raise significant questions about whether the less wealthy party signed the agreement voluntarily. Many courts believe that the embarrassment, humiliation, and expense that some people might suffer if the wedding were canceled can produce a situation that is coercive and can subject the other party to undue duress. Marlene Cooke claimed that she was forced to sign a prenuptial agreement the day before her wedding.[24] Mick Jagger, who compared getting married to "signing a 356-page contract without knowing what's in it," reportedly handed his fiancée Bianca a prenuptial just as she was about to walk down the aisle.[25]

Many divorce attorneys rely on the *invitation mailing rule*; that is, if you want a prenuptial agreement to hold up in court, it should be negotiated and signed before the wedding invitations are mailed. The best approach is to negotiate and sign the prenuptial agreement as soon as reasonably possible, and at least before mailing the wedding invitations. Once significant money is spent on the wedding and the invitations are extended, the less wealthy spouse may be able to assert that he or she did not sign the prenuptial agreement voluntarily and may be able to get a sympathetic court to disregard it.

Take the Emotion out of Negotiating a Prenuptial Agreement

Many people are reluctant to enter into prenuptial agreements, or even talk about them, because they believe that talking about property before marriage somehow tarnishes their love and undermines their trust in each other. Some feel that such agreements predestine the failure of their marriage. (Marla Maples admitted that she did not read the prenuptial agreement given to her by Donald Trump because she believed it was sealing their fate.)

It's time to get real. Marriage is not only the union of two souls; it is also the merger of two economic units. In the old days of dowry, marital partners were chosen on the basis of property. Fortunately, while marriage for property has largely abated, it is Pollyannaish to pretend that the property and liabilities that each party brings to a marriage have no relevance to the success of the marriage. Indeed, most marriage counselors advise that it is crucial to the success of a marriage that each person know and be comfortable with how the other handles his or her financial affairs. Because a valid prenuptial agreement requires full disclosure of all property and debts, each party will have advance notice of the amount of property and debt that the other party has. The process of negotiating the prenuptial agreement will give each party a better understanding of how the other deals with money. Marriage itself is a contract, and all state laws provide for a division of property in the absence of a prenuptial agreement (these laws are discussed in the chapter 3 "Failing to Protect Yourself and Your Children in Divorce"). In other words, when you marry, you enter into a contract that deals with your rights to the marital property. The only question is, Is it a contract that you and your future spouse negotiate, or one that state law provides?

Your responsibility to protect yourself does not end when you get married. It never ends. Unfortunately, Doris Day thought it did when she married Marty. She had saved a lot of her earnings over the years. After they married, Marty suggested that Doris give him power of attorney to handle her business affairs. She did so. Unfortunately, when Marty died years later, Doris found out she was flat broke and in debt. What could Doris have done to protect herself? What could you do to protect yourself in this or similar situations? Read on.

LEGAL MISTAKE #2:

FAILING TO PROTECT YOURSELF AND YOUR CHILDREN IN MARRIAGE

"He taught me housekeeping; when I divorce I keep the house."
Zsa Zsa Gabor

Doris Day, America's sweetheart, teetered on the verge of financial ruin because she relied on her husband, Marty Melcher, to manage their finances. Marty had been her agent and they married in 1951. Sometime thereafter, Doris gave Marty a power of attorney to handle all her investments and other finances. Marty hooked up with lawyer Jerry Rosenthal and the two of them began investing Doris's money in more and more speculative ventures: oil wells, cattle, and big hotels. In her autobiography,[26] Doris Day says Marty was constantly bringing home new investment papers for her to sign, and she became concerned about these investments. She believed she had no business being in such high-risk ventures. When they began building a big hotel in Palo Alto, California, with her money, Doris finally confronted Marty. In a tone Doris describes as condescending, Marty demanded to know "do you trust me or don't you." He declared, "Honey, either you trust Rosenthal and me or you don't." Doris says she agreed with Marty that either you trust a husband or you don't. Despite her apprehension, she decided she trusted him and he continued to control her finances.

Marty died in 1968 and Doris's son Terry was appointed executor of his estate. As Terry dug into Marty and Doris's financial matters, the sorry state of their finances began to unravel. Terry discovered that Doris was flat broke. The hotels were bankrupt, the oil wells were dry, and there were no cattle. He also found that Doris had debts of about $450,000, mostly for past due taxes. Twenty years of films and an estimated $20 million in earnings[27] and it was all gone. Even advances for records Doris had not yet recorded had been spent. Doris was never able to find out whether Marty had conspired with Rosenthal to scam her intentionally or whether Rosenthal had manipulated him into these bad investments. To make matters worse, her film career and her bankability were beginning to wane.

Doris filed a lawsuit against Rosenthal for fraud and legal malpractice. Over the next five years, Doris, Terry, and their lawyers investigated Rosenthal. Rosenthal put up one hurdle after another and resisted turning over his legal records. Finally, in 1974, her trial against Rosenthal began. It lasted one hundred days and, with twelve lawyers participating, cost Doris $250,000 in legal fees — an astronomical sum in that day. This expense was in addition to the legal fees she had already paid during the five years of investigation and preparation. The judge found that Rosenthal was responsible for Doris' losses and awarded her $22,835,646 — the largest amount ever awarded in a civil suit in California at that time. By this time, Rosenthal had nothing — no assets to collect from. Fortunately, Rosenthal had carried malpractice insurance and Doris eventually settled with his insurers for $6 million.

This was not the end of Rosenthal and the hassles that Doris suffered as a result of trusting her husband. In an audacious move, Rosenthal filed a $30 million lawsuit against lawyers he claimed cheated him and Doris out of millions of dollars of real estate investments. He named Doris as a codefendant so that, he claimed, he could seek damages on her behalf without her permission. He alleged that lawyers had given Doris bad advice when they advised her to sell three hotels.[28] This case dragged on for years, but, finally, in 1985 — seventeen years after Doris began her legal battle with Rosenthal — he lost his last appeal.[29] Two years later he was disbarred by the California Supreme Court.[30]

Doris surely rued the day that she decided to trust Marty and go along with his financial decisions to invest her money in high-risk ventures. The power of attorney she granted him to handle her financial affairs proved to be a trust betrayed, and she and her son paid the price. She ended up going through years of litigation, incurred hundreds of thousands of dollars in legal fees, and, ultimately, received a settlement that was substantial but far less than the income she had earned and Marty and Rosenthal had lost.

As Doris learned, there are a number of precautions every woman should make during a marriage to protect herself and her children. Even if your spouse is a devoted husband and father, it is still important to make sure you are protected. Your relationship may deteriorate in later years, or he may die suddenly from a heart attack, become too ill to work, or lack the business acumen necessary to appropriately manage your finances, as was the case for Doris. In a dysfunctional family, the need to protect yourself and your children is even more critical. Don't let yourself be lulled into trusting someone else with your financial and legal affairs. Don't delegate investment decisions to your husband or anyone else or grant an unlimited power of attorney. There are several other legal niceties you need to know in order to protect yourself during your marriage.

Keep Your Separate Property Separate

Let's start with property. In both equitable distribution and community property states, the classification of property as marital or community property, or as separate property, is extremely important. On divorce, in community property states, community property is generally divided equally between the spouses. In equitable distribution states, marital property is divided in the proportions found to be equitable. Separate property in all of these states, however, is not divided. The spouse who owned the separate property keeps it. *Separate property* is property that a person owned prior to marriage, property acquired by the person during marriage by inheritance or gift, income earned on separate property, or property acquired from the proceeds of selling other separate property as long as it is not commingled with marital property. All other property acquired during marriage is *community property* or *marital property.* A married couple can, by a prenuptial agreement, change the character of property. For example, a couple can agree that the money they earn from their jobs will be separate property. Without such an agreement, employment earnings are community property.

Many women presume that if they own property before they marry, that property will always remain theirs, and that, if they divorce, their husband won't be entitled to any portion of their premarital property. Many women are not aware that their separate property won't remain separate if it is commingled with marital or community property. The law of most states presumes that separate property commingled with marital property becomes marital property. This often arises with bank accounts, because cash is fungible, and it is difficult to distinguish separate property cash from community or marital property cash once both are deposited in the same bank account.

Ruth, after she married Earl, deposited a lot of cash that she had saved over the years in their joint bank account. They also deposited both of their paychecks into this same account. From this account, they paid their mortgage and household expenses. When Ruth and Earl began their divorce proceedings, Ruth learned the awful truth about commingling. She found that because she had commingled her separate property cash with their community property cash, the law presumed that all the cash remaining in the account, as well as the property purchased with cash from that account, was community property. Under the laws of the state in which she and Earl resided, Ruth was entitled to try to trace the balance of cash left in the joint bank account back to her separate property cash that she had deposited in the account. To do this, her family lawyer told her she would have to prove that all expenses paid by checks written on the joint bank account were paid from the community property cash in the account, and not from her separate property cash in that account — no small feat when cash is fungible. Because Ruth had not known about the danger of commingling separate property with community property, she had not maintained any records she could rely on to prove this, and therefore, she had to divide the cash balance with Earl.

Carla also learned about commingling the hard way. Carla owned a considerable amount of stock when she married Tony. During their marriage, she sold shares of stock she owned prior to their marriage and used the proceeds to buy additional shares of stock. She deposited the proceeds from sales of her stock in her own individual bank account. Under the general rules of separate and community property, the proceeds from selling the stock she owned before she married would be her separate property, and the stock she subsequently purchased with her separate property proceeds would be her separate property. However, Carla also deposited her paychecks into the same account. From time to time, she transferred money from her own individual bank account into a joint bank account that she maintained with Tony, and from which they paid community expenses. When Carla and Tony later divorced, she believed that the cash in her individual bank account clearly would be her separate property, and that she would not be required to split it with Tony. Tony's attorney believed otherwise. His attorney pointed out that Carla had commingled community property with her separate property each time she deposited her paycheck into her individual bank account. Unless Carla could prove that the cash balance in her individual bank account consisted solely of her own separate property, she had to split the cash with Tony. To accomplish this, Carla had to be able to prove that each time she transferred cash from her individual bank account into the joint bank account, the cash had come from the paychecks — community property — that she deposited into her individual bank account. She had to prove that the cash transferred to their joint bank account had not come from proceeds she made from the sale of her separate property stock, which she also had deposited into her individual bank account. Carla was not able to do this, and Tony got one-half of the cash balance of her individual bank account when they divided up their property.

The problem of commingling is not limited to cash accounts. When separate property is used to improve community or marital property, such as a house, in the event of a divorce, the separate property owner may be entitled to reimbursement for separate property used, or may be entitled to a pro rata share in the appreciated value of the asset. However, the burden is always put on the spouse claiming a separate property share to prove that he or she is entitled to it.

If you have separate property, it is imperative that you keep the property separate and that you not commingle it with marital property. Otherwise, your separate property will be treated as marital property, and will be divided between you and your ex-husband. Even if your husband later fails to make his legally required child support payments, and even if your earning potential is much less than that of your ex-husband, he will be entitled to part of your separate property if it is commingled with community property. Always bear in mind that you and your children may desperately need your separate property for financial support if your marriage is ever dissolved.

Understand Your Husband's Job or Business

It is critical that you know your family's financial circumstances in the event your spouse dies, or becomes disabled and is no longer able to care for or contribute to the financial well-being of the family. This is important whether you work outside the home or not. Married couples should strive for open and complete communication about family finances so that if a spouse dies or is incapacitated, the other is able to go forward with the least amount of financial distress possible.

Ruth's husband, Harry, died in his early forties of a heart attack. His death was totally unexpected, and Ruth was left with two children to raise alone. Harry had operated his own clothing manufacturing business, while Ruth practiced law. Given the demands on Ruth's time to keep up with her law practice, raise two children, and otherwise maintain the household, she had not paid much attention to Harry's business. She knew he contributed significantly to the family's finances, and this was all she felt she needed to know. Harry died before he put into place at his business a contingency plan for his death or disability. Fortunately, several of his long-time employees were able to keep the operation running smoothly enough that customer orders were filled on a fairly timely basis. However, after several weeks, they advised Ruth that creditors were calling about past due bills. Harry's business accountant then informed Ruth that two of Harry's major clients had recently filed for bankruptcy. Harry's business was strapped for cash; it was owed and had counted on large payments from both of these clients. To keep his business afloat, Harry had borrowed a large sum of money from his bank. Harry had not told Ruth about this problem, because he believed the situation was temporary, and he didn't want to worry her.

Harry and Ruth had each taken out a life insurance policy, but the amount of insurance payable on Harry's death was not enough to pay the bank debt. Eventually, Ruth sold Harry's business and the sale brought enough money to pay off the bank debt. However, there was little money left over from the sale, and she was left to raise their children on her salary alone. Ruth had to struggle to meet her family's needs while still grieving Harry's premature death.

If you know about your husband's finances and business affairs, you will be better equipped to protect yourself from unscrupulous persons who may try to take advantage of you while you are grieving over your husband's death. I am reminded of a story. Fran's husband, Lorne, died while involved in several different financial transactions, one of which ended up in a lawsuit. Lorne's attorney falsely told Fran that just before his death, Lorne had decided to pursue the case aggressively, and was not even willing to consider a settlement. Based on the attorney's assurances that this is what Lorne had wanted, Fran agreed to go forward with this plan, even though it would require the attorney and other members of his firm to spend a considerable amount of time on the case and incur substantial legal fees. Fran was not in a position to evaluate the matter, because she and Lorne had not discussed business matters, and, for all she knew, the attorney was accurately informing her of Lorne's wishes. Fran believed that if she did not pursue the course of action Lorne allegedly had chosen, she would somehow dishonor his memory.

Over the next several years, the attorneys billed Fran constantly. Eventually the case settled after Fran agreed to pay some money to the opposing party. The settlement amount turned out to be actually less than the legal fees Fran had paid her attorneys following Lorne's death. After the case was over, Fran learned from a friend of Lorne's who had been out of the country for several years that the other party in the lawsuit had offered to accept the same amount to settle the case immediately prior to Lorne's death. Lorne's friend thought Lorne had planned to accept it, but Fran had not even been informed about the settlement offer from Lorne's attorney. Had she known about it and accepted it, she could have saved hundreds of thousands of dollars in legal fees. Fran now doubts that Lorne's attorney accurately represented Lorne's wishes. She believes the lawyer just wanted to generate more fees, and because Fran and Lorne did not discuss business matters, she just didn't know better.

It's hard enough to go forward with your life when your husband dies or becomes disabled. It's even more difficult when you have several children to raise, and you find out you don't have the financial security you thought you had. It is essential that you get involved, and keep involved, in your family finances. You need to know what your family assets are and what debts you have. Only then will you be sufficiently informed and knowledgeable to make the financial decisions so important to you and your children — decisions you and your children will have to live with for the rest of your lives.

Be Insured

It is always easy to put off buying insurance. When you and your spouse are healthy, the idea of spending money for life and disability insurance is about as attractive as paying taxes — it would seem like putting the money in black hole. Unlike taxes, buying insurance is an option — one too frequently ignored by families, particularly when their financial resources are limited. Often, families rationalize that they will buy insurance later when they have more money. Sometimes, they simply deny the risk of death and serious injury or illness. For families that live paycheck to paycheck, however, the lack of insurance will be devastating if the primary income earner dies or becomes disabled. Even when families do buy insurance, the amount they purchase is often inadequate. It is essential that you maintain adequate insurance. You never know when your family may face the tragedy of death or serious disability. Insurance will help you make it through that difficult time.

Life insurance is available in two basic forms: term and whole life. Under term insurance, a spouse's life is insured for a specific term, generally one year. At the end of the term, the insurance lapses, and there is no residual benefit to the insured or his or her named beneficiary. In other words, life insurance will be payable if the insured dies during the term of the policy, but, if the insured dies after the term has expired, the insurance company has no obligation to pay out insurance on the subsequent death of the insured. The advantage of term insurance is cost; it is much cheaper than whole life insurance. It is sometimes possible to lock in the annual premium over a period of ten, twenty, and sometimes thirty years. In this case, the insurance term will continue to be in effect for each year that the premium is paid. To lock in the annual premium for many years, the annual premiums payable typically are slightly larger in the early years than is the premium you would pay to purchase only a year of term insurance. There are, however, two significant benefits to negotiating a fixed premium for a term of years. First, although the premiums payable in the early years may be higher, the premiums will increase at a much lower rate than if you purchased separate term insurance policies from year to year because term insurance premium rates increase as you get older. Second, you will need to pass a physical examination only in the year you first acquire the insurance, and not each year thereafter. Accordingly, if you develop a noninsurable medical condition many years down the road, you will still be able to maintain your term life insurance for the agreed-upon number of years.

Whole life insurance is much more expensive than term life insurance. Under whole life policies, the insured agrees to pay a set premium for a specified number of years to buy the policy. The insurance company invests the premiums and credits the policy with interest earned. After a certain amount of premiums have been paid toward the policy, the insured can borrow from the policy up to the stated cash value (which is approximately equal to the amount of premiums paid plus interest earned on the premiums). The insurance policy typically has a death benefit — the amount of life insurance proceeds the insurance company will pay to the beneficiaries of the insured, even if the insured dies before all the premiums have been paid. Unlike term insurance, in which the insured and the beneficiaries have no residual interest or rights after the term expires, a whole life policy is an actual asset of the insured against which he or she can borrow. The disadvantage of whole life is the cost. Whole life insurance is much more expensive than term insurance. There is considerable disagreement among financial advisors about whether whole life is worth the additional cost: many say yes, but many also say no.

Some factors need to be weighed when deciding whether to buy term insurance or whole life insurance. For example, can you even afford whole life since the premiums are much greater? Can you earn a higher rate of return than the whole life insurer will credit your whole life policy if you buy term insurance and make your own investments with the amount you save in premiums? Insurance companies are very conservative investors and the rate of return earned on whole life insurance policies is generally low. You may make more money by investing the premium yourself in investments that are not as conservative as those typically invested in by insurance companies. Whole life insurance does have the advantage of investment discipline. If you are the type of person who would spend the premium differential rather than invest it, the discipline of whole life may be just what you need.

A family's need for the financial cushion that insurance can provide is enormous. A woman I know found this out the hard way. June and her husband, Frank, parents of two teenage daughters, had a fairy tale marriage in terms of their devotion to each other. Frank was a salesman, but not an overly successful one. June worked as a secretary on temporary assignments. They lived in a modest house in a modest neighborhood and had little savings. Frank spent much of his leisure time participating in hazardous sports. The core of their social life revolved around these sports activities, but they were quite expensive and used up whatever spare income they had. Tragically, Frank was killed while participating in one of these sports.

Needless to say, June was beside herself with grief. She discovered that Frank had a life insurance policy, but only for $25,000. With the mortgage, funeral expenses, and everyday living expenses, the insurance proceeds were spent very quickly. June continued to work at temporary secretarial assignments, but because of her profound grief and fear, she had difficulty concentrating on and doing her job as well as her employers expected. After years of financial struggle, she wound up in a relationship with a man she did not love, nor want to be with, to get the financial security he provided for her and her children.

At Frank's young age, he probably could have obtained a lot of term life insurance for a modest insurance premium per year. If Frank had not participated in hazardous sports activities, the annual premiums would have been even less. Substantial insurance proceeds would have given June more options following Frank's death. She would have been able to spend more time recovering from her grief before finding employment. She could have gone to school to acquire the skills needed to go on to a new, higher-paying career. In any case, June would have been able to take more control of her as well as her children's future than she was able to do with the limited amount of funds available to her.

Disability insurance is often overlooked, even when the family has life insurance. Apparently, for many people, the possibility of death is more real than the possibility of disability. Disability insurance is important for the family income earner, however, because if he or she becomes disabled and is no longer able to work, the disability insurance proceeds will provide the money needed to pay family expenses. Several different variables must be evaluated when choosing a disability policy. Will benefits increase by cost-of-living adjustments? Will the disability insurance cover partial disability as well as total disability? Will disability be payable if you are unable to work in your chosen field, or must you be unable to work in any field? The biggest difficulty in obtaining disability insurance is cost — it is very expensive. Yet, if the income earner becomes disabled, this insurance may be the only thing standing between the family and welfare checks.

Health care insurance is also essential for families. Many families forego health care insurance because of the cost, but one catastrophic illness or injury can wipe out a family's savings, assets, and future earnings. Insurance can be purchased that covers only catastrophic medical situations and is much cheaper than policies for broader health care coverage.

Many different types of life, disability, and health care policies are available, and you should consult a qualified insurance advisor to determine which policies fit your family's needs and finances.

Domestic Violence: It's Not Your Fault,
But What Can You Do?

I hesitate to include any discussion on domestic violence and child abuse in a book about legal mistakes, because victims of such heinous and inexcusable abuse are not the ones at fault. It is the perpetrator who is solely at fault. However, domestic violence and child abuse are circumstances in which, again, knowledge can be your best defense. Unfortunately, domestic violence is more prevalent than is generally acknowledged. The Federal Bureau of Investigation estimates that one in four marital couples has at least one violent episode during their marriage. In a research project conducted in Minneapolis that studied police visits to scenes of domestic violence,[31] 89 percent of the victims reported that they had been subjected to repeated beatings.

It is often difficult for women who are victims of domestic violence to recognize it for what it is. Generally, the initial abuse is not physical. The husband often starts out by belittling his spouse, criticizing many of the things she does, expressing unhappiness about how she takes care of things, trying to control her every moment and action. He chips and chips away at her self-confidence and self-esteem until it is seriously eroded, and she begins to question her own judgment and comprehension. Actual physical violence often does not occur until later, after she has come to doubt her self-worth and perceptions of the world.

Experts call the evolution of domestic violence in a relationship the *cycle of violence*. June Sheehan Berlinger describes the cycle of violence as:

> cyclical, occurring in three repeating phases. In the tension-building phase, the abuser's behavior starts escalating. For example, he may become moody or overly critical, then yell or swear, then

begin making threats. Knowing what comes next, the victim becomes hypervigilant and tries to keep the peace at all costs. She believes that if she keeps things in order and does everything he expects her to do, she can prevent another crisis. But because she can never be "perfect" in the abuser's eyes, she can't defuse the situation.

The second and shortest phase is the explosion, an emotionally traumatic episode that can include physical abuse. When the abuser loses control, the victim may fight back and call for help.

The third phase, calm, is what keeps the victim stuck in the relationship. Her partner will often apologize profusely, promising never to hurt her again. He may buy her gifts to prove his sincerity. She remembers their courtship and the man she fell in love with. Both believe he won't abuse her again. Mistakenly believing it's over, she may cook his favorite meal. She tells herself, I'm not really crazy, and makes every excuse in the book for his behavior. Even if she called the police earlier, she refuses to press charges or seek help now.

But sooner or later, tension builds again and the cycle repeats.[32]

Those of us who have not experienced domestic violence often find it puzzling that a woman would stay in such a relationship. How many times have we thought, "Why doesn't she just leave him?" Yet a number of factors often prevent abused women from leaving their husbands. First, the risk that a woman will be killed increases about 70 to 75 percent if she tries to leave the relationship, and the greatest risk is within the first two years after she leaves the relationship. During the O.J. Simpson trial for the murder of Nicole Brown Simpson and Ron Goldman, an acquaintance of mine once asked why Nicole had not simply left O.J. Apparently, he had not read the newspaper accounts thoroughly. I reminded him that much of the prosecution's criminal case against O.J. was based on its allegation that Nicole's departure is what drove O.J. to lethal madness.

Other factors may also keep an abused woman from leaving. She may suffer low self-esteem, shame, or blame herself for the abuse. She may have poor coping skills. She may be frozen by depression, passivity, or helplessness. Abused women go through several stages in how they perceive and cope with abuse.[33] In the first stage, the woman feels guilty and blames herself. She believes that the abuse is the result of her own shortcomings or failings. Her abuser's criticism fuels these feelings. At this stage, the woman might try to improve her performance as wife and mother. She might also evaluate the positive aspects of her relationship more highly than the negative. She may rationalize that other women have it worse than she does. In the second stage, she may come to realize that the abuse is not caused by her own shortcomings, but is instead related to the abuser's behavior. She will rationalize that the abusive behavior is an aberration, not the "real him." She may shift from feeling responsible for the abuse to feeling responsible for changing the abuser. She will focus on trying to change his behavior (for example, trying to reduce his drinking) or her own reactions to his behavior. In the third stage, she may see that the abuser is solely responsible for his conduct, and that she can't change him. Typically, she reaches this stage after the abuse has escalated in frequency or severity, and often she is feeling entrapped, depressed, anxious, and frightened. She may try to leave temporarily or have the abuser arrested to motivate him to change. In the last stage, she hits despair. Her only alternative is to leave, and she may consider suicide or homicide as an alternative means of escape.

The woman may believe she can't leave because she has limited employable skills and education, making it difficult for her to become self-supporting. She may lack family support for breaking up the family. She may lack housing and child care.[34] Once in an abusive relationship, it is very difficult to get out. As I noted earlier, in some cases, it can be deadly to try to get out. The severity of the physical violence in an abusive relationship appears to escalate over time. The longer a woman stays in an abusive relationship, the more difficult it will be for her to leave.

Experts in domestic violence have outlined a number of actions women can take to protect themselves against domestic violence. Berlinger[35] recommends that women do the following:

- Learn how to identify your partner's levels of violence in order to assess potential danger.

- Remove all weapons from the home when your partner is nearing a violent state.

- Ask a neighbor to call the police if he or she hears suspicious noises coming from your home.

- Teach your oldest or most responsible child how to call the police from your home as well as from a neighbor's home. Make sure the child can give your name and address.

- Memorize your local battered women's shelter telephone number.

- Implement a safety plan. Plan where you will go in an emergency. Hide money for emergencies either in your home or someplace you can gain access to at any time. Keep enough money to pay for motels, food, gas, and telephone calls. Keep change for pay telephones. Make two extra sets of keys to your home and car. Hide one set in a safe place and give the other set to a friend. Pack a bag of clothing suitable for any season for yourself and your children.

- Copy important paperwork in advance and have a plan for quick access to these documents in case of an emergency. These documents should include social security numbers (including that of your partner and your children), insurance policies, driver's license, birth certificates, protective orders, divorce and child custody papers, pay stubs, bank statements, marriage license, property ownership papers, medication prescriptions, monthly bills, and passport and immigration papers if you are not a U.S. citizen.

- Maintain an up-to-date list of important telephone numbers, such as the local police department, shelters, victims' assistance programs or hot lines, trusted friends, and your social services counselor if you have one.

- Keep extra personal items in a safe place, such as prescription medicines, eyeglasses, and your children's favorite toys.

- Before your partner becomes violent again, make plans to leave when he isn't around. Make plans to stay with a trusted friend whom your partner does not know. Ask your friend to keep your plan confidential.

- During a violent incident, leave the home if possible. If not, get into a room with a telephone and a lock on the door. Stay away from rooms

where weapons are available, such as the
bathroom, kitchen, garage, and workshop.

- If you can't dial 911, ask your children to do so or
  to call your neighbors and have them dial 911. Buy
  your own cellular telephone so you can still call for
  help even if your partner rips out the telephone.

- Call the police if you leave by car. Lock the doors
  as soon as you get in and don't unlock them until
  you reach your destination. If your partner follows
  you in another car, drive to a police station and
  honk for help.

- After a violent incident, check yourself and your
  children for injuries. If you have to go to the
  hospital and leave the children in the home,
  call the police and ask them to check on
  your children.

- File a report with the police and consider
  petitioning the court for a protective order. A
  cautionary note here. Some experts believe that
  seeking a protective order can escalate violence
  and does not provide much protection; other
  experts recommend it. Past cases do illustrate that
  a piece of paper does not necessarily deter
  an enraged partner hell-bent on violence.

- Finally, seek help. There are a number of battered
  women's shelters and victim assistance programs
  staffed with concerned, dedicated professionals
  who want to help you escape your violent
  environment and start a new life free of brutality.

While women who are victims of domestic violence
have many needs, including psychological and financial, there
are a few legal steps a domestic violence victim can consider.

The most common one is a temporary restraining order (TRO). A TRO is granted by a court and forbids the abuser from coming within a specified area of the victim. Sometimes, the children are covered by the TRO as well. Most locations have bar association groups or other community groups that have volunteers to help women obtain such orders. In some states, TROs are called protection orders.

Some women are skeptical about the benefit of a TRO, and for good reason. A piece of paper won't stop someone hell-bent on hurting you. However, a TRO does entitle a woman to get greater police protection than she would probably otherwise receive. A TRO is a court order, and if the woman's abuser violates it, he has committed a punishable offense that the police can act on. Under most state laws, the abuser can be put in jail for violating a TRO, and if he violates it repeatedly, he can end up in jail for a long time. Women who get TROs should keep a copy of it with them at all times and provide copies to their children's schools or day care centers.

Women can also report their abusers to the local prosecutors for criminal prosecution. A victim of domestic violence can civilly sue her assailant. The most important thing, however, is that she escape to safety and freedom. What can society do to help victims of domestic violence and child abuse? Perhaps the most critical help society can give is greater economic opportunity, so that women are able to support themselves and their children and are not forced to stay in unhealthy homes out of financial necessity. Repudiation of the historic view that a woman needs to be coupled with a man — virtually any man — to be complete and valued in our society is also essential. Only then will women have a realistic possibility of leaving men who abuse them before the violence gets deadly. Even in this case, more shelters and more transitional services are needed to help abused women and their children make the shift from an environment of violence to one of freedom and safety.

The laws dealing with domestic violence and child abuse have been significantly strengthened over the last decade in most states. Nevertheless, penalties for family violence are still less than penalties for crimes between strangers. This seems to derive from the historic notion that women and children were the property of the man of the household. Although this misguided and despicable notion is now largely discredited at the societal level and our laws have been significantly changed in accordance, many legal remnants remain.

Even though many women stay in marriages they shouldn't, many do leave bad marriages and many face a divorce they don't want. Maybe he was abusive. Maybe she and her husband just aren't compatible anymore. Maybe her husband leaves her for another woman. Maybe she leaves him for another man. Whatever the reason, their marriage is over and they start the divorce. Divorce is a landmine for legal mistakes. A myriad of emotions — greed, revenge, grief, relief, joy — works to cloud judgment and inspire wasteful expenditures of energy and money. You probably know women who went through a nasty, bitter divorce — women who struggled to make ends meet after they earlier sacrificed their own career to take care of the home and children and now lack essential job skills — and were left with virtually no property to show for a lifetime of commitment. What if you get divorced? Could you end up fearfully looking for a job, any job to pay the rent when you have not worked for fifteen years and don't have marketable job skills? Could you end up trying to raise small children with only the modest wages you can command on the job market? Could this be you? If the answer is yes, it is imperative that you know how to protect yourself from legal mistake of…

LEGAL MISTAKE #3:

FAILING TO PROTECT YOURSELF AND YOUR CHILDREN IN DIVORCE

"I want to get as thin as my first husband's promises."
Texas Guinan

One of the most pivotal and traumatic events that can occur in a woman's life is divorce. The emotional aftermath of divorce can range from devastating hopelessness, despair, self-doubt, and anger, to relief, joy, and renewed optimism toward the future. The financial aftermath can range from the ability to continue living according to a woman's accustomed lifestyle to unanticipated and devastating financial insecurity or poverty. One certainty is that divorce will, in some way, impact the woman's future economic life.

Women generally end up much poorer, and even at the poverty level, after divorce. In the first year of divorce, a woman's standard of living on average drops 45 percent, whereas a man's improves 15 percent.[36] A divorced woman is four to five times more likely to live in poverty than a married woman.[37] The payment rate of child support obligations from former husbands is also dismal. In 1995, the U.S. Census study of children growing up in single-parent households showed that, when support orders existed, only 2.7 million children received full payments, 2 million received partial payments, and 2.2 million received no payments. The study also stated that another 6.8 million children received no payments because either paternity or a support order had not been established.[38] In other words, of the children covered by a support payment, only 39 percent received full payment, 29 percent received partial payment, and 32 percent received no payment at all. When children not covered by a support order are included, the results are even more bleak. The percentage of children receiving full support payment drops to 20 percent, partial support payments drop to 15 percent, and no support payments rise to 66 percent. Despite these dismal statistics, many women still want to believe that their marriage, although failing, is nevertheless different. They are desperate to believe that they did not marry and live with the type of man who would try to cheat them during divorce. However, virtually every couple who gets married does so thinking it will last a lifetime and that their bond and love for each other are indestructible. Reality shows otherwise. The divorce rate continues to hover at about 40 percent to 50 percent,[39] and it is crucial that women be vigilant in protecting their rights to marital assets upon divorce.

The property settlement and agreements about child and spousal support may be the most important agreements a woman facing divorce will ever enter into. Yet many women fail to take the legal precautions necessary to protect themselves even at this most critical juncture of their lives — although their future, and that of their children, depends on it. This can result from many different factors: a trusting nature, lack of business acumen or experience, naivete, guilt, fear, self-doubt, denial, or paralyzing despair.

Some women do successfully stand up for their rights in divorce. Lorna Wendt is definitely the "poster girl" of successful divorce proceedings. She and Gary Wendt grew up in small towns in Wisconsin. She followed him to Harvard Business School, where she worked to support the two of them and helped type his papers. Thereafter, his corporate career took off and he eventually became the chief executive officer of GE Capital. Lorna assumed the mantle of the classic corporate wife. She wined, she dined, she smiled. She read books about what it took to be a "good corporate wife," and she studied the styles of successful corporate wives who preceded her. She could entertain his business associates on a moment's notice, she was active in charitable affairs, and she accompanied her husband on endless business trips, all the time playing the warm, helpful, assured, and stylish corporate wife. Things reportedly began to change when she started taking Outward Bound courses. Gary approved and even accompanied her on the first one. However, as Lorna took more and more courses, she began to assert herself more. She begged out of some business trips, squeezed in more and more Outward Bound trips, and devoted more time to singing in her church choir. A corporate wife to the end, she smiled through a dinner party they threw one week after Gary told her he wanted a divorce.[40]

Lorna did not go quietly. She claimed she was entitled to one-half of Gary's estimated $100 million net worth. She wanted her share of unvested GE stock options and pension benefits that Gary accrued during the marriage but that would not be due until later. She blazed new trails for corporate wives, and the tongue wagging began in earnest. Lorna supporters believed that a corporate marriage is a true financial partnership and that the corporate wife equally contributes to its success. Lorna, as the corporate wife, took care of the home and children so her executive husband could devote his sole attention to his career. She entertained and, through her charitable activities and warm and vivacious spirit, radiated a warmth and humanness that embraced her husband. Without her, he would not have risen to the level of success he did. And studies bear her out. They show that men in traditional marriages tend to earn more and get more promotions than those in marriages in which the wife has her own career.[41] Lorna's detractors believed that, although she certainly contributed to Gary's success, she definitely was not entitled to half the credit. Of course, she entertained and traveled with Gary, but he in turn provided her a life of luxury and financial security. Gary was the one who worked the long hours, fought the corporate wars, and subordinated his personal needs to those of his family so he could "provide" for them. Clearly, their respective contributions were not equal. Gary offered Lorna $8 million plus alimony to settle their divorce. She said no and took him to court. While the court did not award her the 50 percent of their assets she sought (she and Gary lived in an equitable distribution state), it did award her $20 million. The judge also ruled that the stock options Gary got during their marriage but could not cash in until later were marital property, a value had to be assigned to those options, and Lorna was entitled to part of that value.

In 1998, when Vira Hladun Goldman divorced her husband, Robert, a New York banker, she did get exactly one half of their $86 million estate. Robert Goldman and Vira were married for thirty-three years. Vira briefly worked as a schoolteacher, but gave up her career to be the proverbial corporate housewife. She cooked, cleaned, raised their child, entertained, and took care of the ever more expensive homes they moved into. She also refused to settle her divorce for less than one-half of their marital estate, and they fought it out in a three-day trial. Robert's lawyers told the judge that Vira "made minimal and certainly no direct contributions to their wealth by being a spouse." She shouldn't get 50 percent simply because it had been a long marriage. The judge found otherwise. He ruled that "married for 33 years, their fortunes are inseparable," and that Vira "came as close to being a life partner as one could get short of actually being employed."[42]

Not all women fare as well as Lorna or Vira; in fact, most don't. Jennifer was a school administrator. When she ended her eleven-year marriage, she was earning more than her husband — a salesman who had earned good money when they first married but had suffered a number of setbacks in recent years. When her divorce was final, she had lost a large portion of her pension, was ordered to pay alimony to her husband, and had to borrow $50,000 from her parents to buy out his interest in their home and pay the alimony. She has a net worth of about $215,000, mostly from equity in the home, and spends about one-half of her salary on mortgage payments, property taxes, and home repairs. She owes $50,000 to her parents, $30,000 to her ex-husband in property settlement and to her lawyer in legal fees, and has no savings other than her school pension plan. And, her pension has diminished because her husband was entitled to take part of it. Had she not divorced, she would have been able to replace 73 percent of her income at age 60 and 84 percent at age 65. Postdivorce, she will be able to replace only 56 percent of her salary if she retires at age 60 or 73 percent if she retires at age 65. Now Jennifer states: "I'm it, it's just me, and when I'm 65, it's still gonna be me. I should have relied upon myself years ago." Jennifer doesn't foreswear marriage, but claims she will keep her financial life as separate as possible in future relationships.[43]

Kate and Chuck divorced after fifteen years of marriage. There was no big blow-up, no other woman, no other man. They just fell out of love and decided not to live the rest of their lives in that unsatisfying status quo. They owned a modest home and some stocks and bonds. Both worked outside the home, and each had a pension plan where they worked. Kate was a legal secretary and Chuck was the manager of a small hotel. They had one child, Mark. Initially, everything went fine. They split the stocks and bonds, and each kept their own pension plans. Kate bought out Chuck's interest in their home and both agreed she would pay him off over a number of years. Kate would have primary custody of Mark, but Chuck had liberal visitation rights and committed to pay a certain amount of money in child support and one-half of Mark's future college expenses. All went as planned for several years, until Chuck met and married Debra. Debra wanted children too, and before long she and Chuck had their own child, a daughter named Nancy. Debra quit work so she could be home with the baby and the family finances got very tight. On Chuck's income, he was trying to pay the full cost of his new family and household plus child support for Mark. He had less and less time to spend with Mark, and often missed his weekend visitation rights. It seemed Nancy was sick a lot. Debra was complaining a lot too. She thought Chuck paid way too much money for Mark's care. After all, Kate had a good job and could support Mark by herself. By contrast, Debra and Nancy needed all of Chuck's income. Chuck began paying less and less in child support payments for Mark until he paid none at all. Kate complained to the local officials, but not much happened. She talked to lawyers. They would help her sue Chuck, but it would cost her a great deal in legal fees, and even when she won, they couldn't guarantee that she would ever actually collect any past due child support. If Chuck couldn't pay it, he couldn't pay it. "Feel fortunate he at least didn't try to cheat you when you and he split the property," they said.

Do you relate to these stories or do you pretend that divorce is something that only happens to other people, not you? Maybe you avoid business and legal matters because they are too boring and tedious, you are just too busy, and, anyway, your husband takes care of those things. Do you want to know what to do if the awful big "D" comes knocking at your door? You can take action that will protect yourself and your children, help secure your financial future, and help you get through the big "D" with your self-respect intact. In the following sections, I discuss a few basic principles that will help protect you through divorce.

Hire Your Own Divorce Lawyer

Some women don't hire their own lawyer to represent them during divorce. If the couple does not own much property, each spouse works at about the same wage level, they have no children, and neither spouse needs nor expects financial support from the other after the divorce, using a single attorney or "self-navigating" the divorce process will save considerable legal fees. Even in this case, however, most divorce lawyers recommend that the couple use an experienced and qualified mediator to assist them in their divorce instead of relying on a single attorney. However, when the couple has considerable property, either spouse earns substantially more money than the other, or they have minor children, the woman almost certainly will be better off having her own lawyer to represent her interests. The lawyer will be able to evaluate the woman's legal rights to the marital assets, obtain full disclosure of marital assets, and assert rights to child and spousal support.

Why don't some women hire their own lawyer? The husband is often able to assure her that he wants her and the children (if they have any) to be taken care of, and that he will not only be fair, he will be generous as well. He may remind her that they have loved and trusted each other for years, that the impending divorce won't change that, and that lawyers will only make the divorce more contentious and expensive than it needs to be. He may further assure her that *they* are more mature than other couples; that they have had a more trusting, honest relationship than others; and that they won't resort to the petty jealousies, irrational anger, and spiteful acts that so many other divorcing couples resort to. He may remind her of how much more it will cost to pay two lawyers, which will reduce the amount of money and property they can divide. He may play on her low self-esteem and self-doubt to assure her that he is best able to handle the legal matters and will take care of everything for both of them.

If your spouse assures you that he will be fair, should you believe him and not hire your own lawyer? Absolutely not! In most cases, it is absolutely critical that you hire your own lawyer to fight for what is legally yours as well as for what you need to survive financially after the divorce.[44] In too many tragic cases, the wife was led down the primrose path to poverty after relying on insincere and untruthful assurances from her husband. Don't be one of them.

After being married for twenty-two years and raising two children, Loretta's husband told her that he wanted a divorce. Together they had established a very successful business. She handled the creative aspects and left all the financial dealings to her husband. Although they lived quite comfortably, she paid little attention to their actual financial position and assets. Her husband suggested that an old friend of his, a lawyer, handle the divorce for both of them in order to keep the divorce friendly and minimize legal fees. She initially agreed. However, she later discovered that he had closed their bank accounts, taken all of the cash out, and instructed their accountant not to give her any information. Confused, devastated, and filled with despair, Loretta still resisted hiring her own lawyer despite her husband's obvious intent to cheat her. Finally, she consulted a divorce lawyer, who told her that not hiring her own lawyer would be one of the biggest mistakes she would ever make in her life. The lawyer pointed out that she was living in a fantasy world if she believed her husband intended to be fair in dividing their assets. Her husband had already shown his true colors by closing the bank accounts, stripping out the cash, and preventing her from obtaining financial information about their business to which she was entitled. There was no doubt that this man wanted to cheat her out of her fair share of their marital assets.

Susan lived the old-time, traditional marriage. She had been married to Bob for more than twenty-five years and had raised three children. Bob was a successful executive and had supported the family in a very comfortable lifestyle. Susan took care of the home and children and did not work outside the home. Susan and Bob had met and married in college, and Susan had never had a job. They were well regarded in their local community and were invited to all notable civic and charitable events. Their three children were responsible and high achievers. Susan was, she believed, the picture-perfect wife — always supportive, always helping, always there. She believed that she and Bob had a picture-perfect life, until one day he came home in midafternoon and announced that he wanted a divorce. He had been involved with another woman for more than a year — a woman who was also a successful businessperson. Susan's life was shattered. Stunned and in total denial and disbelief, Susan would not hire her own attorney even though Bob urged her to do so. She did not recognize it until later, but deep down Susan knew that if she hired her own lawyer she would be tacitly admitting that the divorce was, in fact, occurring. Initially, Bob tried to be fair, but he soon tired of Susan's refusal to accept the fact that he wanted a divorce, and he began to resent her. He started taking steps to keep as much of their joint assets as possible. He told Susan they should both be represented by the same lawyer in order to save money. Susan still did not want to acknowledge that the divorce was a reality, so she agreed. Because Susan didn't have an independent lawyer to protect her interests, Bob was able to avoid disclosure of some assets and grossly undervalue others.

When the divorce was finalized, Susan left behind a lifetime of devotion to Bob with few assets, very little in spousal support, and only sporadic child support payments. She and her children went from a life of comfort to one close to destitution. Susan was taking primary care of her children alone, and she was terrified that she would not be able to support herself and them. Because most of her social life had revolved around Bob and his position in the community, Susan was left with few friends for moral support and companionship. Eventually, Susan found a job in a local bank where her lifetime of good manners, reliability, and organizational skills served her well. Although she and her children lived more modestly and they ultimately survived their ordeal, she suffered months of anguish. Even if Susan had hired her own lawyer, she would have faced the anguish of divorce. However, Susan's lawyer would have made sure that she and her children received their fair share of the marital property, and she would not have had to suffer from the fear of poverty.

The simple fact is that your interest and that of your children will be better protected if you have your own lawyer. There is another compelling reason to hire your own attorney. Divorce is an emotionally charged event. You will suffer from a number of profound emotions, such as anger, rage, depression, guilt, and self-doubt. It will often be difficult, if not impossible, for you and your estranged spouse to deal with each other in a civil manner, negotiate a property settlement reasonably and fairly, and resolve the myriad of issues that affect your children. Your judgment and your ability to see the long-term effect of your actions may be understandably clouded. Retaining a lawyer will also decrease the amount of time you and your estranged spouse must spend together to decide what to do about property and children, and will reduce the likelihood of making hurtful statements that you may later regret.

Even though most divorce lawyers try to minimize conflict and reach amicable settlements, some divorce lawyers will take their client's case to court, rather than concede so much as a dime to the opposing spouse. This type of lawyer is usually skilled at persuading the client that he or she will be foregoing property he or she rightfully deserves, unless he or she does go to court. You want to avoid this type of lawyer and hope your husband does as well. Regrettably, however, a court trial is sometimes necessary. If your spouse is unwilling to compromise and will not agree to a fair and just settlement, you may be left with little choice but to go to court. In deciding how long to fight, you and your estranged spouse should keep in mind that court proceedings are expensive, contentious, and usually public (unless your attorneys can get the court to agree to nonpublic proceedings). You should always realistically weigh the amount at stake against the monetary and pyschological cost of pursuing the case in court.

Some years ago a prominent government official hired a divorce lawyer with a penchant for court trials. They apparently were loathe to concede or compromise any point. The government official had seriously battered his wife during their marriage. During their divorce trial, the official was undergoing cross-examination by his wife's lawyers about his abusive conduct when an investigative reporter for a major newspaper happened to wander by and recognized him. The reporter stepped into the courtroom to see what was going on and stumbled into what turned out to be a major news story. Once the story was public, the official's highly successful career was over.[45]

Several other factors must be considered in deciding whether or not to take your case to court or accept a proposed settlement. These include the emotional impact of further court proceedings on both you and your children, the adverse consequences of taking additional time and attention away from your business, and the further erosion of your relationship with your husband, which can be particularly important when you have children and will continue to have to interact with him. In some cases, one or more of these factors may be more important than the property settlement.

Sometimes the husband, when faced with competent opposing counsel, will complain to his wife that he and his attorney simply cannot work with the lawyer she has chosen. He will complain that her lawyer is causing trouble and making a reasonable settlement impossible to negotiate. The husband's assessment may be correct, in which case you should seriously consider hiring a new lawyer. However, your husband's complaints about your lawyer may simply indicate that your lawyer is actually doing a good job of protecting your interests and is not allowing your husband and his attorney to take advantage of you. Talk to your accountant (by now, you should have your own accountant as well as your own lawyer) and friends to help sort out whether your lawyer really is being obstructive, or whether he or she is simply representing you well, to your husband's chagrin. If it's the latter, don't let your husband talk you into getting a new lawyer — keep the one you've got.

Nancy had changed lawyers at the request of her husband, Scott. Scott told Nancy that he could not work with her lawyer and that they would never be able to reach a settlement as long as she retained him. Nancy was in her fifties, had spent her marriage working either at home or for a charity at low wages, and needed a reasonable property settlement to have any financial security at all. She complied with Scott's request and went from being represented by a well-qualified, conscientious lawyer who represented his clients well and was not overly contentious or difficult, to being represented by a lawyer who was a nice guy and meant well, but simply did not have the expertise or backbone to stand up to Scott and his lawyer. Nancy's new lawyer eventually conceded some very important points, and she was left exposed to tax liabilities so substantial that she could have lost every asset she received from the divorce. Nancy did not understand (and, apparently, neither did her new lawyer) that she assumed this risk when she signed the property settlement agreement. Consequently, she was completely dismayed and distraught when the IRS assessed more taxes and it looked like the worst would happen. Nancy then had to hire a tax lawyer, who was fortunately able to convince Scott that the tax liability was really his and that he should pick up the tab. (His agreement came after being advised of the extent of his financial affairs that would be introduced into evidence if Nancy proceeded to Tax Court to seek relief as an "innocent spouse"; see Chapter 8 "Neglecting the Tax Man" for a more in-depth discussion.) However, Nancy still incurred considerable legal fees before Scott agreed to pay, and she spent months anguishing over whether she would lose everything. As Nancy learned, when you have a good lawyer, keep that lawyer no matter what your husband says. If he insists that unless you get a new lawyer you will never be able to resolve your differences, don't believe him. It's not true.

Take Off the Rose-Colored Glasses

Cindy married young and supported her husband, Ron, while he attended law school. They settled in Los Angeles, where she worked in the film business as an editor. They were able to purchase their first home with her premarital savings and her income. After a few years of marriage and Ron's graduation from law school, they decided to move. They sold their Los Angeles home and, with the proceeds of the sale, purchased a new home in northern California. Ron set up a law practice and Cindy commuted back and forth between Los Angeles and northern California. While Ron struggled to build his law practice, Cindy provided the primary financial support for the house and their general living expenses. Five years later, Cindy discovered that Ron had had numerous affairs while she was in Los

Angeles working, even going so far as to entertain other women in their own house and to escort other women to social events in their local community. Cindy immediately contacted a divorce lawyer. The lawyer recommended that Cindy file for divorce immediately in Los Angeles. He warned her that if Ron became aware of her intent to file for divorce, he might file first in northern California. Cindy would then be stuck with proceedings in a court in a community in which Ron had more established relationships, since she commuted to Los Angeles weekly to work. In fact, by this time Ron was a well-regarded and well-connected member in the local legal community. Cindy's ability to control the direction of the divorce proceedings would also be limited, and her legal costs would be higher because her lawyer practiced in Los Angeles and would have to travel to northern California for court appearances.

Cindy describes her reaction to this advice as pushing the "dumb button." She ignored her attorney and went back to northern California to talk with Ron about getting a divorce. She put on her rose-colored glasses and believed that they still loved each other, and that Ron would not do anything to hurt her. Cindy hoped he would seek her forgiveness, and they would save their marriage. As she worked hard one night to prepare a special dinner for the two of them, she heard a knock on the door. When she answered, she was met at the door by a U.S. Marshall who served her with divorce papers filed by Ron. Ron had beat her to the punch and gained the upper hand by determining the location where the divorce proceedings would take place.

Cindy says the dumb button stayed turned on. Next, her divorce lawyer told her to continue to live in her and Ron's home, which she largely paid for and which was their primary asset. Alternately, her lawyer suggested that Ron and Cindy both vacate the house and sell it. Cindy again did not follow her lawyer's advice and let Ron stay in the house, while she rented an apartment in Los Angeles. She rationalized that she needed to be near her work and that she and Ron would, in the end, deal with each other fairly. However, the divorce court viewed Cindy's willingness to live elsewhere as evidence that she was less attached to the home than Ron was, and the court awarded the home to Ron. The court required that Ron buy out Cindy's half, but Ron was able to obtain an appraisal for the house that set its value far below its true market value. Cindy eventually received a payment from Ron for her share of the house, but it was even less than the down payment she had made on the house from her own savings. Cindy left years of marriage with less financial security than she had when she entered the marriage. Had Cindy taken off her rose-colored glasses and listened to her lawyer, she might have been able to get the house in the divorce settlement, or at least have sold it to a third party for its true market value.

Like Cindy, many women don't protect themselves in divorce because they hope for a reconciliation and are afraid they will further alienate their husband if they take affirmative steps to protect their rights in the marital property. Others simply don't believe that their multiyear marriage can end in deception or unfair actions by their husband. In Cindy's case, because she did not remain in the house while the divorce was pending, the court held it against her. Although this may not be the case in all courts, there may be other reasons why you would want to remain in the house. With a divorce, your life changes drastically and it helps to keep some stability in your life, such as staying in your own home; it is often easier on the children to remain there, and you simply may not be able to afford a comparable home. You and your husband may wish to try to live together under the same roof while the divorce is pending, and child custody arrangements or the division of property has not yet been worked out. In some cases, this can be detrimental to your mental health. My friend, Stacy Phillips, a highly reputed divorce lawyer in Los Angeles, advises her clients to make *life* decisions, not *divorce* decisions. The divorce will end at some point — your life goes on. The most important thing you need to do is whatever enables you to get through the divorce in one piece and ready to go into the next phase of your life. But before you can do so, you need to take off the rose-colored glasses and really look at what is going on. Only then can you decide what is best for you.

Know What You and Your Husband Own

It is a time-honored tradition in marriage that one spouse takes primary responsibility for financial affairs while the other undertakes responsibility for other matters. Typically, the husband has handled financial matters, although this has become less frequent as more and more women work outside the home. Even if your husband handles the financial matters of your marriage, it is nevertheless critical that you keep informed about your financial well-being and know generally what you and your husband own and where your assets are located. Too often, a woman will face divorce (or the death of her spouse) with virtually no knowledge about how much money she and her husband have, how much money he makes, what other property they own, what debts they owe, and what their regular expenses run. A survey of divorce lawyers taken in the late 1980s found that 52 percent of them said most of their women clients did not have a clear picture of their family assets or income.[46] This puts both the woman and her lawyer at a terrible disadvantage in divorce and makes it much easier for the husband to hide assets where she and her lawyer won't find them. At the very least, lack of this kind of information makes it difficult for the woman to compute how much money she will need to pay for living expenses when she is on her own after the divorce.

Here are some simple "dos" to follow:

• Review bank statements when they come in the mail.

• Keep your own list of banks you and your husband do business with, your bank account numbers, a list of signatories to each account, and the location of safe deposit boxes.

• Review your safe deposit box from time to time and keep an inventory of what is kept there.

• Find out the brokerage houses with which you and your husband maintain your stocks and bonds. Compile your own private list of their names and your account numbers.

• Review property tax bills, credit card statements, and any other documents that look like they have something to do with your marital finances.

• Keep copies of all documents relating to bank accounts, brokerage accounts, your home or other property, such as the deed, mortgage, and insurance, preferably in a safe place in case of divorce or other emergency (some women have found it helpful to store documents at a friend's home).

• Keep copies of your tax returns, pension plans in which you or your spouse have an interest, insurance policies, and estate-planning documents such as wills and trusts, in a safe place.

• Do not sign tax returns, loan agreements, financial statements, or other documents just because your husband asks you to.

• Review legal documents carefully and have your

lawyer review them for you; make your husband explain why he wants you to sign the documents and how they will affect you.

- Don't sign blank documents.

- Review your tax returns carefully for accuracy. You may want your own accountant to review them, particularly if you are filing joint returns, and make sure that the taxes due are actually paid; you can be held solely liable for the full tax if you sign a joint income tax return and your husband doesn't pay the tax.[47]

In the event of divorce, the only way you will be able to make sure that you get your fair share of marital property is to know what you and your husband have. Some states, such as California, legally obligate both spouses to disclose fully what assets each owns or controls. Nevertheless, a dishonest spouse can easily hide money in offshore bank accounts without much risk of detection, unless you have been diligent in watching your assets over the years. If you are not careful, you may find on divorce that your marital assets have been encumbered up to the hilt, that there is little left to divide, and that your dream of financial security in retirement really is just a dream. If this were the case, not only would you face the emotional trauma and adjustment of divorce, but you would also have to find new sources of financial support. This can be particularly devastating if you have children to support. If you watch your marital assets closely, you may be able to prevent such financial insecurity, or at least be in a better position to deal with the lack of financial resources in the case of divorce.

Although your husband may feel threatened or not trusted if you track this financial information, it is critical that you do so for reasons other than divorce. For example you also need to know your and your husband's financial situation in the event that some tragedy befalls him and he dies or becomes incapacitated. Know what you have, what you owe, and what you spend.

So You're Divorcing: How Much Should You Get?

You and your husband have made the decision: you're getting a divorce. Now you fight over who gets what. If you live in a community property state, you should each get one-half of the community property. If you live in an equitable distribution state, you will get whatever the judge decides is equitable or whatever you and your husband can agree to. One thing you should both count on — your standard of living is definitely going to be affected.

Let's say you live in a community property state and you own 50 percent of the assets. Does it matter what assets you get? Should you take the stock and give him the municipal bonds as long as they are worth the same? You love your home; you had all your children in that home. Should you take the home and give him the cash? These are issues you and your lawyer will need to grapple with.

Not all assets are equal. Take, for example, your home. You may love it; you may absolutely adore it. If you take the home, you won't have to move, the kids can stay in their schools, and so on. Absolutely true. However, it is also true that a house is what is called an *illiquid asset*; it doesn't generate any cash which you can use to pay other expenses. Things do go wrong: the house may need expensive repairs. The mortgage is hard to keep up with and, if the interest rate on your mortgage is not fixed, the rate and your payments can increase. You may love it, but can you afford it?

Suppose you and your spouse own stock in one company and tax-exempt municipal bonds that are appraised to be of the same value. Each pays a return of 5 percent on your money. Which one should you take? It depends. You have to consider the amount of tax you would have to pay if you had to sell the investment. You also must evaluate the benefits to you from taking the bonds, in which case the interest will not be taxable to you, compared to the likelihood that the stock has more potential to grow in value and, in the long run, may be worth more.

You have two pieces of real estate. One — a small office building — you and your husband bought ten years ago for $50,000; you have taken depreciation of $28,000 on it. The second was bought only a couple of years ago, also for $50,000. It doesn't have any buildings on it nor have you taken any depreciation on it. Both properties are now valued at $75,000. Which one should you take? Several considerations need to be taken into account. The office building is probably leased out and would provide you with some ongoing rental income, whereas the raw land would not. One piece of real estate may have a greater potential for appreciation, but this is often difficult to predict. One thing is clear: the office building will cost you a lot more in taxes than the land when you sell it, because of the depreciation taken on the office building. If you took the building and had to sell it immediately, you would have a taxable gain on the sale equal to $75,000 less $22,000 (the $50,000 original cost less depreciation of $28,000). In other words, you would pay tax on $53,000. If you took the land instead and sold it, you would pay tax on only $25,000 ($75,000 less $50,000). At least with respect to your taxes, the land is the better deal.

If you and your husband run a business, it will have to be valued. How is this done? Only the appraisers know for sure. To most of us, valuation of businesses seems to be determined more by hocus-pocus than anything else. Take the case of Henry Kravis. He agreed to give his wife, Hedi, 30 percent of his stake in the companies that his investment banking firm, Kohlberg Kravis Roberts, owned. His share had been valued at

$7.2 million the year before. Hedi agreed to $3 to $4 million, based on this valuation. Shortly after they split, the investment banking firm took off, started making major deals, and Henry's net worth far exceeded the valuation of $7.2 million. Hedi filed in court, claiming that Henry defrauded her and that he knew that his share in the companies was worth far more than $7.2 million. Unfortunately for Hedi, the court did not rule in her favor. The judge said that Hedi and Henry had negotiated their agreement for three years, and, during this time, Hedi had ample opportunity to investigate the assets herself and decide what they were worth.[48]

You also need to make sure you think of all the marital assets you and your husband have. His pension plan is a marital asset, and the laws now allow pension plans to be divided among the spouses on divorce. There may be unvested stock options like those Lorna Wendt fought over. There may be life insurance policies, artwork, tax refunds, stock options or warrants, inventions, deferred compensation plans, and many other assets. You and your lawyer need to sit down and thoroughly analyze what assets you and your husband have accumulated during your marriage. You will typically need to employ an accountant to work hand in hand with your lawyer to determine this.

Alimony and Child Support

You and your lawyer also need to negotiate alimony and child support. Taxes are important here: alimony is taxable to you and deductible by your husband, and child support is not taxable to you and not deductible by your husband. The amount of alimony or child support that will be awarded varies greatly from state to state. Whereas historically lifetime alimony has been favored in some states, it is becoming less and less so as more women enter the job market with salable skills, and in more and more cases, no alimony is awarded. Child support is determined in some states through specified formulae, whereas alimony generally is not.[49] You also need to think about ongoing insurance needs for you and your children, including their medical insurance and life insurance that you own on your ex-husband to help you and your children to survive without his financial support should he die.

An important thing to remember, however, is that many men don't pay child support or alimony, even when it's awarded. I earlier noted that the payment rate of child support by former husbands is dismal. In 1995, the U.S. Census study of children growing up in single-parent households showed that, when support orders existed, only 2.7 million children (39 percent) received full payments, 2 million (29 percent) received partial payments, and 2.2 million (32 percent) received no payments. Given these dismal statistics, it is imperative that you get the best up-front property settlement you can to protect both your and your children's future. It may be the only money you and your children will ever see from that marriage.

Forget about Fair; It Costs Too Much

How many times have you heard, "But it's not fair?" It doesn't matter whether the woman or her husband initiated the divorce proceedings. Women generally expect that every item will be divided up fairly, and in accordance with what the woman perceives as fair. In the emotional turmoil that surrounds a divorce, women generally have a hard time appreciating that fair is in the eye of the beholder. However, there are always two views of what went wrong and who fairly deserves what: the woman's view and her husband's. Usually, the party initiating the divorce feels the other drove him or her to it, whereas the party who did not initiate the divorce feels victimized. Both parties feel they contributed more than the other to the marriage. An interminable drive for fairness can be very detrimental to both parties. It exacerbates the resentment between the spouses, prolongs resolution of property division, and skyrockets the legal fees.

I recently heard about a meeting held by a couple undergoing divorce, at which there were three lawyers, two accountants, and the divorcing couple. The squabbles of the divorcing couple eventually centered on several relatively small financial issues. The couple became so contentious about these small matters that the meeting was prolonged by about two hours. The issues they fought over involved a small amount of money — at most, $5,000. The cumulative fees of the five professionals exceeded $1,000 per hour, so more than $2,000 of professional fees were incurred to deal with this small amount. The professionals tried to stop the bickering and end the meeting, but the divorcing couple persisted out of their mutual, but opposing, need to be treated as they each perceived was fair. Their pursuit of fairness, however, was only a needless waste of their money.

Sometimes a woman believes she is not being treated fairly because she is the one who has to pay. One of the lesser appreciated results of greater economic opportunity for women is the fact that in divorce it may well be the woman who is paying spousal support to her ex-husband. This is generally the case when the woman is the primary breadwinner and the husband the primary caretaker of the home and children, a scenario seen more and more often today. Despite the woman's view that she is entitled to equal pay and equal work opportunities, when divorce rolls around she often reverts to tradition and is outraged that *she* has to pay *him*. In her view, it just isn't fair! In the introduction, I stated that new opportunities bring new responsibilities and that new benefits bring new burdens. Exposure to paying spousal and child support is one of those responsibilities/burdens. The divorce laws have largely been gender neutralized, and the woman may end up paying the bills for the divorce.

Barbara was outraged when her ex-husband asked for several hundred dollars a month more in child support, even though it was at her request that he had undertaken primary child-rearing responsibilities for their six children. Again, she did not think this was fair. She raged that "he was trying to make her into the dad." She was reminded by a friend that, because of her own wishes, her ex-husband had taken on the traditional role of mom, and he was legally entitled to reasonable child support. Barbara was eventually dissuaded from spending thousands in legal fees to fight a small increase in child support. The increase in child support was money she could afford, and it was for her children.

Often, the issue of fairness gets tied up with the desire for revenge. Frequently, a woman will go to battle over small money matters because she feels she needs to win that issue, to show her husband and the world what a cad he really is and how badly she was being treated. To this woman, the principle outweighs any amount of legal fees incurred in winning it. As my friend Faith Dornbrand, a prominent Washington, D.C. divorce lawyer, reminds her clients, although the principle may seem important at the time, it is unlikely that it will seem so important in five years, two years, or even six months down the road. But the legal costs will still have to be paid. Revenge, like fairness, is often expensive. When revenge is a woman's motivation, she should try to remember the old saying that "living well is the best revenge," and that prolonged battles over small matters is a waste of money and emotional well-being. Instead, she should wrap up the divorce and go forward into the next stage of her life and live well.

Soraya Khashoggi may say it best. She was included in the *Guinness Book of Records,* 1992 edition, for receiving the highest divorce settlement award ever — a reported $950 million.[50] In 1999, she wrote an article for the London *Times* in an attempt to set the record straight and dissuade divorcing couples from hiring litigious lawyers and feuding over every little thing. She claims that her and Adnan's "war of the roses" began with a bottle of nail polish. An errant secretary of Adnan's had struck the cost of a bottle of nail polish from Soraya's household bill and told her to pay for it herself. Soraya called Marvin Mitchelson, who began a nasty and media-blitzed divorce proceeding against Adnan, and their dirty laundry was aired on worldwide television. Soraya ironically notes that her overseas call to Mitchelson cost her more than the bottle of nail polish. She came to her senses, she says, only when she and her lawyers became so paranoid that they starting having any bouquets of flowers she received swept for bugs. Only then did she and Adnan step back and look at what they were doing to each other and to their children. She and Adnan settled their case, but for far less than the reported $950 million, which she describes as "ludicrous." As Soraya warns, "There is no such thing as a perfect divorce; it is always devastating for the family."[51]

As Soraya found, it is impossible to be totally objective about all financial matters when going through a divorce. Nevertheless, as she learned, you should do your best to keep your eye on the bottom line and the effect of ongoing battles on the family. You need to weigh the cost of getting the exact division you perceive to be fair (and remember your spouse's view of what is fair will almost certainly be different) against the benefit to be obtained. Is it really worth it? Otherwise, you and your estranged spouse can spend undue hours and unnecessary legal fees bickering about small items that ultimately will have little importance to either of you, but in the meantime will create much chaos and grief for your family. The legal costs of doing so will decrease the assets that you have left to divide. Divorce is not about fairness. It is about getting out of an unwanted marriage as financially sound as possible under the circumstances.

Make a Clean Financial Break

In the 1960s, it was popular to believe that married couples could divorce, stay intertwined both emotionally and financially, and live happily ever after with each other and new spouses. Unfortunately, we humans frequently have shown that our spiritual development is not quite so evolved. We often succumb to age-old emotions such as jealousy and greed. It is important that when you separate from your spouse, you cut the financial ties that bound you while you were married. This is imperative if you wish to have control over your new post-divorce financial well-being.

Jackie is paying a high price for agreeing to continue to co-own several pieces of real estate with her former husband, Bill. At the time of her divorce, which took place in the mid-1970s, Jackie and Bill fancied themselves as New Age people. While they agreed to divorce, they would do so as friends and on friendly terms. Bill, being a lawyer, said he would take care of the legal affairs, and Jackie did not hire her own lawyer. They had two pieces of real estate, both of which had potential to appreciate in value. Their residence was located in Bel Air, a spiffy, elite community in Los Angeles, California, and they both believed that the residence had the greatest potential to increase in value. While dividing the property, they talked about giving Jackie sole ownership of the Bel Air property because her father had provided the down payment they used to buy it, and giving Bill sole ownership of the other piece of real estate. However, Jackie thought this would not be fair to Bill, and, instead, she agreed to own jointly both of the properties with Bill. They decided to rent out the properties until they mutually agreed to sell the properties. A deed was recorded that put the properties in their names as equal cotenants (a form of legal ownership in which both owners have an undivided interest in the property).

Years later Jackie discovered that, unbeknown to her, Bill had borrowed a lot of money and used his one-half interest in the Bel Air property as security for the loans. In fact, he had secured loans against his one-half share of the property in amounts far exceeding the value of his share. Additionally, the county assessed additional taxes to pay for local improvements, and these went unpaid because Bill would not pay his share. To make things even worse, Bill then sold his interest in the Bel Air property to another person in what appeared to be a sham sale designed to keep his creditors at bay. Legal title to the property had become so clouded that it was impossible to sell it. As if this weren't enough, Bill used every legal method available to defeat Jackie's attempts to get the liens removed and the property's title cleared, so that she could either buy out his share or jointly sell the property and be rid of it.

Jackie also found out that after their divorce, Bill had migrated from earning his living from a respectable law practice to putting together sham deals and bilking innocent investors out of substantial sums of money. Having crossed the line into criminal behavior, Bill was hardly reluctant to try to cheat Jackie out of their co-owned property. By the time Jackie got the title cleared, she spent more than $100,000 to pay off lien holders, and more than $100,000 in legal fees.

Had Jackie made a clean break with Bill and taken sole ownership of the Bel Air property, he would not have been able to encumber it with liens, she would not have gotten into the legal mess she was in, and she would not have incurred hundreds of thousands of dollars in legal fees. Bill would not have been able to disrupt her life so profoundly. Jackie's retirement fund dissipated as her legal fees and other costs mounted. Had she hired her own lawyer to advise her when she and Bill divorced, it is likely her lawyer would have strongly advised her against co-owning the properties with Bill or would at least have made sure she was protected against the kind of shenanigans he pulled.

Always make as clean a financial break with your former husband as you can. In some cases, it may not be possible to make a totally clean break. For example, if you have children, you will most likely have ongoing financial dealings with your ex-husband. Just do the best you can in your particular situation. Most important, don't stay financially comingled out of some notion of fairness, or because you just know that you and your former husband will stay friends and that he would never do anything to hurt you. Circumstances change, and so do people.

Many more legal issues arise in a divorce that are beyond the scope of this book and are best decided by you and the well-qualified lawyer you should retain after having read some of the discussed principles. The single most important thing to bear in mind is that the law generally will hold you responsible for the choices you make. In the eyes of the law, you are a mature, responsible adult even though you may be traumatized by, and in total despair over, the divorce. Remember, too, that if you have children, they will depend on you, at least in part, to provide for their financial needs. As I mentioned earlier, the rate of delinquency in paying child support is alarmingly high, and you may be your children's sole source of financial support. The property settlement agreement you sign is one you generally will live with for the rest of your life (unless you can show that you were defrauded or otherwise persuade a court to set it aside or modify it — a feat that is never easy). If you realize years later when you are emotionally stronger and more knowledgeable about business affairs that you were cheated in the divorce, it is simply too late. On the other hand, if you protect yourself in divorce, many opportunities will await you. Many women postdivorce start their own businesses. If you do start your own business, you will find an independence like you have never before known, a self-confidence in your own abilities that you would otherwise never obtain, and a pride that you would otherwise never realize. It also could give you a very good income. Since her much publicized divorce from The Donald, Ivana Trump has created a multimillion-dollar home shopping network, a television show, and a new magazine. Your own business plan may be more modest but it will no doubt be as exciting and challenging. In starting a small business, however, there are many potential legal mistakes that can be detrimental. To guard against these, read on . . .

LEGAL MISTAKE #4:

STARTING A BUSINESS: Good Intentions Do Not Protect You from Bad Legal Results

*"Being in your own business is working 80 hours
a week so that you can avoid working 40 hours
a week for someone else."*

Romana E.F. Arnett, president
Romana Enterprises, Inc.

Small business is the fastest growing segment of our contemporary economy. More and more of these small businesses are being started by women. According to the National Foundation for Women Business Owners, the number of women-owned businesses leaped by 103 percent from 1987 to 1999. In 1999, about 9.1 million businesses, or 38 percent of all businesses, were owned by women. Women-owned businesses generated revenues of about $3.6 trillion, a growth of 436 percent from 1987. Employment by women-owned businesses increased by 320 percent from 1987 to 1999. In 1996, one in four employees, 27.5 million people, worked in women-owned businesses. According to Lynn Neeley, former president of the United States Association for Small Business and Entrepreneurship, "The rise of women entrepreneurs is one of the big demographics changing our society."[52]

Why do women start their own businesses? In a 1998 survey of 650 women business owners conducted by Catalyst (a women's research firm) and the National Foundation for Women Business Owners, 46 percent cited greater flexibility as a primary reason for starting their own business, 41 percent a great idea that was closely related to the work they did as employees, 22 percent glass ceiling barriers in the jobs they held, 20 percent the benefit of "being their own boss," 14 percent the lack of challenge they felt where they were employed, and 10 percent said they were downsized.[53] Women business owners continue to diversify into nontraditional businesses. From 1992 to 1999, the greatest growths were in construction (68 percent), wholesale trade (65 percent), transportation/communications (61 percent), agriculture (59 percent), and manufacturing (54 percent).[54]

Unfortunately, many women don't spend the money or take the time necessary to get their businesses in good legal working order. They don't realistically evaluate their own capabilities and needs. They think their hard work and good intentions are all that is needed to achieve success. This attitude can result in the failure of the business, personal liability for business debts, unanticipated tax liabilities and penalties, and employee lawsuits, just to name a few undesirable consequences.

Are You an Entrepreneur?

Several years ago, the *Wall Street Journal* interviewed several small-business experts to discuss the qualities that successful entrepreneurs typically possess. A number of qualities were elicited — creativity, persistence, lack of fear of failure, innovation, tolerance for ambiguity, great endurance, massive physical capacity, long-term perspective, constant focus on business objectives, and the ability to manage people. On the dark side, entrepreneurs, as high-energy people, can become easily bored, and they may have trouble appreciating employees who possess less drive and interest in the business than they have. These qualities may impede their ability to continue to lead the business as it matures.[55]

If you want to start your own business, you must first honestly evaluate whether you have the qualities necessary to be an entrepreneur. These include qualities that go beyond the ability to work hard, and certainly beyond the ability to run your business with good intentions. Ask yourself the following questions. Do I have the personal qualities necessary to be an entrepreneur? Do I have a specific vision for my business? Do I have the energy to put in long hours and juggle many tasks at once? Am I driven enough? Can I deal with not knowing whether I will be able to meet payroll next week without going into a paralyzing panic? Can I manage many people with different temperaments and needs? Do I understand cash flow and other accounting concepts? Can I read financial and bank statements?

Today, women have educational and job opportunities they never before dreamed of. As a group, women have learned that they can do anything that as a group men can do. Individually, however, women still have their own unique set of skills, strengths, weaknesses, and limitations — just like individual men do. Not all women are cut out to be entrepreneurs. Not all men are either. It is critical that you honestly evaluate whether you are the entrepreneurial type before spending your time and resources to start your own business. Many people are simply better suited to be employees. Before trying to start your own business, try to evaluate objectively your personal qualities and shortcomings. To start a business that will fail is expensive, and can be extremely damaging to your self-image and self-confidence.

How Much Capital Do You Need?

It takes money to start a business. Women who start a new business are frequently excited and optimistic about their business, and therefore estimate the amount of capital they need through the proverbial rose-colored glasses. They leave no room for error, the old learning curve, or the unexpected. Then, when they run out of money, they often take drastic measures to keep the business afloat. Some stop paying payroll and sales taxes, and instead use that money to pay other expenses. As discussed later, this is a huge mistake. Some women borrow additional funds from family and friends. This can cause considerable guilt and estrangement if the business fails. Although bank loans are a desirable way to get financing, women entrepreneurs still have more difficulty obtaining financing from traditional sources than do men; however, that trend appears to be improving. A 1998 survey conducted in southern California reported that only 22 percent of women-owned small businesses had access to bank loans, whereas 30 percent of men-owned small businesses did.[56] A survey conducted by the National Foundation for Women Business Owners found that, as of 1998, 52 percent of women-owned business compared with 58 percent of men-owned businesses had bank financing. The survey also found that women-owned businesses have lower levels of available credit than their male counterparts and that women of color find it even more difficult to obtain bank financing, even though women-owned businesses were as financially sound and creditworthy as the male-owned businesses and are more likely to remain in business than the average male-owned business.[57] Fortunately, in this information age, it takes less money to start a business than ever before.

There is no question that it is difficult to calculate exactly how much capital you will need to get a business up and running and make it profitable enough to provide sufficient cash flow to pay expenses. Your budget should include money for contingencies because something invariably goes wrong in the start-up phase. You should also start small and build up. Too often women start with marketing plans really designed for mature, international companies. Most important, you should have a clear idea about how much money you are willing to risk, and promise yourself that once you reach that point, you will seriously evaluate the situation and close up shop if that is your best option. Decide that you *will* cut your losses, and *when* you will cut your losses.

Too many women dig themselves deeper and deeper into debt instead of admitting that their business has failed. Often, they are too embarrassed to admit failure. They are willing to risk their family's financial well-being before risking that other people will know that the business failed. Sometimes, if a woman believes that she should be able to do anything, regardless of her individual strengths and weaknesses — and some feminist rhetoric tells her just that — then her failure at business can take on magnified proportions. Not only has she failed at this single endeavor, she has failed at being a liberated woman. She has provided fodder for sexist men who think women are incapable in business affairs. This is a heavy burden we put on ourselves, and an inappropriate one at that. Equal opportunity means not just the opportunity for women to succeed. It also exposes women to the risk of failure. Be honest about how much capital you will need to start your business, and don't jeopardize your family's financial security just to prove that you can start a business. Many men don't succeed in every venture they take on either. Truly successful people are able to evaluate when they are in a losing venture, and, when faced with failure, they get out as quick and as cheaply as possible.

Form a Limited Liability Entity

If you have decided you have the personality to start

your own business successfully, and have sufficient capital to do so, one of the first things to consider is the types of liabilities that the business might face. You will want to consider whether it is possible to limit your own personal liability for these liabilities by setting up your business through a corporation or limited liability company (LLC). (Appendix D provides sample articles of incorporation used to form a corporation. An LLC is formed by a similar document.) Under the law, corporations and LLCs are treated as legal entities distinct and separate from the owners. Both limit the liability of the owners. If the entity borrows money from a bank, it is the entity, and not the individual owners, that owes the bank. If the entity defaults on the loan, the bank can sue only the entity to collect the amounts still owed (with several important exceptions that are discussed later). Likewise, if the entity enters into a lease agreement with the landlord for the business premises and then cannot pay the rent, the landlord can sue only the entity for payment, and not the owners (again, with several exceptions, as discussed later).

It costs money to set up a corporation or other limited liability entity. Frugal women may often decide against spending the money to set up a legal entity for their business, without really thinking through the consequences of not doing so. It is only after the business has failed, and the creditors look to them personally for payment, that they become fully aware of the adverse results of operating a business without a legally formed business entity.

For example, Alice went to a lawyer for advice about starting a retail business. He advised her to set up a corporation, which, with filing fees and legal fees, would cost between $1,500 to $2,000. Alice decided, however, that she did not want to spend that much money just to form a corporation. She thought the money would be better spent if she bought more inventory to display at her store. So Alice leased space in a retail shopping center and set up shop as a *sole proprietorship* (the legal term for setting up a business owned individually by one person and not through a limited liability entity). She used a combination of her savings and trade credit to buy inventory, furniture and office equipment, and to pay the initial salaries of employees. After struggling to make a go of it for a year, she finally had to close shop. What little profits she made, Alice used to pay her employees' wages. She was unable to pay her trade creditors, and they began calling and demanding payment. By this time, her liabilities exceeded $100,000. Because Alice had not formed a limited liability entity, she was personally responsible for these debts, even though she had closed the business. She had no idea how she would ever pay off a debt this large. Finally, Alice had to hire a new lawyer — this time, a bankruptcy lawyer.

Had Alice used a limited liability company, she would not have been personally liable for the debts she incurred trying to start her business. The company would have owed the debt, and the creditors could have sued only the company, not her. Although the company may have been forced into bankruptcy, she would not have been. This is why most businessmen religiously conduct business through limited liability entities.

There are, however, several situations that restrict your ability to limit personal liability by setting up a limited liability entity. Many landlords require business owners to sign personal guarantees that the limited liability entity will pay all rent called for under a lease agreement. In this case, the landlord can sue the individual owner if the business entity defaults on lease payments. Many banks also require that small business owners personally guarantee loans made to a limited liability entity. Personal guarantees are more frequently required for newly created businesses than for businesses that have been operating successfully for several years. Not all creditors will require a personal guarantee, however, and, even if a limited liability entity does not totally eliminate an owner's personal exposure to its debts (because of required personal guarantees), the entity can at least minimize that exposure for liabilities not subject to personal guarantees (such as amounts owed to suppliers of inventory).

The owner of a limited liability entity may also be personally liable to its business creditors, if the owner does not treat the entity as separate and distinct. If the owner does not maintain separate bank accounts for the entity; does not file separate tax returns; does not hold meetings of the entity's board of directors and keep written minutes of the meetings; drains all of the cash out of the entity for the owner's personal use, leaving it without funds to pay creditors; and otherwise does not act like the entity really is distinct from himself or herself, a creditor can sue in court. The creditor can ask the judge to rule that the entity and the individual owner really are one and the same, and that the individual is personally responsible for the entity's debts. In legal jargon, this is called *piercing the corporate veil*. It is essential to maintain the separation between yourself and your legal entity if you don't want to expose yourself to the liabilities of the entity.

Madge owned a corporation that owed the IRS a huge amount of payroll taxes. Madge also owned several other corporations, which held most of the assets used in the business. The corporation that owed the taxes was the entity that operated the actual business — the operating entity. The other corporations just owned assets, which they leased or licensed to the operating corporation. Madge did not keep up the paperwork, and she moved money back and forth between the corporations any time she wanted to, as though she was just moving money between different bank accounts of a single company. She did not treat the corporations as separate, distinct entities. To collect the delinquent payroll taxes, the IRS threatened to *pierce the corporate veil* and attach the assets owned by the nonoperating corporations. This could have adversely affected the ability of Madge's corporations to get bank loans and other forms of financing. Madge was able to allay this threat only when she agreed to personally pay off all the taxes in installments.

Other problems can come up when the paperwork involving an entity is not maintained properly. Shelly needed help in cleaning up the corporate paperwork of several entities formed by her deceased husband. Stock certificates had not been issued; there was conflicting information about who owned several of the corporations; and minutes of corporate meetings had not been maintained for many years. Shelly wanted to sell a major asset in which more than one of the corporations had an ownership interest. The buyer reasonably wanted to make sure that Shelly had the right to sell the asset, and that no third party could step in and claim that he or she owned one of the corporations and demand more money from the buyer. Shelly paid substantial legal fees trying to clean up the corporate documentation to the extent possible, and was unable to straighten it out completely. The buyer eventually went ahead with the deal, but only after Shelly made several significant concessions, including reducing her price.

You should be aware that for some types of businesses, limited liability may not be possible, even if you set up a limited liability entity. For example, most states have laws that preclude an attorney or doctor from limiting his or her liability for malpractice by setting up a limited liability entity. However, for most types of businesses, limited liability can be obtained.

A limited liability entity does cost money. Generally, it costs between $1,000 to $3,000 to set one up, and most states charge a minimum annual tax. For example, in California, corporations pay a minimum tax of $800 per year. Other costs to maintain a limited liability entity — separate tax returns, preparation of annual minutes, and other miscellaneous costs — run several thousand dollars more. In some cases, the costs may preclude using a limited liability entity. However, if the amount of liabilities you will incur in setting up your business are expected to be substantial and you can avoid personal guarantees, the cost involved in creating a limited liability entity is easily worth it. Think of the limited liability entity as a type of insurance, and the setup and annual costs as equivalent to insurance premiums. Would you pay $3,000 per year in insurance to protect your personal assets from business losses? In many cases, yes. If you do start your own business, consider using a limited liability entity to operate your business. Most men do. They think they are clever to do so — and they are.

Starting a business is one thing, but running it is another. There are employees to manage, orders to fill, creditors to pay, new ideas to implement, strategies to execute. Also, a number of legal obligations must be observed. In a recent survey conducted in southern California, women entrepreneurs had the same chief concerns as their male counterparts: high taxes, burgeoning regulations, and general frustration with the government. Hopefully, you won't encounter laws and regulations that prohibit you from achieving your goals. However, to keep your business healthy, you need to know how to deal with the bane of small business: taxes and government regulations. In the next chapter, I will help you do just that.

LEGAL MISTAKE #5:

RUNNING YOUR BUSINESS: Good Intentions Do Not Protect You from Bad Legal Results

"To open a business is very easy; to keep it open is very difficult."

Chinese proverb

You're working night and day. Your business is growing slowly, painfully, but you hope successfully. What do you do to make sure you stay in business? As I discussed in the last chapter, a recent survey showed that women entrepreneurs share the same chief concerns as their male counterparts: high taxes, burgeoning regulations, and general frustration with the government. Women also cited a tight labor market and tight access to capital as areas of great concern.[58]

Learn (or Try to) the Morass of Government Rules That Affect Your Business

It's virtually impossible to learn all the government regulations that might apply to your business, but you need to try to learn the main ones and, above all, try to maintain a sense of humor as you attempt to do so.

No one escapes the government and the many laws it imposes. The book *The Death of Common Sense*[59] begins with a story about Mother Theresa and the nuns of the Missionaries of Charity who wanted to convert an abandoned building in the South Bronx into a homeless shelter. New York City offered to sell the building for $1 and the nuns budgeted for the necessary construction. However, no one in the New York City government seemed to have the authority to sell the building, at least within anything remotely resembling a reasonable period of time. The nuns spent one and a half years going to hearing after hearing. When the city finally approved the purchase, the nuns found out that the city's building code required that they include a $100,000 elevator. Even though the nuns informed the bureaucrats that they would not use an elevator, the city could not (or would not) waive the requirement that it be installed. The nuns could not afford the elevator and therefore abandoned their efforts. Mother Theresa apparently went back to India, the other nuns went back to their convent, and the South Bronx lost an exceptional opportunity to care for its homeless.

Several years ago I was asked to look into the licensing requirements for an activity in which a client's daughter wanted to get involved. She hoped to make and sell gift baskets during the holiday season. She planned to fill the baskets with toys, coffee mugs, and the like, as well as some nonperishable food items such as nuts, pretzels, coffee beans, and tea bags. My research revealed that, since she intended to include food items, even nonperishable food items, by law she had to maintain her inventory and assemble her baskets at a physical site equipped with refrigeration. Clearly, to lease a facility with the required refrigeration just to make gift baskets was not feasible. We found that she could sublease space from another commercial enterprise that had proper refrigeration permits. She knew of a business that was properly licensed and would let her set up shop. But this was not the end of the bureaucratic obstacles. To transport the gift baskets from the facility where she assembled them to her customers, she could not simply put them in the backseat of her Toyota. She had to transport them in a special truck or wagon attached to her car that met certain refrigeration criteria and was licensed to carry food products. To complicate matters further, once she arrived at her destination, she could not simply carry the baskets into her customer's place of business. The physical act of carrying the baskets into a building required a third license: a "hawker's license." Her customers could come out to her special, licensed truck or wagon and pick up the baskets without her needing to get the third license, but she could not carry the baskets to them. After I explained the labyrinth of rules, she decided to do something else to make a few extra bucks.

Small businesses often complain that they must try to comply with too many rules imposed by too many government agencies. Although these rules may seem silly and unnecessary, unfortunately, you're stuck with them. If you ignore them, you could end up with large fines assessed against you, or, in the worst case, your business could be shut down. Too frequently, women assume that their good intentions outweigh the legal importance of applicable regulations. Sadly, this is not true. Some regulations are not as important as others, and the penalties for noncompliance differ. In some cases, you may incur only a nominal fine and an order to get into compliance within a specified time period. But noncompliance with other regulations may lead to a business shutdown. When safety or the health of anyone is at risk, you must be extremely careful about complying with all applicable laws and regulations.

Pay Those Payroll Taxes

Payroll taxes are one of those things some new business owners just don't get around to dealing with. Business owners often treat their workers as independent contractors, and not as employees, to minimize payroll taxes and employee benefits.

There is a myth out there that you and the worker can elect whether to treat him or her as an employee or as an independent contractor. This is absolutely wrong and can be an extremely expensive mistake.

Whether your workers are employees or independent contractors depends on the amount of supervision and control you exercise — it is not elective. The IRS uses certain criteria to decide which workers are employees and which workers are independent contractors. Generally, the IRS makes its determination based on the amount of supervision you exercise over the way the worker does his or her job. In legal jargon, the test is whether you have the "right to control, not only the result to be achieved, but also the manner in which the services are performed."[60] If you have the right to control the manner in which the worker does his or her job, in the eyes of the IRS, that worker is your employee no matter what you and the worker agree to. This means that your business is directly liable for all income taxes that should be withheld from the worker's wages and paid to the IRS in addition to all social security taxes and unemployment taxes (both employee and employer contributions) that should be withheld and paid. The IRS does not need to look for the worker to collect these taxes; it needs only to look for you. Moreover, if you did not include these workers in your company employee retirement plan and the IRS classifies them as employees, the IRS may also disqualify the retirement plan you set up for your other employees. This too may cost your business a lot in extra taxes.[61]

The IRS historically has taken a very expansive view of who is considered an employee. Almost any worker is classified by the IRS as an employee, rather than as an independent contractor. The IRS is biased toward employee classification because it wants to collect more taxes, and the withholding of employee taxes by business owners is its most successful compliance program. State tax authorities generally take an even more proemployee classification position. They care about the proper classification of workers because employees are entitled to unemployment insurance benefits and workers' compensation benefits, but independent contractors are not. State authorities see employee classification as protective of workers and often apply a definition of employees even more broad than that applied by the IRS, to ensure that workers get these crucial benefits. Both the IRS and state authorities hold employers to a high standard when it comes to reporting and paying payroll taxes, and employer failures are not treated with leniency. Because the amount of payroll taxes owed by employers is quite large, the amount of the liability combined with rigid enforcement by the tax authorities can devastate a business that falls behind.

Delegates to the 1995 White House Conference on Small Business voted employee/independent contractor classification and the catastrophic payroll tax liabilities that can result from an incorrect classification as the most significant problem facing small business today.[62] Congressional representatives have introduced many legislative proposals that attempt to provide a clearer definition of employee and independent contractor. None of these proposals has passed yet. Legislators are concerned that if they make it too easy to classify workers as independent contractors, tax revenues will decline. Statistically, independent contractors simply don't comply with the tax laws and pay their taxes at the same rate that employees do. Too many independent contractors simply don't file tax returns at all or report their income too low and their expenses too high. If the noncompliance rate by independent contractors were not so substantial, the IRS would not be so zealous in its attempt to classify everyone as employees.

The potential threat to your business from potential payroll tax liability is exacerbated by the ambiguity of the test to determine whether a worker is an employee or an independent contractor. As I already stated, the test is one of control by the employer over the manner in which the work is done, as well as the result to be obtained. This is a difficult test to apply because there are no clearcut standards to use. The IRS uses published guidelines to evaluate whether a business owner has the requisite control over workers to classify them as employees, but even these guidelines contain many vague and ambiguous tests. The difficulty faced by a small business is compounded by the all-encompassing definition of *employee* by the tax authorities and the zeal with which they pursue employee classification. The tax authorities think almost everyone is an employee — even those workers you and I would normally think are running their own business and are appropriately treated as independent contractors. If you want to avoid a challenge and the potential liability for tax debts so large that they can sink your business, the safest course of action is to treat all your workers as employees and go through the expense and hassle of withholding and paying payroll taxes, filing payroll tax returns, and all the other administrative tasks associated with employees. In most parts of the country, payroll tax companies are available that will, for a small fee, do all these tasks for you and your business. When in doubt, collect the taxes and pay them out.

Too frequently, small business owners decide not to pay payroll taxes when they incur cash flow shortages. They use that money to pay trade creditors instead. Generally, small busines owners rationalize this choice by concluding that it is more important to keep the business open and to make it profitable. They use the money to pay trade creditors in order to keep the inventory or supplies they need to run the business coming in. These businesses believe they will catch up on taxes later, after they are back on their feet. They often believe that the tax authorities will surely agree that it is more important to keep the business operating and the employees paid than to pay payroll taxes. Wrong! The tax authorities will hold it against you if you choose to pay trade creditors instead of them. They don't care if you go out of business. That is not their problem.

Tammy had a successful business for many years, but it suffered during the recession in the early 1990s. Like many business owners, she thought the bad times would pass. When cash got tight, she used payroll taxes she withheld from her employees' wages to finance operating costs. She thought she would soon be able to pay the delinquent taxes and all would be fine. But this was not the case. The IRS starting contacting her clients to demand that they send any money owed to Tammy's business to the IRS instead, to pay the delinquent taxes. Once Tammy's clients found out she was financially strapped, they began taking their business elsewhere, and her business completely fell apart. She had to close down her business, she underwent foreclosure on her home, and the IRS started its relentless drumbeat for payment. When she sought legal help some years later, her tax problems had still not been resolved, she was living on minimal income, and she lived in fear that the IRS would take even the small amount of money she was able to earn. Because she had no assets and little hope of a substantial income in the future, she submitted an offer in compromise (this type of offer is discussed in chapter 8, "Neglecting the Tax Man: Unexpected Tax Liabilities and Fights with the IRS").

If payroll tax liability is assessed against your business because you treated some workers as independent contractors and did not withhold payroll taxes, and the IRS or state tax agency later determines that they are employees, you can at least argue that the workers are independent contractors and you owe no tax. The IRS now has a settlement program in place that may enable you to reach an agreement without being forced out of business. However, if you treated your workers as employees and collected payroll taxes from their wages, did not pay these taxes to the tax authorities, and used the tax money to pay other business debts, the IRS and the state tax authorities will come after you with a vengeance. They will hold your business liable for the employees' income taxes, social security taxes (both employee and employer portion), and all other forms of payroll taxes. The tax authorities will assess penalties and interest on top of the taxes owed. Frequently, the total amount owed is so large that the business will never be able to get out of debt. There is not much you can do but shut down your business.

Unfortunately, if you withheld the taxes from your employees' wages but didn't pay it to the IRS, you are liable for the withheld taxes even if you shut down your business, and even if you conducted your business through a limited liability entity. Under the 100 percent penalty imposed by the IRS, all the responsible officers of the business (and the owner of a business is always a responsible officer) can be held personally liable for payment of 100 percent of the so-called trust fund taxes. *Trust fund taxes* are the income taxes withheld on employees' wages and the employees' share of social security taxes that should have been paid to the IRS. These are called trust fund taxes because they are withheld from the money employees otherwise would have been paid in wages. They are deemed to be held "in trust" by the employer (who is deemed to be the trustee) for the benefit of the employees and the U.S. Treasury. These monies simply do not belong to the employer. The employer's share of social security taxes, which are payable out of the employer's own money and not payable from wages otherwise due to the employees, are not trust fund taxes, and the responsible officers of the business are not personally liable for them under federal tax laws. However, some states, such as

California, do hold the responsible officers liable for all payroll taxes, including the employer's share. Responsible officers that can be held liable for the 100 percent penalty include more people than just the business owner. The bookkeeper can be considered a responsible officer if he or she has the authority to sign checks and determine which creditors to pay. Several years ago, the IRS changed the nickname of this penalty from the *100 percent penalty* to the *trust fund penalty* as part of an overall program to make itself seem friendlier to the public. Tax practitioners still refer to it for what it is — a 100 percent penalty. In other words, even if you run your business through a corporation, if you don't pay taxes you withheld from your employees' wages, you are personally liable to the IRS for these taxes.

So, what's the worse that can happen? You get behind in your payroll taxes and you shut down your business. If the tax authorities come after you personally, you will simply file bankruptcy. Wrong! Federal bankruptcy laws prevent trust fund tax liability from being canceled in bankruptcy. In this situation, your only resort is to try to negotiate a deal with the IRS and the state tax authority to pay less than you owe. This type of deal is called an *offer in compromise*. Under this type of deal, you agree that you owe the tax, but you demonstrate that you just cannot pay it. Under the old "no blood from a turnip" principle, the IRS and state authorities will sometimes let you off the hook for payment of less than the total amount of tax owed. These agreements are not easy to get. You must prove that you don't have the money to pay off the tax liability, and that you don't expect to get the money to do so in the future. In addition, the tax authorities sometimes require that you agree that if your earnings increase in the future, you will pay a percentage of your higher earnings to the tax authorities.

If an offer in compromise is not an option, the tax authorities may let you pay off your tax liability in installments.

Under an installment agreement, you agree to pay the full amount of tax due, with penalties imposed (unless the tax authority agrees to waive them) and interest accrued on the full amount due. Interest continues to accrue until you fully pay off the tax liability in agreed-upon installments (generally monthly). One way or another, the IRS collects those payroll taxes.

As the owner of a business, it is your legal responsibility to make sure that payroll taxes are properly paid. To the IRS and state tax agencies, it is not an excuse to say that your accountant was supposed to take care of it and failed to. Reliance on a qualified professional may help you persuade the tax authorities to waive penalties, but it will not persuade them to reduce the taxes you owe. Reliance on a good friend or family member who is not qualified for the job is no excuse at all. You have, at a minimum, a duty to make sure that the person you employ to do the job is capable of doing it.

Sandy relied on her unqualified but well-meaning brother, Joe, to handle the tax payments for her business, including payroll taxes. When cash flow tightened, Joe quit paying payroll taxes and used the money they had to continue to pay trade creditors. When the payroll tax liability exceeded $1 million, Sandy became aware that the payroll taxes were delinquent. She took immediate action to straighten out the situation. She contacted the tax authorities before they contacted her and began installment payments. Nevertheless, she was forced out of business. The tax authorities imposed substantial penalties in addition to the tax she owed, and would not waive the penalties despite her obvious good faith attempt to make matters right. One reason the tax authorities gave for not waiving the penalties was their conclusion that Sandy was negligent when she hired Joe to do this job. In the eyes of the IRS, she did not exercise proper diligence in running her business.

Georgia, on the other hand, was able to get penalties

waived even though payroll taxes were delinquent. She relied upon a well-respected accounting firm to take care of payroll tax matters for her medical practice. Georgia retained that accounting firm only after seeking recommendations from other physician groups in the same medical specialty. The IRS felt that Georgia had acted in a businesslike manner. Although Georgia still had to pay the full amount of payroll taxes due, she was relieved of the penalties, which would have amounted to thousands of dollars in additional liability.

Pay Those Sales Taxes

For many state governments, sales taxes are the biggest source of state revenues. Accordingly, most state tax authorities enforce their sales tax laws with a zealousness unknown even to the IRS. Like payroll taxes, sales taxes are trust fund taxes. The sales tax is actually imposed on the seller who sells tangible products at retail prices, but most state laws allow the seller to charge the purchaser for the sales tax. In this case, the amount paid by the purchaser includes both the actual price of the item purchased and the sales tax. Therefore, the sales tax collected is not the seller's money; the seller is only a collecting agent for the state government. Sales taxes are trust fund taxes, so the state governments are as ardent in collecting sales taxes as they are in collecting payroll taxes. And because sales taxes are imposed on the gross sales price of items sold and at rates as high as 8.5 percent in California, the sales tax liability can become a substantial chunk of money for a business to have to pay. Like payroll taxes, owners of a retail business may be personally liable for unpaid sales taxes, even if they conduct business through a limited liability entity, and sales tax liabilities cannot be canceled in bankruptcy.

Jessica and Lilly owned a small restaurant that historically was open only on weekdays. Several years ago, they decided to keep it open on Saturdays and Sundays as well. Through oversight, their sales for the two additional days did not get properly entered into their accounting system, and sales taxes were not reported and paid for a number of months. Jessica and Lilly were subsequently notified that the State intended to audit their sales. The sales tax auditor sat in the restaurant for the entire day on four randomly selected days. She counted customers and reviewed the total sales for each day. Based on that information, a large amount of additional sales tax was assessed against the restaurant. To make matters worse, Lilly had initially misstated the date she had started doing business on weekends. Unfortunately for her, another sales tax auditor happened to be a regular weekend customer of the restaurant and was able to verify that the weekend days began long before the date Lily gave. Lilly's credibility was ruined, and the sales tax auditors would not reduce the penalties.

If you fail to pay payroll taxes or sales taxes and get caught, it is better to be straight with the tax authorities, take responsibility for your failure, and hope they will give you a break and waive penalties. But don't expect to be relieved from the actual payroll tax liability or sales tax liability. They generally don't have the authority to reduce those taxes, except in an offer in compromise case in which they are able to conclude that you don't have the ability to pay the taxes, nor will you be able to in the future. They also cannot waive interest on the amount due.

Not paying payroll and sales tax liabilities is your worst tax nightmare. You are personally liable for these taxes, even if you operate your business through a limited liability entity. And, even if you file bankruptcy, you are still liable for these taxes; they are nondischargeable in bankruptcy. By comparison, trade creditor debt, delinquent rent payments, and overdue installments of bank loans, are dischargeable in bankruptcy. If you used a limited liability company and did not personally guarantee the trade debt or use personal assets to secure the debt, your personal assets will not be liable for these debts. You can shut down the business if you have to and let these creditors sue the defunct company, but there is no escaping the tax authorities when it comes to payroll and sales taxes.

Learn the Labor Laws and Follow Them

Historically, the labor laws have provided for workers much needed protections from abusive and unscrupulous employers. Minimum wages, safety standards, and protection against race, religious, gender, and age discrimination are but a few of these protections. Employee handbooks now must be provided to employees and information about employee rights posted in areas frequented by employees. In this era of victimhood, however, the labor laws that protect employees have expanded greatly — too far according to many employers, particularly small business owners. For example, the American's with Disabilities Act (ADA) appropriately requires employers to alter work premises to provide access to disabled employees, but the expense of doing so can be enormous and some employers question whether the benefits obtained justify the costs. Employers who have no disabled employees in their employ don't happily incur these costs. Moreover, the American Bar Association recently estimated that 90 percent of all lawsuits brought under the ADA are won by employers, and many are downright frivolous.[63] Sexual harassment is now defined so broadly that many men spend their entire workdays nervously on guard that they might slip up and make an offhand comment capable of being construed as lewd or sexist. The U.S. Supreme Court has ruled that employers are absolutely liable for "quid pro quo" harassment. And in a recent case that received a lot of attention in the legal press, an employer settled a case with a worker who claimed she had been sexually harassed. The employer fired the employee who had allegedly committed the harassment, and he in turn sued the employer for wrongful termination — and won! The employer ended up paying damages to both the employee claiming to have been harassed and the employee she claimed had harassed her. Whereas many federal employee protection laws apply only to employers with more than fifteen employees, state laws sometimes lower the threshold of employers subject to the states' comparable laws. For example, New York applies its laws against sex discrimination to employers with as few as four employees.[64] The liability an employer can suffer from employee claims can be substantial. Fortunately, some insurance companies now offer protection against these claims.

For these reasons, it is important that early in the setup of your business, you get advice from a labor lawyer about the labor laws that will apply to your business, and that you diligently comply with these laws. Unfortunately, however, even businesses that comply with the labor laws can find themselves faced with employee-related lawsuits. These days, if you have to fire an employee, the risk of a lawsuit for unlawful termination is significant. Also, if you must fire an employee who is a minority, a woman, older, or disabled, you run the risk of having a discrimination suit filed against your business.

Regrettably, the best actions employers can take to protect themselves from lawsuits for unlawful termination or prohibited discrimination are not necessarily intuitive. Jessica and Daryl started their own accounting business several years ago. One of their employees had been suffering from depression and was taking antidepressants. However, the employee stopped taking her medication, and one day, she angrily threw a book at Jessica, who ducked just in time to avoid injury. Out of compassion for the employee, Jessica and Daryl did not immediately fire her. Instead, they suggested she take several weeks off from work. The employee took some time off, but when Jessica and Daryl talked to her during this period, she reacted to them in a negative and threatening manner. When Jessica and Daryl decided they no longer felt safe working with this employee and wanted to terminate her employment, they received a letter from the employee's lawyer friend threatening litigation if they did so.

Jessica and Daryl retained a labor lawyer who informed them that, because they had been aware of the employee's disability, under the ADA they could be sued if they fired her. Had Jessica and Daryl fired the employee at the time of the book-throwing incident, they would not have been subject to these laws. The termination of employment, in that case, would have been based on the violent incident, not on the employee's disability.

There are several general guidelines you can follow if you believe an employee's performance is not adequate. First, keep written records of the employee's deficient work. Second, give the employee a warning and an opportunity to improve his or her performance. Third, don't give the employee mixed signals. For example, don't give the employee a large bonus if his or her work is unsatisfactory. While employee reviews can be discomforting, particularly when the employee is performing poorly, it is important to give reviews on a regular basis. Then, if you have to fire an employee, it won't be as likely to be viewed as unfair or the result of discriminatory practice.

Your employees can be your greatest asset and your greatest legal exposure. Immediately learn the labor laws that apply to you when you start your business, and follow them to the letter. Keep in mind that not only is your conduct subject to the law, but so is that of your managers and other employees. You must supervise them all, and if you find that any of your employees are acting inappropriately, take action immediately. This will not only reduce your risk of lawsuits, but will also reduce the risk of bad publicity stemming from charges of discrimination. For example, a woman-owned business can be greatly harmed by charges of sexual harassment. The most important rule to remember, however, is that if any legal questions involving your employees come up, immediately consult with your experienced labor lawyer.

Maintaining a Home Office

If you start and operate your own business, you may want to think about running it out of your own home. More and more women are doing so. If you have children, you may find it particularly beneficial. Even if you don't have children, you may want to work out of your home to save the expense of renting an office elsewhere. Or you may want to do so simply because you prefer to work in your pajamas or other very casual attire. Whatever your reasons may be for wanting to work out of your home, you should keep a few things in mind.

First, you should check with your city's zoning office to make sure it is legal to run a business out of your home. Even if it is legal, if your business draws a lot of clients to your home, your neighbors may become annoyed at the substantial foot traffic and the difficulty of finding parking. If you are running a retail operation, you will also need to find out what type of signs the local law will allow you to have.

If you meet certain requirements, you will be able to take tax deductions for a part of your utilities, insurance, repairs, home security systems, and rent. If you own your home, you will be able to deduct part of your cost of the home through depreciation. To qualify for this deduction, you must regularly use the office portion of your home exclusively for business (but it does not have to be a separate room; a corner will do). Also, you must either use your home as your principal place of business, or, if you regularly meet with your clients and customers, use your home to meet with them. If you use your home only for administrative and management activities (for example, if you are a doctor and you see patients only at the local hospital but you do all your billing from your home) and you don't have another office where you do these activities, you can qualify. If you qualify, you can deduct these expenses for the fraction of your house in which your office is located. The total deductions are limited, however, to the actual profit you make from your business. If you make no profit, you get no deductions.

Most people get excited at the prospect of a tax deduction, especially for expenses that have to be paid anyway, but there is a downside to deducting the cost of your home office. Under the tax laws, if you are married and you and your husband sell your house, you can exclude up to $500,000 of the capital gain you made on the house. This means that the difference between what you sold the house for and the amount you originally paid for it has to be greater than $500,000 before you must pay any tax on the sale. If you are single, you can exclude up to $250,000 on the sale. If you take home office deductions, the home office portion of your house doesn't qualify for this exclusion. When you sell your house, you will owe tax on the portion of the sales price that is allocated to the home office. If your house has appreciated greatly in value, you could end up paying more tax on the sale than you saved earlier by taking home office deductions.

Be Insured

Many women don't buy adequate insurance for their business. They believe that nothing bad will happen, so why spend the money on premiums. This misguided act of frugality can ruin your business. Consider all the bad things that can and do happen. What if a fire starts at your business facility? What if you live in southern California and the facility is damaged by an earthquake? What if a customer falls and suffers serious injuries because the floor is wet? What if an employee suffers a work-related injury? You will be truly sorry you did not spend the few extra thousand dollars for insurance.

Every business is required by law to maintain workers' compensation insurance for its employees. This is a legal obligation and an expense you want to bear. If you don't have workers' compensation insurance and one of your employees gets hurt on the job, you could be sued and found liable for substantial sums of money. If you have workers' compensation insurance, your employees are generally limited to recover only the amounts provided for under that policy, which is generally much less than the amount that might be awarded by damage-happy juries in lawsuits.

Although not a legal obligation, you should also carry liability insurance as well as fire, theft, and other casualty loss insurance. Some liability policies will protect you against employee lawsuits, as well as claims against you for purported negligence (for example, slip-and-fall cases). Don't live in a storybook world where bad things don't happen. You have only to watch the nightly news to see the fallacy in that mind-set. Fires, earthquakes, and thefts happen, employees get injured and file claims; employees file groundless lawsuits; customers get injured and file lawsuits; and customers really don't get injured but file lawsuits anyway. It can happen to you. Anyone doing business in the United States can get sued and suffer casualty losses. Forgoing insurance to save a few thousand dollars can be the death knell of your business, if you later suffer one of these losses. Think about it. One employee lawsuit can easily cost you $100,000 or more in legal fees alone. A settlement on top of that skyrockets the cost. How many small businesses can afford a liability of this magnitude? An injured customer can easily cost your business that much. In other words, it can take only one lawsuit to put you out of business. That is also true with natural disasters. It does not take three or four earthquakes to damage your facility beyond usability — it only takes one. Tornados, fires, hurricanes, floods, and many other natural disasters can ruin a business, and none of them are predictable. Insurance will help insulate you from that lack of predictability.

In running a business, good intentions are nice, but they don't cut the legal mustard. This is one aspect of your life where you will clearly be held to the standard of a responsible adult. You are expected to comply fully with the laws. If you don't have time to handle all the legal matters yourself, you are obligated to hire people with the qualifications necessary to carry out your legal obligations. Even after you hire these people, you are expected to oversee their work and make sure they are adequately performing their jobs. The laws that apply to businesses are many and complex. The Chamber of Commerce in most cities can provide materials to acquaint you with the rules that may apply to a new business you wish to start. The Small Business Administration also has helpful materials. In addition, a number of books are available at local bookstores or libraries that help new businesses identify and meet their legal obligations. The paperwork may be boring and tedious and seem never to end. It is important to your business success, however, that you buckle down and get it done.

In the preceding chapters, I discussed several types of legal documents — prenuptial agreements, and divorce property settlement agreements. In later chapters, I will discuss property ownership, tax returns, wills, trusts, and powers of attorney. Many women will sign these documents when they are placed in front of them even though they don't take the time to read or don't really understand what the documents mean. Have you ever signed a legal document you didn't read just because your husband or your father told you to do so? Did you ever find the language in a document so confusing that you didn't really understand what the document meant to you but you went ahead and signed it anyway? Do you know that not reading a document or not understanding what it means doesn't let you off the legal hook if things go awry? Do you know that generally you will be held responsible for all the obligations you committed to in a document even though you didn't really know you were agreeing to obligations? In the next chapter, I will help you avoid the legal mistake of . . .

LEGAL MISTAKE #6:

SIGNING DOCUMENTS YOU DON'T READ OR UNDERSTAND —
Or, Run When Your Husband Says, "Just Sign Here, Honey"

"In trust I found treason."
Elizabeth I

"God is love, but get it in writing."
Gypsy Rose Lee

"Just sign here, honey." Four simple words imbued with trust, benevolence, and assurance. Four simple words that have the power to totally devastate your financial well-being, shatter your life as you know it, and invalidate your trust in those closest to you.

How often has the following situation happened to you? In walks your husband with a loan agreement, real estate deed, joint income tax return, or some other legal document, and he asks you to sign it. Likely, he will give you some brief explanation of what the document is about, why he thinks it's a good thing to do, and why you need to sign it. Maybe he will even have a pen available to make your signing that much easier. Sometimes the significance of the legal documents is highlighted when your husband asks you to go with him to his lawyer's office to sign them. Even then, your husband may try to allay any fears you have by assuring you that your signature is simply a formality and that you won't be responsible for anything. You probably won't even ask him why you are being asked to sign the document if your signature doesn't mean anything. More likely, like many wives, you will sign the document with only a few questions, if any at all, about what it all means. Your husband's reassurances will allay any concerns you might harbor about signing the document. After all, a marriage is built on trust and the commitment to shared lives, and your past experiences with your spouse probably give you no reason to doubt his sincerity and good intentions now. Unfortunately, in some cases your husband's reassurances and your trust in him may result in your financial bankruptcy. Once you sign a legal document, you are legally bound by it and legally responsible for fulfilling the obligations called for in the document.

What happens if you do take legal responsibility by reading and understand legal documents before you sign them? You may be able to avert financial disaster for both you and your husband, you will have a better handle on what the future holds for you as well as your family, and you will be better able to protect your as well as your family's financial well-being. In this chapter, we explore some of the pitfalls and catastrophes that can befall women who do sign legal documents they don't understand and the benefits that accrue when they don't.

Don't Sign Legal Documents before You Read and Understand Them

Betty was a lively forty-two-year-old woman. She had been married to a farmer, Jim, for eighteen of those years. Betty and Jim lived a modest but comfortable life in a small community where they owned their own home, sent their children to good public schools, and were able to save enough to take a nice vacation each year. They were active in community and charitable activities and had a lot of close friends in their community. They had a traditional marriage: Jim made the money and Betty took care of the house and kids.

As is common in farming, Jim financed a significant portion of the capital required to plant crops each year and improve his farm through bank loans. Betty was not active in the farming herself and did not work, she had some separate property she inherited from her parents. Betty was frequently asked to jointly sign the loan documents, or loan guarantees, for the loans made to Jim. The amounts of the loans and guarantees that Betty signed totaled several hundred thousand dollars. She signed these loan documents without reviewing them and, more significantly, without any appreciable thought of the legal liability she was assuming by doing so. The banks later discovered that Jim had given them false financial statements when he applied for the loans. Jim's farming business quickly collapsed, and he was indicted for fraud and other felony crimes. In addition, he was sued by every bank that he owed money to. Other creditors, like the stores where he bought seed and lumber, also started demanding payment of the credit they had extended to Jim.

All along, Betty believed in Jim and had no hint that their life was built on fraud and deceit. When Jim's transgressions came to light, her world shattered. In an instant, she discovered that not only was she no longer financially secure, but the man she had spent much of her adult life with, had had children with, and believed to be honest, trustworthy, and successful, had betrayed her. Predictably, Betty and Jim's relationship quickly disintegrated and divorce proceedings began. As legal proceedings progressed against Jim, Betty learned two devastating facts. First, she had only her separate property on which she could rely to support herself and their children, because all the marital property she and Jim had accumulated was subject to his creditors' claims. Second, she was also named as a defendant along with Jim in numerous lawsuits filed by the banks that had loaned money to Jim and his business. The banks claimed several hundred thousand dollars in damages, and because Betty had jointly signed the loans and guarantees, the banks viewed her just as legally responsible for repayment of the loans as Jim. Moreover, the banks erroneously suspected that she had spirited away considerable amounts of money and was hiding it somewhere they couldn't find it — like in a foreign bank account.

Jim eventually filed for bankruptcy protection, and Betty was confronted with a difficult choice: she could file bankruptcy herself and forfeit the separate property that she needed to support herself and her children to Jim's creditors, or she could legally fight her personal liability to the banks at a considerable cost. She had no chance of saving her interest in their community property because the bankruptcy laws provide that *all* community property is subject to creditor claims, even if only one spouse files bankruptcy. Betty chose to fight. Her lawyers argued that she was not personally liable on the bank loans because the banks had not relied on her personal creditworthiness, or the small amount of her own separate property, to make the loans. Eventually, Betty was able to settle the lawsuits with the banks for far less than the hundreds of thousands of dollars owed, but only after she incurred thousands of dollars in legal fees and endured several years of financial uncertainty and personal anguish.

Unfortunately, Betty's problems didn't end there. She now had the IRS on her back, a creditor far more forbidding and with far more power than the banks. Under the tax laws, a debtor is taxed on the amount of any debt that is forgiven or canceled; this is called *cancellation of debt income*. Once Betty was off the hook with the banks, she had to contend with the reality that the IRS might assess impossible tax liabilities against her based on the thousands of dollars of cancellation of debt income it might claim she realized when the banks agreed that she did not owe them on the loans. The greater the loan amounts that the banks were willing to walk away from, the greater her potential tax liability. Once again, Betty hired lawyers and faced more legal fees and financial uncertainty until a settlement was worked out with the IRS.

What would have happened if Betty had not signed the loan documents in the first place? She still would have suffered a major reversal in lifestyle and would have faced the difficulty of raising her children alone without a secure income. Her capacity to trust people would still have been dramatically shaken. However, the lesson to be learned here is that Betty might have been able to avoid the huge expense in legal fees and the months of anguish and uncertainty she faced in fighting the banks. She might have been able to avoid the daunting potential of astronomical tax liabilities leveled by the IRS. Betty signed the loan documents without any serious consideration and understanding of the potential consequences to her, or whether she really needed to sign for Jim to get the loans. If she had not done so, she could have avoided much expense and turmoil.

Judy Paige Burns, the former wife of high-flying land speculator Robert Burns, faced the same dilemma. Judy met Robert several years after she took second place in a Miss America pageant. At the time, she was trying to launch a career in Hollywood and he was jet setting around, cutting big deals. They were soon married, and Judy became a homemaker. They had a 14,000-square-foot mansion in Paradise Valley with eleven fireplaces, a nanny, an English estate, and much more. Judy left the business to Robert and signed promissory notes, corporate filings — whatever was placed in front of her. Judy says she often read about Robert's deals in the newspapers before he would tell her about them. If she asked questions, "he would just blow up." Robert's financial empire ran into hard times. He defaulted on loans, a bank foreclosed on his assets, and lawsuits started. In 1994, sheriff's deputies and collection agents hauled away jewelry, artwork, televisions, cameras, and other expensive items from their home. Their marriage deteriorated and they started divorce proceedings. The divorce began amicably, but it took a turn for the worse when Judy discovered that Robert had a mistress, and when he decided to treat her like he would any other creditor. Judy is now fighting for her share of their marital estate. As a codefendant in numerous lawsuits brought by Robert's creditors, however, she faces the real possibility that she will lose everything she gets from the divorce. Or as Judy herself puts it, "I'll still be on the hook for millions and millions of dollars, and I didn't do anything. I was just a housewife."[65] The lesson Judy learned, and one you can too, from her experience is that the legal documents you sign have real legal consequences for which you will be responsible.

Sometimes it's a business partner or business advisor who persuades a person to sign documents he or she doesn't understand. Even though this book is about mistakes that women can avoid, I would like to share with you a couple of stories about the mistakes that several famous men have made that can and do happen to women. Kareem Abdul-Jabbar, a former Los Angeles Laker basketball player, was persuaded to sign legal documents by his business manager and lost millions of dollars. In fact, many people speculate that Kareem had to continue playing with the Lakers long after he would have preferred to retire because of the losses he suffered.

What did Kareem's business manager do? He convinced Kareem to invest in hotels and restaurants and Kareem did so without independently evaluating the soundness of the investments; he simply trusted and relied upon his business manager's advice. The Balboa Hotel in Newport Beach, California, was one of these investments. Kareem bought a 19 percent interest in a partnership that bought and operated the hotel. Even though Kareem owned only 19 percent of the partnership, he signed a bank loan for $1.8 million that made him jointly and severally liable for the entire amount borrowed. This means that if the partnership didn't pay back the loan, the bank could make Kareem pay 100 percent of the loan and not just his share. Around the same time, Kareem's business manager spearheaded another investment partnership for a hotel called the Inn at Laguna. The same bank loaned money for this hotel. Kareem's business manager and the bank agreed to consolidate the separate loans that applied to the Balboa Hotel and the Inn at Laguna into one combined loan for a reported $4.5 million. Once again, Kareem's business manager put another promissory note in front of Kareem and he signed it without question. What Kareem didn't know then was that this second note made him jointly and severally liable for the entire combined loan — including the loan for the Inn at Laguna in which he owned nothing. As you can probably guess, the hotels failed and the partnerships filed for bankruptcy. The bank looked around for solvent people who had signed these notes, and it found Kareem. Only then did Kareem become aware that he had signed notes that made him liable for 100 percent of the loan, including that part of the loan for the Inn at Laguna, a property he did not even own. The inevitable lawsuits ensued and Kareem claimed $55 million of damages. He told the court that he had not read any of the notes or other documents that his business manager had him sign because of his "complete faith and trust" in the business manager.[66]

Mike Douglass, a former San Diego Charger linebacker, had a similar experience. He claims he was tricked into guaranteeing $90,000 of real estate loans for his lawyer/agent, who later failed to pay the loans. Mike says he signed the guarantee of the bank loans because his lawyer/agent was a college friend whom he had known for eight years and he trusted him. "No matter how long you know someone, I learned that you need to rely on other people to see if there is truth in the relationship," Douglass said.[67] He sued his lawyer/agent for $3 million.

The lesson that Kareem and Mike learned is that you can't afford to completely trust your professional advisors when it comes to your legal affairs. If you delegate this authority, you are the one that's left holding the bag when things go wrong.

Angela didn't rely on trust. Angela was a take-charge kind of person and never left anything, including her business and legal affairs, to chance. She acknowledged the significance of legal documents and knew she should never sign a legal document she did not understand. Her husband, Terry, appreciated this quality about her and frequently relied on her to handle much of their business and legal matters. One day Terry gave her a loan document and security agreement to sign. Finding the language incomprehensible, Angela consulted her lawyers, and it was a good thing she did. Terry thought the only security he was giving to the bank was the real estate that the loan funds were going to be used to acquire. He also thought it was a nonrecourse loan, meaning that the bank, if Terry defaulted on the loan, could only foreclose on the property. It could not take other property owned by Terry and Angela. However, when Angela's attorneys reviewed the loan and security agreements, they found that the bank reserved the right to seize other properties and did not limit its recourse only to the property being acquired. Had Terry and Angela signed the papers as they were initially drafted, they would have obligated themselves to much more risk to their financial security than they intended. Because of Angela's vigilance, a significant misunderstanding that could have been very costly to her and Terry was averted.

When you are faced with signing a legal document, think about Betty, Judy, Kareem, and Mike and the financial disasters they faced; think about Angela and the financial disaster she averted by legal vigilance. Keep in mind that if you sign documents you have not read or don't understand, financial peril can raise its ugly head in many different situations. You could sign a loan agreement and mortgage not realizing that your home has just been put up as collateral and that you and your family will lose your home if the loan is not repaid. You could sign a joint income tax return with your husband, not realizing that signing it makes you individually liable for 100 percent of the taxes due. You could sign one of many other types of documents, each of which can expose you to financial disaster — real estate deeds, leases, contracts to buy or sell goods or services, indemnities, guarantees, and partnership or corporate buy/sell agreements.

Any type of legal document carries with it some form of obligation. Before you sign it, you want to make sure that you understand what the document means, what the consequences of signing it are, and what your responsibilities will be from signing the document. Don't be misled into believing that your execution of the documents will not expose you to any liability or consequences. If there are no real legal obligations being imposed on you, your signature is not needed. You would not be asked to sign the document.

Don't Sign Business Documents until Your Lawyer Reviews Them

You may find the legalese in the document totally incomprehensible. What do you do when there is no possibility of understanding this thing on your own? Hire a lawyer to explain it to you. You may not want to spend the money to do this, but spending a little now may save you considerable heartache, financial disaster, and enormous legal fees down the road. If you simply cannot afford a lawyer, your community may have a legal clinic where you can get low-cost legal help, or you may be able to find a helpful law book.

Women who are uneducated, too poor to hire a lawyer, or unsophisticated in the ways of business are not the only ones who sign documents they don't understand. The number of highly successful, sophisticated, and rich women who sign legal documents without having them carefully reviewed by their own lawyer to make sure their personal interests are protected is surprising. Like Kareem and Mike, they often rely on the assurances of their business partner or employer, or on the advice of their business partner's or employer's lawyer, that they are well protected and should simply sign. Most often, these women fail to hire their own lawyer because they don't want to spend the money (even if they are wealthy), or because they are concerned that hiring their own lawyer might be misconstrued as a lack of trust in their business partner or employer. Neither reason justifies their failure to exercise self-responsibility and make sure they are protected before signing any significant legal documents.

A very successful and well-known musician had been in business with a promoter for a number of years and had signed several agreements with him. She never hired her own lawyer to review these documents and instead relied upon the advice of the promoter's lawyer. Obviously, the promoter's lawyer worked for him and strived to get the promoter the best deal possible, without necessarily alerting the musician of his actions. After they had worked together for some years, the promoter was approached by someone who wanted to buy his company. At the buyer's insistence, the musician retained her own lawyer to represent her interests in the sale. Her new lawyer found that she had previously signed legal documents in which she had unknowingly signed away to the promoter a substantial portion of her most valuable assets. As a result, her share of the sales proceeds was significantly less than she thought she rightfully deserved. She saved a few thousand dollars in legal fees in the early years, but lost millions on the sale.

Beverly was neither rich nor famous. She also didn't have her lawyer review an agreement she had signed, and she paid a huge price later. Beverly inherited one-half of the stock ownership of a company from her father, and the son of the other co-owner, Eric, inherited the other half. Beverly and Eric subsequently decided to sell a one-third interest to Kevin, who was not related to either of them. Kevin and Eric convinced Beverly to enter into a buy-sale agreement, which gave the shareholders the right to buy the shares of any of the three who died or became disabled. They also agreed that if any of them wanted to withdraw from the company, after two years elapsed from signing the agreement, the other two would buy out that person. The written agreement, however, was not drafted to specify this. Instead, the agreement provided that the right to withdraw and make the others buy out the shares of the with-drawing shareholder existed only *during* the first two years after the agreement was signed, instead of providing, as they intend-ed, that the buyout right started *after* the two-year period and continued indefinitely. It may well be that the agreement was just poorly drafted, and that Kevin and Eric did not purposely mislead Beverly. However, she did not hire her own lawyer to review the agreement, and did not realize that it did not match her understanding or expectation.

After Kevin got involved in the company, Beverly's role began to diminish. She was often left out of the decision mak-ing, and she became unhappy. Beverly decided she wanted to sell her interest in the company. Because she thought the buy-out right did not become effective until after two years from the date they signed the buy-sale agreement, she quietly waited for the two-year period to end. When two years had expired, she hired a lawyer to help her proceed with the buyout process. In reading the agreement she had signed, her lawyer quickly realized that the time period for exercising this right had already come and gone. Beverly's lawyer nevertheless told Eric and Kevin that she wanted to sell out her interest and anticipated doing so according to what she had understood the agreement to be. Eric and Kevin refused to buy her out. They claimed that the parties always intended to limit the buyout right to the first two years after the agreement was signed, that the agreement was correct, and that they were under no obligation to buy out Beverly or pay her anything at all. It was a classic case of "he said, she said" in a business context. Eventually, Beverly and her lawyer settled this case for a much lower monetary amount than Beverly would have been entitled to under the buyout provision she thought she had agreed to, and thought she had complied with by waiting for the two-year period to elapse.

If Beverly had retained her own lawyer to review the buy-sale agreement before she signed it, she would have known about the two-year limitation from the outset and could have negotiated for a longer buyout period. At the least, she would have been made aware of the two-year limitation on the buyout and could have submitted her buyout demand to Eric and Kevin within the two-year period. Beverly learned the hard way — don't sign documents that affect your business or legal affairs until your own lawyer has reviewed them for you.

Don't Sign Blank Legal Documents

Jane was a nurse. She married her high school sweetheart, Alex, who, after college, went into real estate and became a very successful real estate developer. Their marriage had lasted twenty-four years without any major difficulties. They had a nice home in the suburbs, their children were out of college and making their own way in the world, and Jane and Alex were headed toward a quiet and pleasant retirement. Most of their wealth was tied up in Alex's real estate projects. One day Alex asked Jane to sign a number of blank quit claim deeds. He told her it would make it easier for him to conduct his business if he didn't have to get her signature all the time — he could have it "on file" as it were, and he wouldn't have to bother her as much. Jane signed the deeds without thinking twice about it. After all, she had been married to Alex for years and he had always taken good care of her and the children. (Legally, signatures on real estate deeds must be notarized, but someone in Alex's position typically has a notary in their employ and has no problem getting signatures on blank deeds notarized.)

Eight months later, Alex announced that he was leaving Jane for the proverbial younger woman — a thirty-year-old who worked in his office. During the divorce proceedings, Alex produced lots of quit claim deeds, all signed by Jane, that now had been filled in for each of the real estate properties and purported to transfer 100 percent of their many real estate properties entirely to him. These deeds were the blank ones Jane had signed earlier. Alex's lawyer argued that with these deeds, Jane had intentionally and knowingly made a gift of all these properties to Alex, that Alex owned them entirely, and that Jane had no legal right to any of the properties. Jane's lawyer argued that Jane had not knowingly signed over her rights to the property, and that she had been duped. Months of bruising legal battles ensued. Eventually, Jane agreed to settle for far less property than she really was entitled to. She wanted to end the fighting, and given that she had signed the quit claim deeds, her lawyer could not assure her that she would win in court. As Jane learned, signing a blank legal document is tricky business. You never know what it will be used for and how it could come back to haunt you.

For example, Constance and Patricia Kiesewetter never

thought for a moment that the blank promissory notes they signed for their father would later be used by their brother, William, in his attempt to cut them out of their mother's estate, purported to be worth millions. Shortly after their mother's death, William filed what he claimed was their mother's last will. It left everything to him and nothing to his two sisters. An earlier will had divided up the mother's estate equally between the three children. At first things appeared to go amicably. The three met at their mother's home several weeks after her death to divide among themselves silverware and jewelry. After Constance and Patricia left, William called the police and reported the property stolen. Their relationship disintegrated from that point and numerous lawsuits ensued. Among other claims, William claimed that the promissory notes reflected numerous loans that his father and mother had made to Constance and Patricia and that his father intended for William to collect on them. Constance and Patricia claimed otherwise. They said their father had asked for the notes only to provide an accounting of how much each child got.[68]

As these stories show, you should never sign blank legal documents, particularly ones that can be used to transfer ownership of your interest in the primary assets that make up your financial security. Your husband or business partner may tell you it will make it easier to do business. But, remember, signing blank documents is not always a tool of expediency — it can be a setup.

Don't Sign Loan Documents You Don't Want to Be Liable For

Betty faced phenomenal difficulties when her husband, Jim, defaulted on millions of dollars of bank loans she had co-signed. In this particular case, Jim had borrowed the money based on fraudulent representations made to the banks of his financial worth. However, if you co-sign loan documents, you can encounter substantial liability even when your husband has done nothing wrong. Your husband may not be able to repay a business loan even when he has acted with the best of intentions toward you and the bank. Many things can cause a business to be unprofitable and loans not to be repaid: mismanagement, too rapid growth, unanticipated competition, or simple bad luck. In these cases, it is still better if you are not personally liable, along with your husband, for the loan. If you have your own assets, you may be able to protect them against attachment by the bank. If your husband must file for bankruptcy protection, you may be able to preserve your own good credit. In this way, you and your husband will together be in a much better position to make a fresh start.

Sara wanted help getting out from under a large bank loan her husband, Jack, had taken out to expand his business. Since shortly after they were married, Jack had owned and operated a retail store. Sara helped out at the store part-time and, when not at the store, took care of their children and home. Although the income from the retail store was not substantial, it was steady and provided them with an enjoyable lifestyle. They owned their own home and had managed to put away some money toward their retirement. Sara had also inherited some money from her parents, which she kept in a separate mutual fund.

As their children approached college age, however, Jack felt he needed to increase their income so they could help the children with college expenses. Jack opened several additional stores in nearby cities. He secured a loan from his longtime banker to finance the improvements needed in the new retail stores, to purchase inventory and the office furniture and equipment needed to run the stores, and to provide working capital for the startup period. He operated his business as a sole proprietorship and was personally liable for repayment of the loan.

Because Jack and Sara's business was small, the banker asked that Sara sign the loan as well as Jack and that they give the bank a security interest in the existing business, their home, and in her separate inheritance. Sara trusted Jack's decision to open the new stores and willingly agreed to cosign the loan and put up her own assets as collateral.

Unfortunately, the new stores were not successful. Jack became despondent and his self-esteem disintegrated as he realized that not only was he going to lose the new stores, but he also was going to lose the old one he had successfully operated for years. Shortly thereafter, he suffered an emotional breakdown and required hospitalization. When Jack was released from the hospital, his doctor kept him under heavy medication. Sara was confronted with not only taking care of a very sick husband, but also having to deal alone with the financial crisis that resulted when their bank eventually began to foreclosure on their assets, including her separate inheritance.

In this case, it might not have been possible for Jack to obtain the loan without Sara's agreement to be a codebtor and the posting of her separate inheritance as security for the loan. However, Jack and Sara never challenged the bank on these conditions and did not check with other banks to see if they could get the same loan without Sara becoming jointly liable and without putting up her separate inheritance as security for the loan. It is possible they could have at least protected her separate inheritance, and possibly their home. Although they still would have faced financial difficulties, particularly during Jack's recovery, they at least would have had some savings to fall back on.

If you are asked to cosign a loan or personal guarantee with your spouse, find out if the lender will make the loan on the sole basis of your husband's creditworthiness, or on his separate businesses and assets. Your personal liability might not be required. You will have to be a tough negotiator, however, because lenders strive to get the most security they can for their loans. If the lender absolutely refuses to make the loan without your personal liability, carefully weigh the benefits of the loan to you and your family against the potential liability you are assuming. (As discussed in chapter 4, "Starting a Business" you and your husband should both try to limit your liability for loans through the use of a limited liability entity.)

Even if the lender does not demand your personal liability, it may require that a loan be collateralized by a security interest in marital property. If so, it will require that you and your husband both sign a mortgage, deed of trust, or other document giving the lender the right to foreclose on your marital property if the loan is not repaid. Nevertheless, you can give the lender a security interest in your marital property without also committing yourself to personal liability and may be able to do so without committing your separate property as security for the loan. Your goal is to minimize your exposure and the exposure of your assets to liability for repayment of the loan. In all cases, make sure you understand what is going on and that you and your husband mutually agree that borrowing the money is the right course of action. The law will assume that you knowingly consented to legal liability when you signed a loan document, or when you let your share of marital property be put up as collateral for repayment of a loan.

Never (or Almost Never) Deed Your Interest in Your Home to Your Husband

Barbara's husband, Glen, was very controlling and domineering. During their marriage, he had slowly and methodically undermined Barbara's self-confidence and self-esteem. When he presented her with a quitclaim deed to sign that assigned her interest in their home to him, she did so without question. (A quitclaim deed is a legal document that transfers your interest in real estate to whomever you assign it to in the deed on an "as is" basis; this and other types of deeds are explained in "Failing to Protect Legal Title to Your Property.") She could not face another angry, nasty confrontation with him. When he subsequently filed for divorce, she was dismayed to find that the quitclaim deed she had signed could be legally binding on her. She had, in her view, only signed it under duress. Glen disputed her version of events, and the judge hearing the divorce case did not readily accept Barbara's claim that she signed the quitclaim deed only under duress. Eventually, she and Glen reached an out-of-court property settlement. However, like Jane, the terms Barbara settled for were far less favorable to her than she likely would have been able to negotiate had she not signed the quitclaim deed in the first place.

The most substantial asset many couples own is their house. When a couple is buying their house, they generally acquire the property in both their names. Joint ownership in this case is appropriately based as much on emotional needs as legal niceties. And for couples whose primary asset is their home, their lender will typically require joint liability on the home mortgage. Sometimes the husband or wife may later ask the other to sign a quitclaim deed transferring sole ownership to the other spouse. If you are ever asked to do this, consult a lawyer first. Sometimes you may be asked to sign a quitclaim deed for a totally appropriate purpose. For example, married couples often transfer their ownership to their own home by quitclaim deed to a trust established for both of them in order to avoid probate. (This type of trust is discussed in chapter 10, entitled "Failing to Plan for Your Death or Incapacity.") In this case, the wife is not transferring over her interest to the husband. Both the husband and wife maintain their joint interest in the home; only now it is held in a trust. In other cases, however, a husband may ask his wife to do so with the intent of subsequently divorcing his wife and trying to take complete ownership of the house. The husband often feels justified in doing this if he has been the sole wage earner of the marriage. He reasons that it was his hard work that bought the house, and his wife should not benefit from it. The husband may use threats of violence to coerce his wife to quitclaim her interest in their home. Or he maybe able to cajole her into doing so by convincing her that the transfer is simply a formality that will make their record keeping easier. He reassures her that he will, of course, always take care of her and the children.

There may be a few legitimate reasons to quitclaim your interest in your home to your husband so that he alone owns it, but they are hard to envision. If your husband asks you to quit-claim your interest in the home to him, you should generally assume he is up to no good, particularly when you are jointly liable on the mortgage. Typically, when this situation arises, your husband is looking ahead and is planning to leave you. He is taking steps to improve his position in the inevitable proper-ty settlement dispute. When he leaves you, he will assert that the house is entirely his. Your husband will insist that your quitclaim to him evidences that you have no interest in the property — that it was his separate property all along, or that you gave him your interest in exchange for something else. He will contend that you are now claiming ownership in the house only because of your distress and anger over his decision to divorce you. The quitclaim deed will support his claim. Although you may be able to persuade a judge that you were tricked into signing the quit-claim deed and that it should be set aside, there is no guarantee. At the very least, you will be put into a far worse bargaining position than you would have been without the quitclaim deed. This will result in greater legal fees and, most likely, a lower property settlement than you would have obtained had you retained your legal interest in the home. As a general rule, there is no good reason to deed over your interest in your home to your husband, so that you no longer have an express ownership interest, and he alone owns it. There may be exceptions to this rule, and there may be situations when it in fact makes sense, but they will be few and far between. You should never sign a quitclaim deed without first getting advice from your own lawyer. Don't let your husband railroad you into it. Otherwise, on divorce settlement day you and your children may be literally homeless.

The stories in this chapter all emphasize how important it is that you not sign legal documents that you haven't read or don't understand and never sign blank documents. Any time you are presented with a legal document such as a loan document or a quitclaim deed, remember that if you sign it, the law will assume that you read the document, understood it, and agreed to the legal consequences of signing it. Even simple agreements can contain legalese that may be difficult for a non-lawyer to fully understand. If you can afford it, you should always have your own independent lawyer review legal agreements for you before you agree to incur the legal consequences. And always keep in mind this basic principal: if there aren't real legal obligations being imposed on you, you would not be asked to sign the document in the first place.

So far we have talked about a lot of legal documents. We have also talked about the need to read and understand the legal documents you sign and to have a good lawyer help you review or prepare these documents. Although many people may feel that working with a lawyer is a fate worse than death, as we have found in this book, it is at times extremely important that you do so. Have you ever hired a lawyer? Did you feel that he or she listened to you? Did the lawyer do a good job for you? Did you ever wish you could get rid of the lawyer but didn't know how to do it? The next chapter helps you deal with your fears, apprehensions, and uncertainty about dealing with lawyers and gives you guidelines to think about when hiring a lawyer or deciding whether you need to fire a lawyer.

LEGAL MISTAKE #7:

FAILING TO HIRE AND
(WHEN APPROPRIATE)
FIRE LAWYERS

"There are three reasons why lawyers are being used more and more in scientific experiments. First, every year there are more and more of them around. Second, lab assistants don't get attached to them. And, third, there are some things that rats just won't do."

Anonymous

Many people try hard to avoid lawyers. Over the years, we have gained the reputation of being abrasive, untrustworthy, arrogant, and unprincipled. Regrettably, I have to agree that some lawyers have done much to deserve their reputation. I am reminded of the definition of *lawyer* provided in *White's Law Dictionary:*

> *lawyer:* someone who is trained in the manipulation of the law. For corporations, there are two distinct types of lawyers: "in-house" and "outhouse," the latter term accurately suggesting the nature of what lawyers produce.[69]

While the public may be skeptical, there are still many fine lawyers who do their work honorably, professionally, and truly with their clients' best interests at heart. And when things go wrong, your lawyer may well be your best defender and protector. Earlier I talked about hiring lawyers to represent you in divorce in chapter 3, "Failing to Protect Yourself and Your Children in Divorce." In this chapter, I talk more generally about hiring lawyers.

Hiring lawyers is one area where women are markedly different from men. Women are much more reluctant than men are to hire lawyers. There appear to be two basic reasons. First, women are generally more reluctant than men to incur the high cost of legal fees. Second, women are more intimidated by lawyers. The first concern is real. Lawyers do cost money. However, the cost of hiring a lawyer and getting the work done right in the first place can often save you much more in dollars and aggravation in the long run. The second concern is not real. It seems to evolve from the deep-rooted pedestal of authority that our society has granted lawyers and doctors. It ignores the true role of your lawyer — to provide legal services to you and to advise you to the best of his or her ability. Finding the lawyer with the expertise that you need, and whom you can also trust and feel comfortable working with, may seem difficult, but will be more manageable if you do your homework.

Hire a Lawyer and Do It Right

Lawyers are unquestionably expensive, but the real question you should ask yourself is, Are legal services worth the cost? The answer is frequently yes. In many cases, payment of legal fees up front to get the job done right can save many times the amount of fees that might have to be paid later to fix a matter that has gone legally astray. Hiring a lawyer can also save you from unnecessary heartaches and headaches and the irreparable loss that can result from legal messes.

Ruth's husband, Mac, had formed several corporations through which he conducted various investments and activities in the entertainment industry. The corporations were legally formed by the proper filings with the office of the Secretary of State, but not much else was done according to proper legal form. Stock certificates weren't issued, and minutes weren't prepared to authorize corporate actions or elect directors or officers. Money was funneled from one entity to another and to the owner without any documentation whatsoever. Because Mac failed to observe the legal formalities of treating each corporation as a separate, distinct legal entity, it was not clear which entity owned what asset, which entity owed money to others, or which entity earned what income. Long after Mac died, Ruth wanted to sell one of the corporate assets for a lot of money. The buyer (or, more precisely, the buyer's lawyer) demanded proof as to which entity actually held legal title to the asset, and who was a duly appointed officer of that entity and had the legal authority to act on its behalf. Because of the mess in which Mac had left the corporations, there was no way to tell. Ruth had to hire a lawyer to straighten out the mess, and it cost her thousands of dollars more in legal fees and other costs than it would have cost Mac to pay a lawyer to do it right in the first place and to maintain the corporations properly after that. In addition, because it was not possible to truly know the ownership of each corporation or who had legal authority to act on behalf of each of the corporations, the buyer seriously considered walking away from the deal. The buyer was legitimately worried that some unknown third party might later claim legal ownership of the corporations or the asset the buyer wanted to buy and sue the buyer to get it back.

Katie had a much different experience when she was selling her business. Her buyer also asked for copies of all the corporate documentation. The buyer wanted to see for herself that all major corporate actions had been appropriately approved, and that the legal ownership of the company was exactly as Katie represented. Fortunately, Katie had been nothing short of scrupulous in making sure her corporate records were kept right and up to date. And she paid her lawyer only several hundred dollars a year to do so. As a result, her corporate records were pristine. Her lawyer simply took the corporate minute book to a copying service, had the contents of the book copied in its entirety, and mailed the copies to the buyer's legal counsel. Done! The buyer's lawyer got all she needed to evaluate the ownership, and no angst or suspicions were triggered that might have caused the buyer to hesitate on the deal. Katie's foresight, and her willingness to pay some up-front costs to make sure her business's legal affairs were in good order, saved her a lot in legal fees later when she decided to sell her business. It saved more than just dollars, however — it saved time, trouble, and anxiety. There were no questions or suspicions to be resolved to the buyer's satisfaction that could have delayed or, even worse, cost Katie the deal. There was no scrambling to find lost documents or to find other ways to verify ownership. And there were no gaps or discrepancies that made the buyer wary of going forward with the deal. It was straightforward, clean, and beneficial to all involved. It was the way to do business.

It almost always pays to hire a lawyer who can do the job right. Although you will incur up-front legal fees, doing it right legally at the outset can save you thousands of dollars in legal fees that you might otherwise have to pay in the future to straighten out a legal mess, and it may even save a business deal. If you are not able to afford a lawyer, legal self-help books are available, and in some communities, legal clinics provide low-cost legal services. But before embarking on your own journey through the legal maze, you should question whether you are prepared to take the time to learn the law and to handle every time-consuming detail to represent yourself, such as filing items in court, drafting documents, and researching arcane legal issues. You may conclude that it's cheaper to hire an experienced lawyer to represent you, while you continue to devote your time to what you do best — running your business and adding value to it.

Hire the Lawyer Who Fits Your Needs and Works with You

When you decide to hire a lawyer, consider only lawyers known for the particular expertise you need. In fact, you may need different lawyers for different purposes. For example, the lawyer who handles your business legal matters will probably not have the expertise needed to defend you in a lawsuit. It has been decades since lawyers could adequately practice in many different legal fields. The law has simply become too complex, and most lawyers specialize in one or at most a few areas.

If you need a lawyer, you should ask friends, acquaintances, other businesspersons, and family members for referrals. Many local bar associations have referral services, but more experienced attorneys often don't participate in these services. Your accountant or other lawyers you know may also be able to refer you to a suitable lawyer. However, keep in mind that professionals often refer clients to other professionals who refer clients back to them, and you may not be referred to the lawyer most equipped to work with you and deal with your specific needs. On the other hand, other lawyers and professionals have the broadest experience in dealing with lawyers and have had the opportunity to work with many. This vantage point often makes them terrific referral sources, as long as they make the referral based on your individual needs and not as a payback.

Meet with the lawyer you think you might want to hire, and see how you feel about him or her. Do you feel this is a person whom you would be comfortable calling and talking over your problems? Do you feel you could trust him or her to give honest evaluations of your legal matters and to keep you timely informed of developments in a timely manner? Always keep in mind that you ultimately call the shots. Your lawyer's job is to advise you about the benefits and hurdles you may encounter in a particular situation and to recommend what he or she thinks is the best course for you. You want an advisor, not a dictator; you pay the fees, not vice versa.

You want a lawyer who is tough enough to stand up to your opponents. Lawyers often play the role of warriors without weapons. In other words, don't hire someone just because he or she is nice, or expresses great sympathy for your situation. You want a lawyer that is competent, experienced, knowledgeable, and tough. I personally don't think you should seek a lawyer based on gender. There are capable men and women lawyers in all fields. Unfortunately, many women lawyers still encounter potential clients who fear that a woman lawyer won't be tough enough to stand up to their opponents, even when she may be the best choice for other reasons. Undoubtedly there are some women as well as men lawyers who find tough negotiating difficult, but most women lawyers are more than able to be tough and withstand offensive tactics from the other side. It is ironic that women lawyers were perceived as weak by some people because of the general perception that women are nurturers, not warriors. When you hire a lawyer, you are hiring someone to take care of your legal needs — to take care of you. And who better than a woman lawyer with a strong maternal instinct? On the other hand, you don't want a lawyer who is so hell-bent on winning that he or she loses sight of your best interests. Your warrior lawyer also must be capable of being a compromiser — someone who can judge how far to push to get you the best deal and when it is in your best interest to back down. A lawyer should also focus on what is best for you and, usually, that means compromise and not winning at all costs. It is not the lawyer's ego or winning streak that counts — it is you.

Lawyers come from big firms, medium firms, small firms, and solo practioners. In addition to your personal compatibility with a specific lawyer, you should evaluate whether the environment in which he or she practices law is compatible with your needs and your budget. Large firms are generally perceived as the most powerful and are most frequently hired to work on mega deals. Most large law firms will only represent clients who will generate an estimated amount of legal fees — usually quite large — for the firm. They simply don't think it is worthwhile to represent smaller clients. (All lawyers have some threshold of size and estimated fees for deciding whether or not to take on a client, but the thresholds generally are lower for small law firms and solo practitioners.) For huge business transactions and litigation cases that require many lawyers to handle the matter properly, a large firm may be the best choice. Smaller firms have more difficulty providing the people power needed to handle large matters. However, a large firm is typically much more expensive. They tend to layer lawyer on top of lawyer in their cases, all billing away at fairly high hourly rates. In addition, the specific lawyer you selected may not do much of the work on your case. Most large firms assign a significant portion of the work to less experienced, and sometimes very inexperienced, lawyers and paralegals. You can, of course, inform your lawyer that you expect him or her to closely monitor and supervise the work done on your behalf. Some people believe that all lawyers who work in large law firms are the best of the profession. Although many of the best lawyers do work in large firms, this is not always true; some lawyers in large firms are not the best, and some of the best choose to work in other environments.

Medium and small firms tout their ability to give you greater hands-on attention than you will typically get at a large firm. If your business is not a Fortune 500 company, that claim is often true. You also are more likely to be able to hand pick the lawyers who will actually do your legal work. Although the billable rates of the attorneys in the medium to small law firms may equal rates charged by attorneys in the large firms, the cost is typically less. Smaller firms don't layer the job with lawyers as large firms do. Fewer hours on your case does not mean they are doing a lower-quality job. Large law firms are notorious for looking under every rock in a case, even if the rock has no significant effect on your legal matter. Cost/benefit analysis is a principle largely unknown, or at least generally not followed, in large law firms. Lawyers in smaller firms tend to be more cost conscious on your behalf, and will undertake only those tasks they think will significantly impact you and advance your case. The disadvantages of the medium to small law firms are their lack of people power for cases that really do require many lawyers, their lack of lawyers with different specialties for cases requiring that, and their lack of support services, such as an extensive word processing and secretarial base. Smaller firms often don't have the same clout as the large firms do, although some of the notable ones certainly do.

Sole practitioners probably give you the best and the worst. The specific lawyer you select will definitely do your work, and you will probably pay the least in legal fees. Again, this is not necessarily because sole practitioners charge a lower hourly rate. Indeed, some sole practitioners charge as much, or more, than lawyers in the larger firms. For some matters, you may pay more because sole practitioners do all the work and do not have lower-priced associates to whom they can delegate some of the work, but usually they will bill fewer hours to your case. However, sole practitioners certainly lack the breadth of legal expertise that a firm with more lawyers can provide. A sole practitioner simply cannot handle legal matters that require many lawyers, or that require lawyers with many different areas of expertise.

There is no magic formula for choosing the lawyer who is right for you, just as there is no magic formula for finding the perfect doctor, accountant, or other service provider. You should seriously listen to and consider the recommendations of your family and friends, but in the end, the choice is yours. Each client has his or her own individual needs and personality preferences. Find the lawyer that is right for you.

If You Hire the Wrong Lawyer, End the Relationship and Move On

Many women hire lawyers they become unhappy with, yet, for one reason or another, they won't fire that lawyer and move on. Their reticence to do so seems to be based on several different perceptions and fears. For example, some women are scared of their lawyers. They give their lawyers so much deference and control, it would seem that the lawyers are paying them, rather than vice versa. This is most frequently seen when women hire male lawyers. Some women fear that they will gain their lawyer's disapproval or rebuke if they dare to question or criticize him, much less terminate his services. If this is you, you need to do some serious soul searching. Remember, you are paying him to help you. He is the service provider, not you. He should do his best job for you and keep you informed about your case. He should listen to you and follow your direction (unless, of course, you are directing him to do something illegal or unethical). If you are not getting the services you are paying for, why keep that lawyer? In fact, if you are scared to approach him, this is a definite sign that you need a new lawyer.

In some cases, women feel that the cost of hiring a new lawyer will be too high. They reason that their current lawyer knows the case and that the time it would take for a new lawyer to get up to speed is would be so great that it would cost them more to move on. Of course, this may be true in some cases. If there is only a small amount of additional work to be done, it may be less costly to keep the lawyer you have, even if you don't feel comfortable with him or her or are not completely satisfied with how the work is being done. In many cases, however, staying with a lawyer you don't like may be the most expensive decision you can make.

When a client is unhappy with his or her lawyer, the client is usually dissatisfied with the quality of the work being performed and/or the results being obtained. In some cases, the unhappiness flows from the unprofessional or offensive conduct of the lawyer: for example, the lawyer's failure to return the client's telephone calls, to keep the client informed of progress on the legal issues, or the lawyer's personal conduct toward the client. The conduct of bad lawyers can range from abusive — screaming and demeaning the client — to sly — misrepresenting the case or lying about a significant issue. If your attorney is this bad, do you really think you are better off clenching your teeth and going forward? If he or she has done a bad job in the past, or has treated you in an unprofessional manner, ask yourself why you think this behavior will get better, or become tolerable, in the future. In many cases, when your lawyer is not working out, you will be better off financially and emotionally to terminate that representation and start fresh. Few legal matters are so complex that a good lawyer cannot get up to speed on the matter within a reasonable time. If you get a better lawyer, you will probably get a better result, and the additional legal fees will be well spent.

Wanda hired a corporate lawyer on the advice of a friend. He did an inadequate job for her, screamed at her, and otherwise failed to fulfill his professional obligations to her, all the time ludicrously protesting that his work was the equivalent of "slam dunk." Nevertheless, Wanda refused to fire him and hire a new lawyer. She reasoned that her case was so complex that a new lawyer would have to spend considerable time learning about it, and that would cost her thousands in additional legal fees. As it turned out, Wanda's bad lawyer failed to send her any bills at all for many months, and she had no clue about the amount of legal fees he was accruing. When he finally did send a bill, it was for several hundred thousand dollars. Wanda protested the fees and, after months of haggling and paying other lawyers to fight with her first lawyer over his legal bill, the case was settled. Even then, Wanda paid him more than she might have had to pay a good lawyer, who likely would have produced a better result. In addition, Wanda had to pay legal fees to other lawyers to fight the bad lawyer. Wanda now regrets that she didn't get rid of him earlier. She would have had to pay a new lawyer several thousand dollars to educate himself or herself about the legal issues involved, but she would have saved herself tens of thousands of dollars in legal fees and considerable heartache.

You must bear in mind that a lawyer is not a miracle worker. Some clients are not happy with their lawyer unless they can get the client out of situations that not even Houdini would be able to escape. The fact is that sometimes a lawyer cannot completely get you out of whatever fix you are in. What you can expect of your lawyer is that he or she will work hard, do his or her best, appropriately advise you as to your options, and deal with you in a professional manner.

Read and Negotiate Your Fee Agreement

Most lawyers prepare written fee agreements with new clients. These agreements should set out the hourly rates, costs, and other financial arrangements between you and your lawyer. Some lawyers will agree to a flat fee for certain types of projects. And, of course, some trial lawyers are willing to take on lawsuits on a contingency-fee basis. This means that they get a percentage of any money they make for you, and if you don't win anything in the lawsuit, you pay them nothing. In some cases, you may have to pay out-of-pocket expenses. In other cases, the lawyers bear these costs.

The most important step in negotiating a fee agreement is to read it before you sign it. It is amazing how many people simply sign these agreements without a close review, or any review at all. Many people think a lawyer's fee agreement is essentially boilerplate and nonnegotiable. Whereas many lawyers will not negotiate their fee, others will and you may want to try to negotiate the hourly rates charged.

Whatever the hourly rate you agree to pay, if legal services are rendered over a long period, you should anticipate that the lawyer will raise his or her hourly rate from time to time. Like everyone else, lawyers raise their prices occasionally to keep up with inflation. Most lawyers don't raise their fees without prior notice, and most don't raise them above the going rate, in accordance with professional standards and market realities. However, a lawyer friend recently told me about a client whose prior attorney had doubled his fee in a single hike, without any notice at all. In addition, the monthly bills did not clearly state the hourly rate, and until my friend reviewed the bills and calculated the hourly rate for her, she did not even know her lawyer had increased the hourly rate. All she knew was that she was getting astronomical bills from her lawyer that seemed far in excess of the amount of work done (and they were).

You may want to inquire which other lawyers will be assigned to your case and the hourly rate each will charge. For example, a young associate attorney could be quite capable of doing some of the work, and you could talk to your lawyer about assigning that work to the lower-cost associate. In most cases, work is allocated so that the lowest-cost professional who is capable of doing the work is assigned to that task. However, some firms, particularly those that are not working to capacity, will assign the work so as to maximize their revenues, not keep your fees down.

Whereas it may be difficult to negotiate hourly fees, you

may be able to negotiate the costs that you will be charged. There are some costs that virtually all lawyers bill to clients. These include long-distance telephone calls, mileage, parking, and photocopying. You should anticipate little negotiation on these. However, some firms (particularly large ones) have begun charging clients for many costs that were historically considered overhead and absorbed by the firm, such as word processing and secretarial costs. Instead of charging clients the actual out-of-pocket costs incurred in working on their matter, some firms compute their costs charged on a percentage of the client's bill. For example, these firms may charge every client they have 5 percent of legal fees billed to that client for photocopying, facsimile, and postage costs, even though a particular client did not require those services. In large matters, the percentage charge method can add thousands of dollars to your legal bills. It is certainly more convenient for the firm to base its cost charges on a percentage of billings, rather than actually keeping track of each client's use. In some cases, this formula may result in your being charged for costs far in excess of the costs actually incurred by the firm on your behalf. You may be able to exclude costs (such as secretarial and word processing) that, appropriately, should be considered overhead and included within the hourly rate you pay. You should also clarify whether a percentage of billings method is being used by your lawyer, and, if so, decide whether that is an acceptable method.

A few lawyers insert an *availability fee* in a fee agreement. This is a minimum fee you will be charged just because the lawyer is willing to make himself or herself available to you. Do these fees make sense? I don't think so. If the lawyer isn't available to do your work, he or she shouldn't even be entertaining the idea of taking on your matter. The lawyer obviously has to be available to do your work in the first place in order to take on the matter, so why should you pay for it? This is like paying a lawyer an extra fee because he or she has gone to law school and is licensed to practice law, when in fact that's why they charge high hourly rates. You should keep in mind, however, that your lawyer is not always available at your beck and call. Most lawyers represent several different clients on a number of different legal matters at the same time and therefore must divide their time accordingly. You should not wait until the last minute to talk to your lawyer about a legal matter, expecting him or her to drop everything just for you. Your lawyer simply may not be able to do so. Of course, if you really want a lawyer to be at your beck and call, you can probably get that — at a huge price. You can simply pay your own lawyer enough so that he or she will agree not to work for anyone else. (This would be a true availability fee.) Most clients — other than corporations large enough to justify hiring their own in-house lawyers — don't want to pay the price to do so.

A lawyer may also require a retainer when he or she first begins representing you. This is an advance payment that the lawyer will apply against legal fees subsequently charged to you. Some clients seem to take great offense when a lawyer asks for a retainer. The client may think this implies that the lawyer believes the client is a deadbeat, or not true to his or her word. The client might instead worry that the lawyer will just take the money and not do the work. Regrettably, lawyers have found that some clients (and it seems to be a growing number) refuse to pay their legal bills even when the work was done professionally and efficiently, and then threaten to sue for malpractice if the lawyer tries to collect the fees rightfully owed by the client. If lawyers did not encounter this, they would not ask for retainers. So, when a lawyer asks for a retainer, remember that this request is based solely on the lawyer's experience with many clients and is not a personal affront. Lawyers have a rule of thumb: if a client objects to payment of a very reasonable retainer, that client will more likely become a credit risk than other clients. Most clients who pay their legal bills on time don't object to payment of a retainer and, in fact, even expect to pay one. They know it's just business.

Some clients complain about every cost and every hour charged on a legal bill. Although you should certainly raise legitimate questions about your legal bill, you can't expect to get first-class work at discount prices. Contrary to popular belief, lawyers are human and most really want to do the best for their clients. However, they react negatively to undue and persistent harping about legal bills that are fair and honestly reflect the costs and hours needed to serve the client. If you constantly complain, your lawyer's commitment and dedication to you will slowly erode. At some point, your lawyer will suggest that you take your business elsewhere. You want a lawyer who treats you with respect, but you need to treat your lawyer with respect as well. The keys to a good attorney-client relationship are mutual trust, mutual respect, and realistic expectations.

Few things in life are considered as distasteful and boring as taxes, and few things can so totally devastate your life as unpaid taxes. If you fail to comply with the tax laws in your business or when filing your personal income tax return, you may encounter months and years of time-consuming negotiations with the IRS, punishing penalties and interest on unpaid taxes, and expensive legal and accounting fees. Ask Leona Helmsley, Heidi Fleiss, or Willie Nelson. In the next chapter, I tell you how they ran afoul of the tax laws and the high prices they each paid. Leona and Heidi intentionally violated the tax laws and paid the high price of jail time. Willie Nelson did not intentionally violate the law, but nevertheless faced tax liabilities so steep that his personal fortune was wiped out. A few basic legal principles can help you traverse the gloomy reality of taxes.

LEGAL MISTAKE #8:

NEGLECTING THE TAX MAN: Unexpected Tax Liabilities and Fights with the IRS

"People who complain about taxes can be divided into two classes: men and women."

Anonymous

Perhaps Leona Helmsley found taxes too boring to deal with, or perhaps she found them just a nuisance that she believed she could simply ignore. Leona and her husband, Harry, had a real estate and hotel empire worth more than $5 billion. In 1986, the *New York Post*, tipped off by a disgruntled former employee, ran a series of articles detailing their alleged tax violations. Unfortunately for Leona, federal law enforcement officials read these articles and took action. They investigated the Helmsleys' tax filings and were dismayed. Personal expenses, such as a swimming pool and home outdoor stereo system, were paid for by the Helmsley companies and deducted as business expenses. The Helmsleys did not, however, report these payments as income on their personal returns. They found that Leona received kickbacks in cash and TV sets from liquor salesmen and other suppliers. The investigators found so much fraud that they brought criminal charges against the Helmsleys. Leona's trial highlighted her imperious personality, fits of temper, and abusive treatment of employees. When a former housekeeper testified that Leona had once yelled at her "We don't pay taxes. The little people pay taxes," the public was both captivated and incensed. The jury of "little people" decided that they shouldn't be the only ones paying taxes. After deliberating for only four days, they found Leona guilty of thirty-three felony counts, including tax evasion, filing false returns, and mail fraud. Following the trial, one of the jurors told reporters that "Mrs. Helmsley and her friends didn't have a chance. Their fingerprints, their signatures, were on every piece of paper. Whether they knew what they were signing or not, their names were on everything."[70]

Like Al Capone, Heidi Fleiss, the "Hollywood Madam," was done in by the tax man, not the vice squad. Fleiss was Hollywood's leading madam and supplied call girls to some of the richest men in the world. Fleiss was first tried on pandering charges. She didn't take the charges too seriously at first, and often brought an entourage of call girls with her to court bearing hats that said "Heidi-Ho." In Superior Court, jurors initially found her guilty of felony pandering but not guilty on a more serious drug charge. They later recounted on the pandering charge when they learned that this carried a mandatory prison term. Based on juror admissions that they had traded votes to avoid a deadlock, a state appeals courts threw out the conviction and ordered that her case be retried. This is when the Feds stepped in. The IRS claimed that Fleiss had avoided paying taxes on hundreds of thousands of dollars by funneling her cash into savings accounts of different relatives and into a Benedict Canyon house that had been bought by her father, a prominent local pediatrician. Her father pled guilty to conspiracy to evade taxes and making false statements on loan documents and was sentenced to three years probation, 625 hours of community service, and was fined $50,000. Fleiss was later convicted of conspiracy to evade taxes, tax evasion, and money laundering. She was sentenced to thirty-seven months in federal prison.[71]

Although not many people do what Leona Helmsley or Heidi Fleiss did and end up in jail, many people find it difficult to pay their taxes on time or find that they (unintentionally) did not pay the amount of taxes they really owed and are liable for much, much more. Have you wondered just how much of your income goes to pay taxes? Between income taxes, sales taxes, and property taxes, taxes can easily consume more than 50 percent of your income. Have you ever thought about what your largest single expense is? You guessed it — taxes! Tax delinquencies can be the most distressing and catastrophic liability a person will ever encounter. Interest on federal tax liabilities, and most state tax liabilities, compounds daily, so it accrues very rapidly. In fact, your total tax and interest liability doubles about every five years that it remains unpaid! Even when you are totally broke and contemplate filing bankruptcy, you may not be able to escape your tax liabilities — many tax liabilities cannot be discharged in bankruptcy.

To make matters even worse, the IRS has little motivation to resolve tax cases quickly, or to settle for less than the full amount of tax it claims is due. A dispute with the IRS is different from a dispute you might have with a private vendor to whom you owe money. The private vendor might be willing to settle for less than the full amount due in order to get a quick resolution and a quick payment. With taxes, you are dealing with government employees. It's not their money, and they don't feel the same urgency to collect the money as most private vendors do. They have no reason to reduce the amount due. Also, you generally have the burden of proof in tax cases, not the IRS. In other words, you have to prove that you reported all of your income and that all the deductions you took are appropriate. There has been much talk about a change in the burden of proof passed by Congress in the summer of 1998, which purports to shift the burden to the IRS to prove that you owe taxes, rather than you proving that you don't owe taxes. However, under this new law so many conditions must be met before the burden of proof shifts, you should not count on it and should always assume that you have the burden of proof. What are some of the basic things you should watch out for when it comes to taxes?

File Joint Income Tax Returns with Great Care and Caution

Do you file a joint income tax return with your husband? More than 95 percent of married taxpayers do. Yet, few understand the implications of filing jointly; it is only when the IRS knocks on their door that they find out.

What is a joint income tax return? It is a return married couples can file that reports their income and deductions on a combined basis. Married couples are not required to file joint income tax returns and can file separate returns in which each spouse reports his or her own income and deductions. Joint income tax returns are generally favored, however, because they provide more tax benefits to the married couple. The tax rates that apply are generally lower and other tax breaks are given to joint returns. This is the upside. On the downside — and it is a very serious, but greatly underappreciated downside — joint income tax returns impose joint liability and separate liability for taxes that are reported on that return. This means that if you and your husband owe the IRS $10,000 and don't pay it, the IRS can hold you separately responsible for the full $10,000, it can hold your husband separately responsible for the entire $10,000, or the IRS can collect a portion of the tax due from each of you. The only restriction observed by the IRS is that it will not collect the $10,000 twice. There are exceptions to joint liability — referred to as the innocent spouse defense — that I will talk about later. However, it is quite difficult to qualify as an innocent spouse and you must file for this relief within certain prescribed time periods. You will probably have to hire a lawyer to help you do this. You should never file a joint return assuming that you will be able to qualify as an innocent spouse.

By filing a joint return, you are responsible for its accuracy even if you are not familiar with the business engaged in by your husband, even if you relied on a professional accountant to advise you and correctly prepare the return, and even if you did not carefully review and scrutinize the return because you relied upon your husband to handle that part of your mutual family obligations. You are also responsible for making sure that the tax is actually paid to the IRS.

As long as you and your spouse remain married, joint filing (and hence joint liability) generally doesn't pose a problem. Typically, your assets and your income will be pooled and used for the benefit of both of you. The trouble tends to arise after death or divorce, when you may be struggling financially, coping at the margins to maintain a supportive and nurturing home for your children, or suffering through the devastation and psychological turmoil of divorce or the death of your husband. This is when the income your husband earned but failed to report on your joint income tax returns, or the crazy tax shelter in which he invested in order to deduct large losses against other income, will come back to haunt you and threaten whatever financial security and emotional center you have. Although the IRS may try to collect from your ex-husband first if he was the family wage earner, it will readily turn to you if it can't collect from him. Your ex-husband may have moved to another state or skipped the country. He may have hidden his assets or simply be broke. Or he may mount such a rigorous defense to liability that the IRS simply finds it easier to pursue you. If your husband dies, you will be the only person whom the IRS can possibly collect from, and it will not hesitate to call on you.

The consequences of filing a joint income tax return is an important issue and bears repeating. If you sign a joint tax return, you can be liable for the entire amount of tax liability due on that joint return, even if the tax relates to income you did not earn, to a business you had nothing to do with and knew nothing about, or to income earned by your spouse that you did not even know about. When you sign a joint return, you are jointly responsible for paying the taxes the return says you and your husband owe. You can also be forced to pay the full 100 percent of the tax due. Even though joint tax returns have been a primary feature of the federal income tax laws since 1948, many married women have come to loathe the potentially dire tax consequences they face by signing one.

Martha, a schoolteacher, was married to an attorney, Jeff. Their marriage eventually grew distant, but like so many people of Martha and Jeff's generation, they stayed together for the sake of their two sons. After more than twenty years of marriage, Martha learned that Jeff had, in the mid-1980s, embezzled funds he held on behalf of several of his clients. Jeff had not reported the stolen money as income on their joint tax returns. He was apprehended and pled guilty to several felony counts of theft and tax fraud. Martha had no knowledge of his embezzlement, because Jeff maintained all his law practice records at an outside office. The money he had stolen from his clients was used to try to start a new business of which Martha was unaware. The stolen money was not used to increase their standard of living, which had remained unchanged throughout this period. Shortly after Martha found out about his criminal activities, she and Jeff separated and divorce proceedings were initiated. Because of monetary liabilities and his disbarment as a result of his criminal acts, Jeff was unable to provide Martha with alimony or other support, and she was left with only their modest home and wages from her own job.

Unfortunately, Martha had signed joint federal income tax returns for the years during which Jeff embezzled the money, just like she had every year of their marriage and just like most married couples do. Although she would do a cursory review of their joint returns, she relied on Jeff and their certified public accountant (CPA) to complete their returns accurately. After all, Jeff was an attorney, and she had no reason to suspect that he was not complying with the law. Her education and experience as a teacher did not familiarize her with tax matters, and she did not feel the least bit knowledgeable about such matters. Nevertheless, the IRS assessed taxes against her for the income Jeff embezzled and failed to report on their tax returns. The IRS did so, even though it acknowledged that Martha did not participate in the embezzlement, did not know about the embezzlement, and did not personally benefit from the stolen money. In addition, the IRS assessed interest and penalties. On the advice advice of her lawyer, Martha claimed that she was entitled to relief from liability for these taxes as an *innocent spouse* — a defense to liability for taxes due on a joint income tax return sometimes permitted under the federal income tax laws.

What is an innocent spouse? To be classified as an innocent spouse, a woman must show that she did not know, and had no reason to know, that tax on a joint federal income tax return was understated. She also must prove that the failure to report all taxes owed is due to her husband. In addition, she must show that it would be unfair to hold her liable for the taxes. This generally requires showing that she did not financially benefit from the tax savings. A luxurious standard of living is often seen as a benefit that precludes innocent spouse status. In other words if a woman has an expensive wardrobe and travels abroad a lot, it is unlikely that she would be viewed as an innocent spouse.

The IRS and the courts look at other factors as well when they evaluate innocence. If a woman is educated, or has some business experience, she will have tremendous difficulty qualifying for innocent spouse status. A college degree in any field will make it much harder to persuade the IRS that she had no knowledge of the errors on the joint tax returns, even if her degree is in a field totally unrelated to taxes or general business and financial matters. Few excuses are accepted. Naivete or lack of knowledge help qualify for innocent spouse, but are not always enough. A too busy schedule will not suffice. Even physical violence in the marriage may not be sufficient to avoid legal responsibility. Bear in mind, too, that each condition of the innocent spouse test must be met for relief to be granted. Not only must the innocent spouse show that she did not know, and had no reason to know, about the errors on the return, she must also show that she did not benefit from the tax savings, and that it would be unfair to collect the tax from her.

To make things even tougher, the IRS and the courts often take a very broad view about what the innocent spouse should have known. In Martha's case, the IRS agent believed that she should have known that Jeff was not reporting all of his income. The IRS agent thought that, because Jeff reported so little income from his law practice on their tax return, Martha should have realized that something was amiss and that there had to be more money somewhere. In other words, the IRS agent thought that a teacher should have known that a tax return prepared by an attorney (who was also her husband, whom she trusted and relied on) and a CPA was inaccurate. She should have known something was amiss, even though the IRS agent herself admitted that Martha did not know about the embezzlement and did not benefit from the stolen money. Eventually, the IRS agreed that Martha was an innocent spouse for the embezzled funds. However, during the months it took to negotiate that agreement, Martha incurred substantial legal fees and suffered considerable anguish for something she did not do, nor even know about, before the IRS relented and granted her innocent spouse status.

The legal casebooks are littered with tragic stories of women left to face the tax authorities alone, without the financial wherewithal to pay off tax liabilities they and their former husbands are deemed to owe because they signed joint income tax returns. In many cases like Martha's, husbands were involved in illegal activities the wives didn't know about: drug dealing, embezzlement, and outright robbery. Husbands have used illegal or unreported income for uses and diversions their wives didn't share in and didn't know about. They have supported mistresses and drug habits with this money, and then the wives were liable for the income taxes on the money used for such recreations. In other cases, the income was earned legally, but husbands simply did not report the income on their tax returns. Frequently, many of these husbands did not have the financial means to pay the taxes either, particularly in cases in which they were caught engaged in illegal activities. They may be in jail or otherwise stripped of their ability to earn an income. They may have left the country. They may have substantial assets that are hidden in foreign bank accounts. In cases such as these, the IRS may decide not to go to the trouble to find those assets because the wives are a much easier target.

In a number of cases, the problem created by filing a joint income tax return is not unreported income, but improper deductions. For example, your husband may have invested in a flaky tax shelter, which was supposed to generate substantial tax deductions to offset other income on your joint tax returns. (Tax laws passed in 1986 sharply curtailed tax shelters, and many tax shelter cases seen today are for tax returns filed many years ago; given the length of time these cases have been outstanding, the accrued interest and penalties on the eventual tax assessment are staggering.) Or he may have simply picked a number out of the air and deducted it as a loss from some fictional investment. (Seriously, I've seen this done.) It is more difficult to prove that you qualify as an innocent spouse in these cases than in cases in which income was simply omitted from the joint tax return. Omitted income is not visible on the tax return, so it is more likely that the innocent spouse will not be aware of it. By contrast, a phony tax deduction appears right on the face of the return, and therefore it is more difficult to prove that you did not know about a large deduction.

Beth had been married for a number of years to David, a television industry executive who earned high salaries and bonuses. David had invested in some flaky tax shelters and had deducted huge losses attributable to these tax shelter investments on their joint income tax returns. Several years after their divorce was finalized, the IRS audited their joint tax returns. David alone had made the decision to invest in the tax shelters, and he alone had arranged and supervised the preparation of their joint income tax returns. David was a domineering and angry husband, and Beth simply signed all of the joint tax returns presented to her without question and without any serious review.

The IRS determined that the tax shelters in which David had invested were shams and were invested in solely for the purpose of reducing his income taxes. The IRS concluded that, under the applicable tax laws, the losses were not deductible, and Beth and David owed a great deal in additional taxes, interest, and penalties.

Generally, when divorcing couples reach a property settlement agreement, or even when they don't, and the judge divides the marital property, some kind of agreement is reached about which spouse will be responsible for paying additional taxes if the IRS later decides more is owed. For a couple, with one wage earner, the spouse who earned the income generally assumes this liability and, in the property settlement agreement, indemnifies the nonearning spouse against taxes that may arise from income tax returns they had filed together. In other cases, each spouse will agree to be responsible for additional income taxes attributable to their respective businesses and will indemnify the other against such additional taxes. There is no set rule for who will bear the additional tax liabilities in the event of a subsequent audit. Tax indemnity is an important part of any property settlement agreement and should be vigorously asserted on your behalf by your divorce lawyer. However, these agreements *do not*, I repeat, *do not* bind the IRS. Only you and your ex-husband are parties to the agreement. The IRS is not, and it can pursue both or either of you for full collection of the additional taxes, regardless of what your property settlement agreement states or what the court ordered. Some states, such as California, do provide a procedure in which the state tax agency can approve a tax responsibility provision, and once it approves the provision, is bound by it. However, such provisions are available only in a few cases, and there is no equivalent procedure that applies to the IRS. All that the property settlement gives you is the right to sue your ex-husband if he does not pay the tax liabilities he agreed to pay, but the IRS can still come after you.

In Beth and David's property settlement agreement, David had agreed to indemnify Beth only against any taxes that might be assessed against them from joint tax returns, in cases in which the IRS might claim that their joint returns were fraudulent. Although the tax shelters were shams, David's deduction of the tax shelter losses on their joint return did not rise to the level of fraud, and Beth had no recourse against him. She had no recourse against the IRS, either because, as I stated, the IRS was not bound by their property settlement agreement.

The amount of tax they owed, when combined with interest and penalties, was so large that Beth's entire property settlement would have been wiped out had she been forced to pay it. Beth argued that she was an innocent spouse and should not be liable, but the IRS did not agree. The IRS agent thought Beth should have known their tax had been understated, because the deduction was clearly visible on their joint tax returns, which she had signed. Beth was required by law to review all the tax returns she filed with David and to make sure they complied with the tax laws. The fact that David was domineering, that he was the primary breadwinner in the family, and that she would encounter an angry and possibly violent showdown with David if she dared to question him did not reduce her responsibility. In addition, the IRS agent believed Beth had benefited from the tax they saved from the deduction. The agent believed Beth got a larger property settlement in the divorce than she would have gotten had the taxes been paid. In the end, the IRS refused to grant Beth innocent spouse status.

In some cases, you can never qualify as an innocent spouse — when the tax reported on the return as due is simply not paid or the return is prepared correctly but is not filed. You can find yourself faced with joint liability even when you reviewed the return and found that it was prepared correctly but relied on your husband to file the return and pay the tax and he failed to do so.

This is exactly what happened to Lisa. She and her former husband, Tony, signed joint tax returns for calendar years 1983 and 1984. They separated and divorced in the mid-1980s. In 1996, Lisa was contacted by the IRS. The joint income tax returns she and Tony had signed for 1983 and 1984 reported their income and expenses correctly (at least the IRS did not dispute the accuracy of the returns). However, Lisa had relied on Tony to mail the returns and pay the taxes. Now, more than ten years later, the IRS was telling her that Tony had mailed the returns, but he didn't pay the taxes they owed. The IRS was now looking to Lisa for payment. Interest and penalties had accumulated so much over the years that the total amount due now exceeded five times the original tax due. Lisa was now elderly, terminally ill, and surviving on very modest savings. It was impossible for her to pay the taxes. She was able to find out where Tony was living, but by the time the IRS tried to contact him, he had moved to another state. The IRS was not willing to undertake further efforts to collect from him when Lisa was nearby. The IRS agent focused his sights on Lisa instead. Because the tax liability did not arise from omitting income from the return, or from taking too many deductions, but because Tony failed to pay the tax owed, Lisa couldn't even assert that she was an innocent spouse. She asked the IRS to consider an offer in compromise (again, this is the procedure whereby the IRS will sometimes agree to reduce your tax liability if you simply cannot pay it). Because Lisa was so ill, it took her quite a lot of time to compile the financial information about her living expenses and sources of income that she had to submit to the IRS for an offer in compromise. Before she was able to get it all together, the IRS seized her bank account — her sole savings on which she lived. Lisa was penniless. Checks she had written before her account was levied began to bounce. She was not even able to purchase much-needed medicine for the pain she suffered from her terminal illness. She rapidly descended into despair over how she would continue to live without the few funds she had in the now seized bank account.

Lisa's attorney demanded to know why the IRS seized the bank account without first giving a thirty-day notice, which the IRS is generally required to do before it levies on a bank account. This gives the taxpayer time to either pay the taxes due or work out a payment schedule. (If, however, the IRS reasonably believes that its ability to collect the taxes will be jeopardized if it does not seize the account immediately — a so-called jeopardy assessment — it can dispense with the thirty-day notice.) This notice would have given Lisa the opportunity to complete the offer in compromise and show that she did not have the ability to pay the outstanding taxes. The IRS agent told her attorney that the IRS had sent her a notice ten years earlier, in 1987, and, as far as the agent was concerned, that fulfilled the IRS's thirty-day notice obligation. Lisa appealed this ludicrous decision up the chain of authority within the IRS, but lost. The higher authorities in the IRS agreed that a notice issued ten years earlier was sufficient. Eventually, Lisa submitted a hardship order request and most of her seized assets were released; however, Lisa spent days in total despondency and fear before this was accomplished.

Lisa's attorney also tried to find out whether Tony had paid any of the taxes. Until a few years ago, the IRS had no obligation to tell you whether it had collected any of the taxes from your ex-husband even on a joint return, or whether it had made any attempt to locate him and collect taxes from him. However, the Taxpayer Bill of Rights 2, which was enacted in 1996, requires that the IRS give you that information if you request it in writing. Unfortunately, the law does not require that the IRS actually try to collect taxes from your former spouse — only that the IRS disclose to you whether or not it made an effort to do so. The IRS informed Lisa that it had made no attempt to find Tony.

Although many innocent spouse cases involve women who are not highly educated or experienced in business, they are not limited to these women. Even high-earning career women often delegate their tax return responsibilities to their husbands. Take Eleanor Norton Holmes, for example. A lawyer and former chief of the U.S. Equal Employment Opportunity Commission, Eleanor was campaigning to be elected as the congressional representative from Washington, D.C., when an anonymous fax to news organizations tipped them off that she and her husband had failed to file their tax returns with the District of Columbia for 1982 through 1989. Her husband had always handled the family's tax returns, she had signed returns for each of those years, and she had assumed that he filed the returns they prepared and signed. Not so. Apparently, Mr. Norton disagreed with an assessment he received from the District of Columbia for 1982 and dealt with that by not filing in subsequent years. He also claimed that through income tax withholding on Eleanor's salary and estimated tax payments he made quarterly, they owed no additional taxes. While the public debated whether she qualified as an innocent spouse or not, Eleanor stepped up to the plate and got all returns filed and paid all outstanding taxes and penalties. The voters of the District of Columbia, a forgiving group, elected her as their congressional representative, and she has sponsored several pieces of legislation to reduce the District's taxes.[72]

In 1998, Congress enacted new law that is supposed to make it easier to qualify as an innocent spouse.[73] More than 63,406 claims for innocent spouse relief from 33,006 taxpayers (some claims cover several tax years) have been filed with the IRS since Congress passed this new law. While the new law purports to make it easier to qualify as an innocent spouse, it is not clear how much easier it will be. As of April 2000, the IRS had fully reviewed 31,258 claims and rejected all but 15,692 as technically deficient or not qualified for innocent spouse treatment. Of the 15,692 cases it considered, it granted innocent spouse relief to 44 percent and partial relief to another 7 percent. The IRS claims that this percentage is considerably higher than it would have granted under the old law.[74] Only a few cases in which the IRS refused to grant relief have proceeded to court since the new law passed, and the courts have not ruled in favor of the spouse claiming innocent spouse status in most of these cases.[75]

The new law provides two other alternatives that may, in some cases, help women avoid unfair tax liability resulting from their ex-husband's improper reporting. Under the second alternative, if the IRS tries to hold you responsible for taxes not paid when you and your husband filed a joint return, the new law allows you to retroactively elect to pay your share of taxes as though you filed a separate tax return.[76] In other words, you can eliminate your joint liability for taxes due from the joint return and elect to be responsible only for the taxes that you would have owed had you filed a separate return in the first place. This would include your own wages and salary and income from your separate property. Income from joint property in some cases, according to the IRS, may be taxable to either or both of you; that is, such income can remain subject to joint and several liability. Deductions are allocated equally or pursuant to some other allocation method, such as proportionate ownership in a business.[77] If you live in a community property state, you are taxed on your community property share of your ex-husband's income. If your spouse elects separate return reporting but you do not, you remain jointly and severally liable for the full tax due.

You can make this separate return election many years after the return has been filed, when the IRS is trying to collect taxes based on the joint tax return you filed. Time limits are imposed, however, and you need to contact your tax advisor immediately when you receive a tax assessment from the IRS. But, the burden is on you to prove what your separate liability for taxes would have been, so it is critical that you maintain and keep proper records for many years (it is usually many years after the return has been filed that the IRS audits the joint return and actually starts trying to collect the taxes).

In addition, there are several restrictions on who can make this election. You must be divorced or legally separated from the spouse with whom you filed the joint tax return. The election is not available if the IRS can show that you knew taxes were being underpaid when the return was initially filed. In addition, the election does not apply to the extent that you and your ex-husband transferred assets between each other in an effort to avoid taxes. This new election will provide new ways to avoid paying the taxes your ex-husband rightfully owes, but it is not foolproof.

Moreover, whereas the new law eases the rules for obtaining relief from joint tax return liabilities in some ways, the new law makes it tougher in other ways. For example, the U.S. Tax Court recently held that if one spouse tries to limit his or her liability as an innocent spouse or has made the separate return election, and the case ends up in Tax Court, the other spouse is entitled to challenge the electing spouse's right to innocent spouse or separate return treatment.[78] The new law has similar rules for administrative proceedings before the IRS before the case reaches court.[79] Under the old law, if you filed for innocent spouse, your husband wasn't entitled to do this. It was believed that this matter was solely between you and the IRS. As the law is further interpreted by the courts, it is likely that other limitations on its use will likely develop and what was initially believed to be a panacea to many distressed women may turn out to be false hope.

Under the third alternative, when a joint return filer either doesn't qualify as an innocent spouse or can't take advantage of the separate return election, and the IRS, after taking into account all the facts and circumstances, finds that it would be inequitable to hold one of the joint return filers liable for any unpaid tax, the IRS can grant relief to that joint return filer from liability.[80] The IRS can give this relief when the liability results from the tax just not being paid — a situation in which innocent spouse relief can't be given. The IRS has considerable latitude in whether or not to grant this equitable relief, but its actions so far are not at all promising. Congresswoman Nancy Pelosi wrote the IRS in February 1999 and asked that it use its new equitable authority to reverse its long-standing practice of trying to collect premarital and separate property tax liabilities of one spouse by seizing community property assets of both spouses. She told of one of her constituents who was faced with this problem. The U.S. Attorney's Office was trying to foreclose on the personal residence of an elderly widow to collect the tax debt owed by her now-deceased husband — taxes he owed long before they were ever married. Even though the house was in the widow's name alone, the U.S. Attorney's Office presumed this was community property because although the two were married, the deceased husband was the sole income earner.[81] The IRS responded a few months later, saying that it was sorry, but nothing could be done since the widower herself didn't owe the taxes; her husband did. Remarkably, the IRS said it would be more likely to help people keep their property if they were the tax miscreants than it would if the property owner were an innocent victim of someone else's tax dereliction.[82] If this is the IRS's idea of equity, you should not count on getting relief under this third alternative. So what can you do to protect yourself from staggering tax liabilities that can surface long after the marriage is over and the divorce papers are final?

First, you can exercise responsibility and review the returns carefully. Ask questions about anything you don't understand. Better yet, have your own accountant review the returns and advise you about whether they are correct. Of course, there is a cost involved in having your own accountant review the returns, both in actual dollars and in potential marital turmoil if your husband takes offense. It may, however, save you considerable heartache down the road. Make sure the return is actually filed and the taxes are actually paid. You could file the returns yourself, check for filing receipts or at least confirm with your husband that it has been done. If taxes are owed, review your check register. Was a check written to pay the taxes? Has the canceled check been returned?

What do you do if you hire your own accountant, and he or she advises you that the return contains phony deductions, and you should not sign it? You should, of course, first discuss this with your husband to see if you can persuade him to amend the errors and file a correct return. If he refuses, your best course of action is to file a separate return. Married couples are not legally obligated to file joint returns; they can file separately. The tax brackets and rates that apply to married persons who file separate returns are higher than when filing jointly (and are even higher than if you were unmarried and filed as a single person). But paying more tax now and filing a return that you know is right can save you tons of liability and misery later. As I mentioned previously, tax liabilities that are assessed by the IRS years after the return was originally filed will be increased by interest, and often penalties. The total tax liability can grow to astronomical proportions.

On a separate return, you report your own income and related expenses. Your husband's income and related expenses are reported on his own separate return. If you live in a community property state, each spouse reports one-half of the community property earnings, and one-half of any other community property income earned by each spouse. If your husband deducts expenses on his separate tax returns and those deductions have no legal basis, it is his problem, not yours. You did not sign that return, and you have no liability for it. Of course, as a practical matter, as long as you are married and pool your resources with your husband, you will be negatively impacted if the IRS assesses tax against your husband based on his separate return. However, if you have separated before this occurs, the filing of a separate return will relieve you of considerable expense and aggravation if your husband files incorrect tax returns.

A separate return provides added protection against tax liabilities for omitted income. If it is not your income, then your husband's failure to report it on his own separate return exposes him, and only him, to criminal and civil liability for the omission. Even if you hire your own accountant to review the joint returns, it is doubtful that he or she will be able to warn you about omitted income, because it simply doesn't show up on the joint tax return.

Report All — I Mean All — of Your Income and Don't Deduct Personal Expenses

Some of the most common mistakes made on tax returns are the most basic — not reporting all income or deducting expenses that are not deductible. Many people think the only income they are required to pay taxes on is the money they earn from their regular job. If it's not reported on a Form W-2, it's not income. This is absolutely not true. The Internal Revenue Code states that *all* income, from whatever source derived, is taxable.[83] This means even those shares of stock in the company you were given to persuade you to work for it. Property you receive as compensation for services or payment for something you sold is generally taxable to you at the value of the property you receive. For example, if you get stock in the company you work for that is worth $20,000, you generally have taxable income that you must report on your income tax return of $20,000. There are exceptions to this general rule. For example, if you have to forfeit the stock if you quit within a certain number of years, then you don't have to pay tax on the value of the stock now. However, you do later when the risk of forfeiture ends and the stock is absolutely yours. You also may have income if you trade one type of property for another. For example, if you own ten shares of stock in XYZ company and you trade it for 10 shares of ABC company, you have taxable income equal to the difference between the value of the ABC stock when you got it and the amount you paid for the XYZ stock. The money you make from selling that antique chest your grandmother gave you, the money you make from selling eggs your chickens lay, or the money you make mending clothes from time to time are all taxable. In other words, taxable income comes in all forms and types. As a general rule, if you get something that's worth something, it's taxable and it's taxable in the year in which you receive it. There are exceptions. For example, gifts you receive are not taxable. Money you borrow is not taxable so long as you have to pay it back, but if the lender decides not to make you pay it back, it is taxable at that time. If you think something of value that you have received is not taxable, you should talk to your accountant or tax lawyer before you decide not to report it on your tax return.

While most cash and other property you receive is taxable, not all of your expenses are deductible. An area in which many mistakes are made is personal expenses. Whereas business-related expenses are generally deductible, personal expenses are not deductible unless a specific provision in the Internal Revenue Code says they are. For example, interest on your mortgage is deductible because Section 163 of the Internal Revenue Code says it is. Property taxes on your home are deductible because Section 164 of the Internal Revenue Code says they are. Repairs to your home and insurance on your home are not deductible. These are considered personal expenses and nowhere does the Internal Revenue Code say you can deduct them. Likewise for vacations even if your job drives you crazy and you absolutely need to get away. Sometimes there is a fine line between what is business and what is personal, but you need to be careful not to deduct personal expenses.

Some famous people have not followed these basic rules and consequently have landed in hot water. Pete Rose admitted to underreporting his income by $355,000. He paid $366,000 in back taxes and penalties, was fined $50,000, and spent five months in prison and three in a halfway house. Al Capone was done in not by gangster activities but by tax evasion. He was convicted of failing to report $1 million of income and served seven years in prison. Marvin Mitchelson, the famed divorce lawyer, failed to report $2 million of income. He was ordered to pay $2 million in restitution and sentenced to thirty months in jail. Lyndon LaRouche had his personal expenses paid by corporations he controlled and did not report these payments as income to himself. He received a fifteen-year sentence. [84]

Although you won't go to jail if you fail to report income because of a mistake or because you sincerely don't think something is income, or if you think an expense is properly deductible and it turns out not to be, you will have to pay the back taxes, interest, and possibly penalties. This can be quite expensive. If your failures are intentional and you purposely cheat Uncle Sam out of his fair share of taxes, you should read the preceding paragraph again.

File Your Tax Returns on Time
Even if You Cannot Pay All the Taxes

Have you ever found that you didn't have the money to pay your taxes when your tax return was due? What did you do? Many taxpayers run into financial problems at some time in their life and cannot pay all their income taxes. Unfortunately, at times like this, many panic and don't file their tax returns at all.

They think that if they can't pay, they are better off not filing their returns. Wrong! In fact, this is not only wrong, it is probably the worst thing you can do. It is a felony not to file tax returns. You can be prosecuted and put in jail. However, if you file your returns on time, but cannot pay all your taxes, you will not go to jail. We don't have debtors' prison in the United States. (But, if the return you file is fraudulent, that's another story.) The IRS will generally let you pay off what you owe in installments. Sometimes, if you really don't have the assets and no potential to earn enough money to pay off the tax liability, the IRS will reduce the amount of tax you owe. This is called an *offer in compromise*. Generally, to qualify for an offer in compromise, you must clearly demonstrate that you don't have money or other assets to pay the tax, that you cannot borrow the money to pay the tax, and that your financial situation probably won't get much better in the foreseeable future. Even if you can prove all that, the IRS frequently requires that you agree to give it a percentage of your future income in the event your financial circumstances improve.

Too often, when a taxpayer misses one year of tax returns, he or she doesn't know what to do the following year. The taxpayer believes that if he or she files a return in the later year, the IRS will figure out that he or she did not file a return in the earlier year. The tazpayer is right; typically, they will. Unfortunately, this starts the snowball of returns not being filed year after year, until the taxpayer lives in constant fear of IRS agents hauling him or her to jail in the middle of the night. Obviously, it is best not to get behind in filing your tax returns and paying your taxes. However, if you cannot pay all your taxes in a particular year, file your return anyway. You can work out some payment arrangement with the IRS. It may not be easy, but if you don't file your returns, thinking it is better to lay low, the IRS will probably find out, and it will be a lot worse than if you had filed your return without making your tax payment. You could be prosecuted. Even if the IRS does not go after you for fraud, it will throw every civil penalty it can at you, and the penalties that are imposed for not filing returns are extremely costly. The cost, both financially and emotionally, of not filing your tax returns can be devastating. Betsy certainly found that out. So did Richard Pryor.

Betsy worked in a creative job and did not enjoy, nor have any particular aptitude for, bookkeeping and preparing tax returns. For many years she was involved with a man who suddenly, and without warning, dumped her for another woman. Betsy was devastated and depressed. That year she simply did not get around to filing her income tax returns. The next year, she worried about filing her returns because she had failed to do so the previous year. She reasoned that filing her return now would bring attention to the fact that she had missed filing the previous year. Betsy decided not to file the second year either. This led to not filing in the third year, or the fourth year, until she had failed to file returns for six consecutive years. During these years, she was self-employed and, as an independent contractor, did not have taxes withheld and paid to the IRS from the money she had earned. Neither was Betsy making quarterly estimated tax payments as self-employed people are supposed to do. Unfortunately, the IRS discovered that she was not filing returns and it contacted her to demand that she file tax returns for all the years in which she had failed to do so, and that she pay her past tax liabilities. The IRS also levied substantial penalties. By the time the IRS finished adding up penalties, interest, and past due taxes, Betsy's tax liability exceeded $300,000 — a huge debt for a young woman to try to deal with.

If Betsy had filed her tax returns timely, even if she could not have paid her full tax liability, she would have reduced her total tax liability by about $75,000 — the amount in penalties imposed for not filing returns. In addition, she may have been more disciplined about paying at least a portion of the taxes she owed, so the interest assessed would have been much less. The IRS may also have imposed less penalties for not paying the taxes on time (a much lower penalty than is imposed for not filing returns on time), if the IRS agents believed she was honestly trying to comply with the tax law requirements. Although IRS agents cannot reduce interest on delinquent taxes, they have some discretion about the penalties they impose. The more it appears that you have intentionally attempted to flout the tax laws, the more likely you will face substantial penalties when you get caught.

Richard Pryor faced even more serious penalties. He was originally charged with four felonies for failing to file tax returns from 1967 to 1974, during which time he made $250,000. In a plea bargain agreed to in 1974, Pryor pleaded one count of willfully neglecting to file a return. He was fined $10,000 and spent ten days in jail.[85] He was lucky; he went on to a successful comedic career. Most convicted felons have no hope of a successful career following their conviction.

As these stories illustrate, you should always file your tax returns on time even if you cannot pay all the taxes you owe. If you don't, you may let the years roll by before you face the music; when you do, you could not only face a mountain of tax debt that you will never be able to overcome, you could face jail time as well. Heidi Fleiss, Pete Rose, Al Capone, and Leona Helmsey are but a few of the more famous taxpayers who have spent time in prison for failing to observe the tax laws.[86] The prosecutors don't limit their sights to the rich and famous, however. Many ordinary taxpayers are convicted of tax fraud each year and spend months or even years in jail.

Carefully Review Your
Tax Return for Accuracy before Filing

Do you prepare your own tax return? Does your husband prepare your tax return? If so, do you even bother to review it before signing? Do you carry boxes of receipts and canceled checks to your accountant and let him or her prepare it? Do you bother to review the return your accountant has prepared or do you just assume it's correct? After all, your *accountant* prepared it. No matter who prepares your return, whether that person is qualified or not, you must review it carefully to make sure that it accurately reports your income and expenses. Your accountant, even though a professional tax return preparer, can only prepare your return based on the information you have given. Your accountant may not be intimately familiar with your financial life and may miss income you are obligated to report or deductions you incurred and are entitled to deduct. Ultimately, you bear the primary responsibility for making sure the tax return is accurate.

What can you do to make sure your tax return is prepared correctly? Before meeting with your accountant, you should carefully think about everything you did during the taxable year that generated income or expenses, so that you are able to give your professional a comprehensive rundown of your activities. You should compile and review your receipts and canceled checks, as well as credit card charges. This may remind you of other expenses you are entitled to deduct. Many taxpayers present their accountants with boxes of unsorted receipts and expect him or her to sort them out, determine which are deductible expenses and which are not, and otherwise make some sense out of the heap of papers. Often, these taxpayers are the first to complain about the amount of fees they are charged by their accountant. Apparently, they expect the accountant to sort through the mass of paper for free, but it takes time for the accountant to do this, and therefore he or she should charge for the extra time. You will get the most accurate, and the least expensive, tax return possible if you spend time organizing your tax return information before you deliver it to your accountant. Not only will sorting through the receipts yourself save you in accountant's fees, it may also help you remember other activities or costs you incurred that you can deduct or other income you earned that must be reported.

Beware of Cocktail Party Tax Tips

You are at a cocktail party and one of your friends starts bragging about how her accountant told her about a certain loophole that could save her thousands of dollars in taxes. Surely your accountant is using the loophole too, she says. When you say your accountant has never mentioned it, she gives you this knowing look. It's sad that you aren't as clever as she, that you employ this mediocre accountant while hers is sharp, cutting-edge, and brilliant.

Always beware of cocktail party tax tips. Many people in our society brag about their alleged tax plans to demonstrate their bravado, cleverness, and ingenuity. They are smarter than most because they employ the most clever accountants or lawyers. Their cunning in the tax arena is just one more example of their financial prowess and success. Instead of surpassing the Joneses by buying a bigger house, these people express their purported superiority through their brilliant gimmicks to beat Uncle Sam.

The poster boy of tax schemes is the popular country western singer Willie Nelson. As Willie's fame and wealth grew, so did his spending. He embraced a philosophy of spend now, live for the moment. Unlike many newfound celebrities, much of his spending was to help old and new friends, those who helped him on his way to stardom, and those in need. Nelson relied on his manager to handle his taxes. Unfortunately, his manager had a prior conviction for embezzling stock and was not too diligent about paperwork himself. Money turned up missing. Tax returns were not filed. The IRS claimed at least $2 million in taxes was due. Willie was put in contact with one of the so-called big five accounting firms, which advised him that he needed to get into tax-sheltered investments in order to avoid paying a lot of taxes each year. The accounting firm recommended that he borrow money to invest in government securities issued by a San Francisco-based firm, First Western Government Securities. Willie claims he argued with his professionals and told them this scheme did not make sense. If he was going to borrow money, why not use it to pay the back taxes the IRS claimed he owed, rather than invest in tax shelters? The accounting firm persuaded him that this was the right thing to do. The firm later became concerned that something about First Western wasn't right and advised Willie to drop his investment there and go into cattle. The plan was to buy cattle and feed at the end of the tax year, deduct the cost of the feed, and then sell the fattened cattle in the next year for enough to cover the cost of the cattle and the feed. The problem was that the price of cattle dropped drastically and the accounting firm allegedly failed to advise Willie of a method he might have used to protect himself against actual losses — by selling cattle futures. Willie and his new manager lost $2 million on that deal, and to top it off, the IRS disallowed $3 million of cattle feed expenses for one of the years. It said the cattle didn't eat that much. Things continued to get worse. The IRS issued notices of deficiencies, it disallowed all of Willie's tax shelter losses, and Willie lost a case in U.S. Tax Court in which he contested the IRS's disallowance of some personal expenses in earlier years. According to Willie's tax attorney, Willie's tax liability had climbed to $32 million by 1990. The attorney was able to negotiate this down to $6 million in taxes, plus $9 million in interest and penalties. But Willie had to pony up a significant amount — $2 million —

for the settlement to be good. The IRS seized his property but no one bid on it. Willie eventually produced a CD especially for the purpose of raising money to pay off his tax liabilities and gave the IRS a large percentage of royalties earned on this CD. Its title — "Who'll Buy My Memories?: The IRS Tapes."[87]

Willie Nelson is not the only taxpayer who has lost a lot more by investing in tax shelters than they ever dreamed they would save in 1970s and 1980s. Tax shelter investments have included everything from real estate to cattle to windmills to chinchillas. In some cases, the promoters told the investors they were entitled to take deductions on their tax returns as much as eight or nine times greater than the actual amount of cash the investors had put into the deal. Tax shelters were an extremely popular cocktail party topic until Congress passed a new law in 1986 that shut down most of these shelters that were then popular. However, even before Congress acted, the IRS challenged the propriety of the more egregious tax shelters, and it won hands down. Court after court ruled in favor of the IRS, and ruled that tax shelters were shams and the deductions from investing in the shelters were disallowed. In these cases, the investors often were allowed to deduct the actual cash they invested, but no more. In other cases, they were not allowed to deduct even the cash they had invested and now lost. The investors faced substantial tax liabilities, plus interest on past due taxes. In addition, they often were assessed substantial penalties. In the end, many investors were liable for taxes, penalties, and interest, totaling as much as four to five times the initial taxes they had saved from the investment.

My friend Kelly is a case in point. She had been encouraged to invest in a tax shelter by a financial advisor. Unfortunately, the tax shelter turned out to be a complete sham. The promoters of this sham told investors that their investment would entitle them to take big tax deductions against their other income, which would greatly reduce their overall tax liability. In Kelly's case, the question of whether the deductions were valid deductions did not even arise. The promoters had outright stolen the money from her and the other investors, and had not used the money to make the investments the promoters represented the money would be used for. Under the tax laws, you never can take deductions from an investment you did not make. Of course, the promoters did not tell the investors that they had stolen the money instead of buying the properties as represented. Each year, the promoters sent out tax forms that advised the investors how much they were entitled to deduct for that year. It was only after the IRS found out about the scam that the investors learned the true story. The investors sued the promoters, who, predictably, no longer had the money. The IRS assessed taxes, penalties, and interest against all the investors, including Kelly, who simply had no defense. Many years had elapsed since Kelly initially had invested in the shelter, and, consequently, the interest and penalties had gone through the roof and her investment of $15,000 had turned into a tax liability of more than $100,000. Her finances had also suffered in recent years, and the added tax liability almost drove her to bankruptcy. So much for cocktail party tax tidbits.

As Willie Nelson learned the hard way, your legal obligation to correctly report your tax liability and pay the amount of tax you legally owe is one of the most significant legal obligations you have. If you delegate the responsibility to someone else, you are still on the hook. If you don't comply with the tax laws and you get caught, your financial well-being can be so devastated that you will never recover. If you intentionally violate the laws, you could be looking at jail time. The IRS is the most expensive and most powerful creditor you can have. It charges more interest than most creditors (because of daily compounding), and it can do all sorts of things to collect taxes from you that regular creditors cannot do. For example, the IRS can levy against your wages and bank accounts, and seize other assets without having first to go to court and get a judgment against you.

Most clever tax dodges are not legal or, at best, are very questionable, yet they continue to proliferate. Congress has many smart tax lawyers and accountants to shut down tax schemes. The IRS and the Treasury Department likewise are populated with extremely bright professionals who are able to discern the wheat from the chaff. And the IRS and Congress have enacted laws that virtually eliminate taxpayers' ability to minimize taxes through tax shelters and other tax schemes. Nevertheless, as one shelter is shut down, new ones are created. A popular form today is the use of trusts to inflate business deductions or to attempt to make nondeductible personal expenses into deductible business expenses.[88] Others are more sophisticated and use elaborate techniques that employ currency swaps and other obscure financial instruments to generate tax deductions and losses where they did not exist before.[89] Like in the old tax shelter days, the IRS is challenging these shelters and winning hands down. The new shelters are as risky as the old ones were. The tax laws refer to these types of schemes as lacking *economic reality* or lacking a *business purpose* — an investment primarily made to get tax deductions and not to actually make money, or just shams. If a friend at a cocktail party tells you about some great scheme, you should presume that either he or she is making it up and really doesn't use the device on his or her own returns, or that your friend is cheating on his or her taxes. If it sounds legitimate, you certainly should ask your tax accountant or lawyer to review the merits of the plan. After all, you are not under any legal obligation to pay more tax than you rightfully owe. But you should not automatically believe that the tax schemes you hear about are valid. Remember, if it sounds too good to be true, it probably is.

Having the IRS come after you is not the only scary legal thing that can happen to you. Have you ever read a story in the newspaper about how someone paid good money for a house only to later find out that the paperwork didn't state that he or she owned it and the person ended up losing it and all the money he or she paid for it? Do you worry that this could happen to you? Do you even know if you legally own your own home? Do you know how to make sure that the property you own is absolutely yours and no one can sell it out from under you? Do you let your husband or business partner handle all the paperwork for your property? You may morally and rightfully own the property, but you need to make sure you also *legally* own your property. In the next chapter, I will help you make sure you do.

LEGAL MISTAKE #9:

FAILING TO PROTECT LEGAL TITLE TO YOUR PROPERTY

*"Whoever said money can't buy happiness
didn't know where to shop."*

Gertrude Stein

The honeymoon was definitely over. A week from now they had to be out of their home — the cute white house with the white picket fence and French windows, lined by rows of tulips and framed by roses crawling up the trellis. The house Sara had always dreamed of. She and Ben had moved there as soon as they returned from their honeymoon. For the first two years of their marriage, she could not believe her good fortune. Ben was her high school sweetheart and they had married shortly after they both graduated from college. He worked for a major company and was steadily working his way up the corporate ladder. Sara taught fourth grade at a ritzy private school. Both of their parents lived nearby, and the three families got together frequently. Ben's parents helped them buy the house. Ben's father, Bill, put up the down payment and both of Ben's parents helped pay part of the monthly mortgage. Bill handled the purchase for them, because neither Ben nor Sara had bought a house before. The deed to the house was put in Bill's name temporarily, since he contributed the down payment and escrow was scheduled to close while Ben and Sara were on their honeymoon. It didn't seem to matter because they all knew that the home belonged to Ben and Sara.

Fixing up their home was great fun. They wallpapered, painted, dug and planted, moved furniture back and forth until it was in the perfect position. To complete their home, they went to the local pound and brought home a robust and playful brown and white spotted puppy. At night, they often stayed at home for a quiet dinner with just the two of them and their puppy. Life was very good.

But now they were losing their home. Sara knew it wasn't Ben's fault and she was trying to be understanding. But she was devastated that they were losing their home — the home they had spent so much time and love fixing up to make it just perfect. Ben didn't know that Bill's business was failing. He didn't know that Bill's creditors would start foreclosing on all of Bill's assets, including their home. Ben and Sara tried to convince the bank that the house really was theirs, not Bill's. The bank was out a lot of money, however, and because it was legally entitled, it started foreclosure on their home.

Could this happen to you? Could your dream home be taken even though you did nothing wrong? The American dream is to own your own home, to have that place you can call your own and raise your children in, to have a significant asset that will help finance retirement. Unfortunately, many women find their American dream thwarted when they fail to make sure the property they do own, and their ownership in that property, is legally protected. Do you want to know how to protect your property so this won't happen to you? Protect your property, your retirement, your home? This chapter discusses some of the most basic things you need to watch out for. Most of this chapter focuses on real estate, but most of the principles discussed apply to other types of property such as intangible property and personal property. Intangible property includes shares of stock in corporations, trademarks, copyrights, and franchises. Personal property is tangible property such as cars, boats, jewelry, and artwork. But, first, we need to learn about the types of documents used to evidence ownership in real estate and other types of property, the public records in which these documents are recorded and the effect of recording these documents, and the different forms of ownership by which property is typically held. This may be the most technical chapter in this book, but it is also one of the most critical.

Documents That Transfer Ownership

Disputes about who owns legal title to property can arise in unexpected situations. When the Atlantic City boardwalk was being overtaken in the late 1970s by developers who wanted to build casinos, the State of New Jersey disputed their legal title to millions of dollars worth of the land along the boardwalk. One of the largest properties in dispute was a $25 million parcel owned by Resorts International. New Jersey relied on a legal doctrine governing *riparian* land, that is, land adjoining water. Under this legal doctrine, the state owns this land unless it expressly sells it to someone else. New Jersey used sophisticated aerial infrared photography as well as old deeds, maps, and land descriptions to support its case. Homeowners became fearful that they too might lose their property to New Jersey's riparian rights and, in 1981, amended the state constitution to radically limit these rights. [90]

In the late 1980s a small church in Georgia that had left the fold of the Assemblies of God over differences in doctrine and policies ended up in a bruising battle over who owned the small church and the property on which it was located. In 1986, one year after the small congregation cut its ties with the Assemblies of God, the Georgia Council of the Assemblies of God filed suit, seeking to regain control of the church property from the 125-member congregation. The Georgia Council claimed that it had built the church. The local congregation countered that they had saved the church from foreclosure some years earlier without any help from the Georgia Council. The case turned upon whether the Assemblies of God organization was hierarchical in nature, in which case the Georgia Council would own the church, or congregational, in which case the local congregation would own it. Two years and $22,000 in legal fees later, the parties agreed to drop their suits and countersuits, and the small congregation kept the church.[91]

Most questions of legal title to property are far less esoteric than the riparian rights of the state or congregational/hierarchical character of a church. Most center on the more basic issue of whether you own it or somebody else owns it. Have you ever wondered how the law determines who owns what property? Unless you already own a home, probably not, and even if you own a home, you may have relied on your husband or someone else to make sure everything was done correctly. However, you may buy a home in the future by yourself and you will need to know how property ownership is accounted for. This is the only way you can protect your own property.

Ownership of real estate is evidenced by a legal document called a *deed*. In the deed, which is signed by the seller, the seller declares that he or she is selling all of his or her rights in the property to the buyer; this is commonly referred to as *conveying title to the property to the buyer*. The deed also describes very specifically the property to be sold so it won't be confused with other real estate. A deed is filed (*recorded* in legal jargon) in a government office located in the county in which the property itself is located. Typically, the county recorder's office or the county courthouse is the appropriate place to file the deed.

Several different types of deeds are used to evidence that a seller of real estate has sold his or her legal title and ownership to real estate to the buyer. The protections provided to a buyer under each form of deed is determined by the laws of the state in which the property is located. I will describe general rules that usually apply, but you need to check the specific laws of your state before buying property.

The type of deed that gives the buyer the greatest protection, and is the least commonly used, is a warranty deed. Under a warranty deed, the seller promises the buyer that not only has he or she not given an ownership interest or security interest in the property to anyone else, but neither has any prior owner. If some third party later claims an interest in the property, the seller is obligated to defend the buyer's title to the property. This type of deed is rarely used because buyers generally buy title insurance to protect against third-party claims.[92]

A grant deed provides the buyer with some protection against third-party claims, but less than that given under a warranty deed. Under a grant deed, the seller warrants that he or she has not conveyed any right to the property to a third party, and that the seller has not given anyone else a lien against the property to secure a debt of the seller. The seller in this case does not protect against actions of prior owners. Grant deeds are the form most commonly used to transfer property.[93]

A quitclaim deed does not include warranties. Under a quitclaim deed, the seller conveys whatever interest he or she has in the property, but does not warrant against third-party claims. Basically, the buyer agrees to buy the property "as is" and takes it subject to any claims that a third party had against the seller or a prior owner.[94] Quitclaim deeds are commonly used to transfer title to real estate in a divorce, or to transfer property to a revocable trust used for estate planning purposes (revocable trusts are described in chapter 10 "Failing to Plan for Your Death or Incapacity"). Appendix A provides an example of a quitclaim deed.

Recording Deeds and Liens
against Property in Public Records

Do you know how the law works to prevent other people from selling your home out from under you? Do you know what can happen to you if your ownership in your home is not recorded correctly? When the owner of property signs the deed to property that states "I sell this to the buyer," legal title, (that is, legal ownership) is transferred from the seller to the buyer. To prevent a dishonest property seller from selling the same property to several buyers, deeds are recorded in a government office in a manner that allows potential buyers to verify that the seller still owns the property and has not sold the property to someone else. Generally, real estate deeds are recorded in the county recorder's office in the courthouse of the county in which the real estate is located. This puts everyone on *constructive notice,* which means that the buyer has purchased the property and rightfully owns the real estate. If the seller persuades another person to buy the real estate a second time after the first buyer has recorded his or her deed, and the second buyer does not check the public records, the second buyer suffers the loss.

Buyers are protected in another way. Liens against the property are also recorded in the public records. For example, most people borrow money from a bank to buy their home. The bank will lend them money only if they agree to grant the bank a security interest (also called a lien, a mortgage, or a deed of trust) in the property. If the property owner defaults on the loan and doesn't pay it back to the bank, the security interest permits the bank to take the property as repayment for the loan. The bank's security interest will be documented in a deed of trust or mortgage, which is also typically recorded in the public records. If deeds of trust and mortgages were not recorded, and the bank could not determine whether the property owner had given other people liens against the property, the property owner could borrow money from several banks using the same property over and over as security and cheat the banks out of large sums of money. Appendix B provides an example of a deed of trust.

Prospective buyers and lenders generally don't go to the government office and check the public records themselves to confirm that the seller still owns the property, and that the seller has not previously sold the property or granted liens against it. There are companies that, for a fee, check the records for you. For example, in many states *title companies* check the records, confirm that the owner still owns the property or has not given other parties an interest in it, and, for a premium, will issue an insurance policy to the buyer which insures against losses and damages the buyer will incur if something goes wrong and he or she does not get good title to the property. The insurance covers losses only up to the face amount of the policy and may not cover all losses and damages. Title insurance is widely misunderstood as to what it does and does not do.

A basic title insurance policy ensures that there are no liens or other claims to the property that are recorded in the public documents or on "record." It may also insure against some "off-record" risks such as whether the seller was mentally competent to sell the property. Title insurance, however, does not protect against a whole host of "off-record" problems. For example, it does not protect against loss if the property is not properly described on the deed.

Legal descriptions of real estate are very difficult to read and can easily be described incorrectly in the deed. The accuracy of the legal description can only be confirmed by an actual survey done by a qualified surveyor. I recently heard about a multimillion dollar home being built in a very expensive neighborhood that had to be partially torn down. The deed described the property line as starting twelves inches farther out that it really did. The new owner started building this very expensive home only to find out later that part of his new home encroached on someone else's land. It cost the new owner a lot of money to tear down that part of the house, and he ended up with a smaller house than he wanted. And he had to pay for it himself because his title insurance policy did not cover this type of loss. In another well-known case in California, a home owner found out that his swimming pool and concrete deck was built on adjacent property and not his own. He spent a lot of money to move his swimming pool and deck. He then sued his title insurance company to recover the money spent fixing things, but lost in court. The court said that title insurance does not insure against incorrect property descriptions.

Title insurance policies also include a lot of exceptions and don't insure against a number of risks that can restrict your right to use your property however you choose. For example, title insurance policies generally don't protect you against losses from certain tax liens for delinquent property taxes, easements granted to the public or someone else to use part of your property (for example, a hiking trail or the right of your neighbor to go across your property to get to his or her property), zoning regulations, or easements granted to the city or county where the property is located to put in telephone lines, water lines, and the like. The title insurance policy will list these exceptions, but you won't know how much they will affect you unless you ask the title insurance company to get you the underlying documents for each exception. For example, the city may have an easement to install telephone lines on your property. While you probably want a telephone, you won't know whether the city can install telephone lines at the same place you want to build a house unless you look at the actual documents that give the city the right to come in and install the telephone lines. The title insurance company can provide these to you, but you generally have to ask for them.

It is possible to get more protection from title insurance than basic policies give you. There are more expensive policies available, and you should talk to the title insurance company to find out about the different policies and the risks that each type of policy will protect you against. You should also confirm the amount of losses that the policy covers. Typically, the seller will pay the cost of a basic title insurance policy and the buyer pays the additional premium to buy a better policy.

In some states, the use of title insurance is not commonly used to protect buyers of property; lawyers' opinions are used instead. Before buying real estate, you need to find out what is common practice in the state where the property is located.

Legal ownership of other types of property can, and should, be recorded in the appropriate government office to give everyone notice that you now own it. Ownership of cars is generally handled by recording appropriate documents with the Department of Motor Vehicles of the state in which you reside, airplanes with the Federal Aviation Administration, copyrights with the U.S. Copyright Office, and trademarks and patents with the U.S. Office of Patents and Trademarks. In some cases, there is no government office to record the transfer of ownership. In these cases, you must be extremely careful to make sure that you have, in your possession, whatever documentation is required to prove ownership. For example, stock ownership in privately owned corporations is evidenced by physical possession of the actual stock certificate. Shareholders in privately owned corporations should always make sure that a stock certificate is issued in their name for the correct number of shares they own. In the case of larger corporations whose stock is publicly traded on the New York Stock Exchange, NASDAQ, or other exchange, actual share certificates typically are not issued to each shareholder. A designated transfer agent maintains records of the shareholders and the number of shares held by each. Any and all legal documents that evidence your legal ownership in property should be kept in a safe place, such as a safe deposit box.

The actual sale of property is often accomplished through the use of an independent third party — usually an escrow company or an attorney. The buyer gives the money to buy the property, and the seller gives the deed conveying ownership to the buyer and a title insurance policy to the escrow company. The escrow company properly records the deed, gives the money to the seller, and gives the buyer the recorded deed and the title insurance policy. Typically, the buyer and seller split the escrow company's fee for their services.

Legal Forms of Ownership

If you already own a home or other property, do you know how legal title is recorded? Is your property owned in joint tenancy, cotenancy, or community property? The form of ownership will have vastly different consequences to you and you need to know what they are.

Owning Property in Fee

There are several different types of property ownership. If you own property in fee (also referred to as fee simple or fee absolute), it means that you and you alone own that property; nobody else has any legal right to it. Even if you are married, you can hold and acquire property that you and you alone own. In the marital context, this is generally referred to as separate property. Property that you own outright in fee is property you can sell, give to someone else as a gift, leave to anyone you choose by will on your death, and otherwise deal with as you alone decide.

Common Forms of Co-Ownership

Two or more people can own property in several different forms of legal ownership. One of the most common forms
of co-ownership is called *joint tenant* or *joint tenancy*. In joint
tenancy, you and your co-owner own equal but undivided
shares in the property. Generally, the percentage of ownership
of each owner is determined by the number of owners. For
example, if there are two owners, they will each have a 50 percent interest; if there are four owners, they will each have a 25
percent interest, and so on. Each joint tenant can use the property at any time and in any way and neither has exclusive right
to it. Income earned from the property is divided equally. The
most significant feature that distinguishes joint tenancy from
other forms of property ownership is referred to as the *right of
survivorship*. This means that if a co-owner dies, the surviving
joint tenant solely owns the property automatically (or, in legal
jargon, by *operation of law*).

For example, if Mark and Jane own a house together as
joint tenants and Jane dies, on her death Mark becomes the sole
owner of the house. Even if Jane leaves a will stating that when
she dies, her share of the house is to go to her sister Beth, Mark
will still own the house by himself, and Beth won't own any part
of it. If Jane has children and would like her share of the house
to go to them on her death, Jane's interest in the house will still
go to Mark as the surviving joint tenant. The joint tenancy form
of ownership overrides all other claims of ownership.

The joint tenant form of ownership is evidenced by the
language used on the deed. For example, the deed to a house
owned by two people as joint tenants will include language similar to the following: "Seller transfers the property to Mark and
Jane as joint tenants." Alternatively, it could read: "Seller transfers the property to Mark and Jane in joint tenancy."

There is only one good reason to hold property in joint

tenancy. When a joint tenant dies, the survivor does not have to go through the probate court to get the title transferred to him or her. The deceased joint tenant's interest automatically transfers to the surviving joint tenant. Probate proceedings can be time-consuming, and expensive. (Probate proceedings are discussed in more detail in chapter 10, "Failing to Plan for Your Death or Incapacity.") When a joint tenant dies, the transfer of sole legal title to the property to the surviving joint tenant is generally evidenced by simply recording a copy of the deceased joint tenant's death certificate and a document called something like an Affidavit of Surviving Joint Tenant in the office having jurisdiction over the type of property subject to the joint tenancy. For real estate held in joint tenancy, an Affidavit of a Surviving Joint Tenant is recorded in the same office in which the original property deed was recorded.

Although avoiding the maze of probate is a plus in favor of joint tenancy ownership, there are disadvantages to this form of ownership. Sometimes it does not make sense to use this form of ownership, especially because it is possible to achieve the main benefit of joint tenancy — avoidance of probate — through the use of a living trust (also called, for example, family trust or probate-avoiding trust), which I explain later in "Failing to Plan for Your Death or Incapacity." The primary disadvantage to joint tenancy is also the form's primary distinction — the right of survivorship. You should only own property in joint tenancy with someone you want to inherit your share of the property upon your death — the person to whom you would give your share of the property anyway. If you are married, this would likely be your spouse, and married couples are the most common users of the joint tenant form of ownership. However, if you live in a community property state, there are tax reasons for owning property in community property rather than in joint tenancy. (This is also be discussed in chapter 10, "Failing to Plan for Your Death or Incapacity.") If you own property in joint tenancy and you sell your interest to someone else, the joint tenancy is broken and your former co-owner and the new co-owner thereafter own the property as co-tenants.

In many states, you can unilaterally break a joint tenancy by simply recording a document that says you hold your interest in the property as co-tenant rather than a joint tenant. You need to check the laws of the state where the property is located to find out what works. Joint tenancies can also be broken when co-owners don't intend to do so. For example, if a creditor of one of the co-owners gets an interest in the property, joint tenancy will be broken.

A variant of joint tenancy is tenancy by the entirety. This is joint tenancy between a husband and wife. Under this form of ownership, the husband and wife effectively own the entire property, not just an interest in the property, and neither can deal with the property independently of the other. Some states require that married couples own property in this form, while other states don't recognize it at all. Because tenancy by the entirety depends on marriage, if the couple divorce, the ownership of the property automatically coverts to tenancy in common or joint tenancy with each party owning one-half, depending on the applicable state law. On the death of one spouse, the other automatically owns the entire property.

If you co-own property and you don't want that other person to get your share on your death, the joint tenant form of ownership is the worst form possible. On your death your share will automatically transfer to your co-owner, no matter what you intended and no matter what you provide for in your will or trust. (There is one exception to this general rule: if your co-owner murders you, he or she does not get the property. You shouldn't count on this one.) If you want your share to go to somebody other than the co-owner, you want to co-own the property as tenants in common.

Tenants in common or *tenancy in common* is co-ownership without the right of survivorship in which two or more persons can own property. Tenants in common each own only a portion of the property, but are entitled to the use of the entire property. They may own their interests in unequal shares. In legal parlance, this is called an *undivided interest*. For example, if Mark and Jill own their house in equal shares as tenants in common, they are both entitled to reside there and use the entire property. If they sell the house, they will each be entitled to one-half of the sales proceeds. If Mark wants to sell his share in the house and Jill doesn't, Mark is legally able to sell his undivided interest to someone else. As a practical matter, it is really difficult to find a buyer for only an undivided interest in a house. You generally see this only when the tenants in common are relatives and one sells to another relative.

Tenants in common can own equal shares or unequal shares in the property. For example, if Jill put up 70 percent of the money to buy the house and pays 70 percent of the expenses and Mark put up the other 30 percent, then Jill would have a 70 percent co-tenant interest and Mark would have a 30 percent co-tenant interest. On the sale of the house, Jill would get 70 percent of the sales proceeds and Mark would get 30 percent.

Unlike joint tenancy ownership, if Mark dies, his co-tenant share in the property is transferred to the person he designates in his will or trust. It won't automatically go to Jill. This is the primary distinction between co-tenancy and joint tenancy. If Mark does not leave a will or trust, his share of the property still won't go to Jill. Mark's tenant in common interest will be transferred to a member of his family as determined by the intestacy laws of the state in which he resides. (Intestacy laws are also discussed in chapter 10, "Failing to Plan for Your Death or Incapacity," but, briefly, in the absence of a will or trust in which the deceased gifts his or her property, the intestacy laws of the state in which the decedent lived will determine who will inherit his or her property. Typically, this is the deceased person's closest relatives.)

Ownership as tenants in common will be evidenced by language on a deed such as: "Seller sells to Mark and Jill as equal tenants in common" or "Seller sells to Mark and Jill as common tenants." In most states, if the language in the deed is not very clear about whether it is a joint tenancy or a tenancy in common, the law presumes that the ownership is a tenancy in common, unless the co-owners are married, in which case the presumption is joint tenancy, or if the couple resides in a community property state, community property. However, this is not always the case because each state has its own peculiar set of laws dealing with property ownership.

Community Property

Community property was discussed in the chapter 1 "Failing to Protect Yourself in a Prenuptial Agreement." Community property is the law of nine states, and under this law, property acquired during a marriage is owned one-half by each spouse unless it is the separate property of one of the spouses or unless the husband and wife have agreed to convert it to some other form of ownership, such as a joint tenancy.

Partnership

Co-ownership of assets can also be by partnership. (There are several types of partnerships: general partnerships, limited partnerships, joint ventures. Here I provide only a general overview of this type of ownership.) A partnership is generally formed so that individuals can conduct a business together and share the profits and expenses of that business. A partnership can also own property and other assets. In many ways, a partnership is similar to the tenants in common form of ownership. However, with tenants in common ownership, the individuals directly own the property or assets; the deed to the property will say "to Mark and Jill as equal tenants in common." In a partnership, the legal entity of the partnership will own the property or assets. The deed to the property will say "to M & J Partnership" or "to M & J Limited Partnership."

Another important difference between a partnership and a tenant in common ownership is that partnerships are generally used for business activities and are not formed for ownership of a personal residence or other personal property. Tenant in common ownership is more frequently used for personal use property. However, for tax purposes, any co-owned property (whether held in partnership or a tenancy in common) used in an active business generally will be considered by the IRS to be held in partnership. Calling the co-ownership a tenancy in common, a joint venture, or any other name does not change the tax rules. If the co-owners pool their money and actively conduct a business, the ownership of assets and property is taxed as though owned by a partnership.

Many special tax rules apply to partnerships (the eye-glazing details of which I only briefly summarize here). A partnership must file a partnership return, which reports the income earned and expenses incurred in running the business, as well as how much of the partnership's income is allocated to each partner. The partnership itself does not pay taxes. The partners pay taxes on their proportionate share of partnership income. Tax matters for partnerships can quickly become complicated, and it is best to consult a tax professional to assist in these matters.

In a general partnership, any partner has the legal authority to sell or otherwise dispose of the partnership property unless there is a contrary agreement among the partners and each partner is responsible for debts incurred by the other partners in conducting partnership business. For example, some partnership agreements provide that the property cannot be sold without the consent of all partners Whereas these restrictions will be binding against each of the partners, third parties are not subject to such restrictions if they don't know about them. Before third parties are bound by any such restrictions, such restrictions must be recorded in the public records. In other words, third parties must be put on constructive notice of the restrictions for them to have any legal effect.

You now know about the different forms of property ownership and how legal ownership is protected. What kinds of mistakes do you need to watch out for? Where can you go wrong?

Identify Your Ownership Interest on the Deed

In the introduction, I stated that many of the legal mistakes women make derive from their propensity to readily trust other people. Property ownership is a glaring example of how too much trust can unravel your financial security and faith in others. A surprising number of people allow the property they own to be recorded in someone else's name, or solely in the name of a co-owner, generally a spouse or other family member.

Madge and her brother Pat worked in the construction industry. For more than a decade, they acquired "fixer-upper" homes to restore and sell for a profit. In a couple of cases, they built completely new homes from the ground up. Most of the money they made on a given sale was used to purchase the next house, and they progressed to more and more valuable homes. Madge handled most of the actual construction. She would hire and supervise crews and order materials and arrange for delivery. Pat handled the financial end. Pat persuaded Madge to let the deeds to the homes be recorded in Pat's name alone. Pat said that would make it easier for him to deal with the finances. They talked about formalizing their joint ownership in a partnership agreement, but just never got around to it.

After many years, they started having disagreements over how to deal with the property and what projects should take precedence. Their relationship became more and more acrimonious. Finally, Madge proposed that they sell the project they had just completed, divide the profits as partners, and go their separate ways. Pat then denied that they ever had a partnership. He also denied that Madge owned any part of the projects they had worked on and sold over the years. Madge was only an employee, Pat said. To add insult to injury, Pat claimed that Madge, who was the younger of the two and female to boot, could not have made it out in the world on her own and that he employed Madge to work with him only out of brotherly concern and support.

Because Madge had trusted Pat to handle their financial and legal affairs properly, Madge had almost no documentation of any sort, much less a deed, to support her claim that she owned one-half of the project and the built-up capital invested in it. Some very nasty litigation ensued. As family disputes often go, the other family members eventually took sides and most sided with Pat. They saw Madge as the instigator of the problems, because she originally proposed the breakup, and faulted her for the disruption in the family. In the end, not only did Madge lose her rightful share in the property, she permanently damaged her relationship with her family.

A letter to a mid-west newspaper describes the following case. The writer's husband had opened a CD certificate and, for no particular reason, put his and his brother's names on it. His brother had given his daughter a power of attorney. When she learned of the CD, she immediately marched down to the bank, cashed in the CD, and closed the account. When the writer's husband found out and tried to get his money back, the bank said there was nothing it could do. The account was a joint account between the writer's husband and his brother, and his brother's daughter had a legal power of attorney. She had acted within her legal rights.[95]

As these two cases illustrate, even when you co-own property with a family member, it is crucial that you always make sure your ownership in the property is properly documented. This can prevent disputes with your familial co-owner and can avoid the havoc that such disputes have on the rest of the family.

Record Your Ownership Interest

You must make sure that your legal ownership is recorded correctly. Mary and Paul had one piece of property from their marriage, which they divided in their property settlement but continued to own together after their divorce. At the time of their divorce, the market value for the type of real estate they owned had dramatically declined, and they would have lost a lot of money had they sold it then, so Mary and Paul agreed to continue to own the property together until the value appreciated. Then, they would sell the property and split the proceeds. Mary and Paul both remarried and had children with their new spouses. Many years after their divorce, Mary consulted an attorney, who found that the deed to this property described their co-ownership as joint tenancy, and not as tenants in common. Under such form of ownership, if either Mary or Paul died, their share would automatically go to the other under the right of survivorship. Their share would not go to their new spouse and children. This was quite a surprise to both Mary and Paul because it was not what they had intended. Because they were in agreement, it was fairly easy to correct the form of ownership by simply recording a new deed that described their holdings as tenants in common. Even if Paul had not agreed, Mary could unilaterally have broken the joint tenancy. However, if she had not found out that title was held as joint tenants before she died, her spouse and children would have faced a formidable hurdle in proving that the deed was wrongly drafted and that it did not accurately reflect Mary and Paul's true legal ownership.

The courts are filled with cases of demoralized people who trusted their property co-owners to take care of the legal niceties of property ownership and to do the right thing. Too often, these trusting souls later find themselves fighting with their co-owners for the property and condemning themselves for their own naivete. Don't let this happen to you. Make sure you are properly named as a co-owner, that the form of ownership is properly described, and that the deed or other ownership document is properly recorded. Your financial security depends on your wise and careful handling of your property.

Record Restrictions on Co-owners' Rights

Have you ever owned property with somebody else and you both agreed you wouldn't do certain things with the property? If so, was your agreement verbal and known only between the two of you? Did you think this verbal agreement prevented your co-owner from doing something contrary to your agreement?

Frequently, co-owners agree to restrict their individual right to deal with the property. In fact, it is generally advisable to impose some restrictions on each other. For example, you may agree that neither of you will sell your interest without first offering it to the other. You may agree that neither of you will use your interest as security for a bank loan without the prior written approval of the other. In the case of bank accounts, you may agree that neither of you will withdraw funds nor write a check against the account in excess of a certain dollar amount. If you don't have these agreements, your co-owner can enter into deals that will adversely affect you. For instance, your co-owner might sell his or her interest in the property to a third party who has totally different views about how to use the property than you do. Your co-owner might use his or her interest as security for a bank loan. If he or she fails to pay the loan and the bank forecloses on his or her interest, the bank will be your new co-owner and you will have to deal with it. The bank's goal may well be contrary to your own. Most likely, the bank will want to sell the property as soon as possible and get its money out as fast as possible. If you co-own a bank account, you might wake up one day to a zero balance.

If you have private agreements that restrict both you and your co-owner as to how you can use the property and they are known only to the two of you, you will be limited in what you can do if your co-owner violates those agreements. You may well have solid legal grounds for suing your co-owner, but if he or she is in financial straits — and often financial despair under-lies a co-owner's violation of agreed-upon restrictions — your ability to sue is a right without a practical remedy. Even if you win your lawsuit, your award will only entitle you to collect damages from someone who probably cannot pay them. You won't have legal claims against an innocent third party who believed your co-owner's assurances that he or she could sell the property.

If you and your co-owner do agree on limitations concerning the co-owned property, it is imperative that these limitations be recorded in the appropriate public record, thereby putting the world on constructive notice of the agreement, which enables you to enforce your rights against third parties as well as your co-owner. For example, if you and your co-owner of real estate agree that neither of you will sell your interest without first offering it to the other, and that neither of you will use the property to secure a loan, you need to record an agreement that outlines these limitations in the same government office in which the deed to the property was recorded (as previously mentioned, this will vary by state, but is often either the county recorder's office or the county courthouse in the county where the property is located). If this agreement is recorded and your co-owner nevertheless violates it by selling his or her interest to a third party, or gives a bank a security interest in the property for a loan, you will have a good case for getting the sale or the secured interest set aside, even though the third party will be harmed. The third party and the bank are on notice of the restrictions and are subject to your rights under the agreement. Likewise, if you jointly own a bank account with someone else, the bank records should reflect that withdrawals of any funds, or checks written on the account, or checks in excess of a specified amount must be approved by all co-owners.

Rose did not heed this advice when she and her husband, Robert, divorced and continued to own a piece of real estate together as tenants in common. They agreed that neither would sell their interest, nor give it as security to a lender, without the other co-owner's consent, and this agreement was included in their property settlement agreement on their divorce. They did not record an agreement listing these restrictions in the public real estate records. Years later, Robert put up his interest in the property as security for several loans, without first obtaining Rose's consent and without even informing her of his intent to do so. By the time she found out, Robert's interest, and hence her interest indirectly, was so tangled up in liens, fraudulent conveyances, and sham transactions that it took Rose years and thousands of dollars in legal fees to straighten out the title to the property. Even though Rose had a very good legal case against Robert for breaching their property settlement agreement, by that time he was flat broke. If their agreement had been properly recorded, Rose probably could have been able to get the sales and liens set aside. The buyers and lenders would have been on notice that Robert could neither sell his interest nor post it as collateral for a loan without Rose's prior consent.

Choose Your Co-owners Carefully

Have you ever had a bad experience with a business partner? Did someone you trust ever cheat you? Considering the importance of protecting your legal and financial health, it is imperative that you carefully choose the people with whom you do business, own property, or enter into an agreement. This principal may seem obvious, but it is extraordinary how many people believe that someone reputed to be deceitful and dishonest will, for some reason, be honest and trustworthy with them. It seems they are convinced that the dishonest person was not really dishonest, and instead believe that the person was mistreated or falsely maligned by his or her former acquaintances or business associates. Or, alternatively, these people believe that their venture with the dishonest person will be so successful that the risk is worth taking. As often happens, after they buy property with or go into business with this dishonest person, they are genuinely surprised when they too get cheated.

A case in point. Melanie, an aspiring film producer with a fair amount of personal wealth (fresh meat to unscrupulous producers) came to Hollywood not only with stars in her eyes but with her head in the sand. Melanie agreed to contribute a considerable amount of money to the financial operations of two veteran film producers in exchange for a profit participation and producer credits for involvement in certain film projects. The producers she planned to join up with were reputed to be fast and slick, of which she was aware. Nevertheless, she would not make them enter into a detailed written agreement spelling out her profit participations and other components of their deal. She thought they wouldn't do business with her if she was too pushy. Instead, the producers drafted and signed a short letter of agreement detailing the amount of money Melanie was to contribute and little else. Needless to say, after Melanie contributed her money, the other two producers began to slowly cut out her participation in the film projects. They had her money and felt no moral compulsion to live up to their end of the bargain. They also had no clear legal obligation to live up to either, because the three of them had not entered into a comprehensive agreement that clarified Melanie's rights.

Whereas some potential problems can be avoided by detailed written agreements and by recording restrictions in the public record, problems such as dishonest dealings cannot always be foreseen. If your co-owner has no moral reservations about stealing from you, it is highly unlikely that he or she will be disturbed about breaching a contract. The best way to protect yourself in this case is to know your co-owners and their reputations. Take off the rose-colored glasses and scrutinize your potential colleagues through the lens of reality and past behavior. Don't do business with people who have previously demonstrated dishonest and untrustworthy conduct. If, for some reason you must, do so with your eyes wide open and protect yourself as much as possible.

In the preceding chapters, I talked about property — how to hold title to property and how to protect your legal right to property. I talked about protecting property in prenuptial agreements, during your marriage, and in divorce. I talked about building a business and running it successfully and making sure you comply with all your tax obligations. In the next chapter, I talk about wills, trusts, and other documents you need to prepare in case you become incapacitated and to ensure that your property is distributed as you wish on your death.

LEGAL MISTAKE # 10:

FAILING TO PLAN FOR YOUR DEATH OR INCAPACITY

*"It's not that I'm afraid to die. I just
don't want to be there when it happens."*
Woody Allen

"DEATH, n. To stop sinning suddenly."
The Devil's Dictionary, by Ambrose Bierce

Do you have a will, a trust, a power of attorney for health care? Have you ever thought about preparing one? Do you think you're too young to worry about this? Do you question why you should plan for your death? After all, you won't be around to deal with the issues that may come up, as your children and heirs try to deal with your property and other matters. Most people, however, have a deep psychological need to leave a personal legacy of some sort in this world. Most of us don't wish to impose unnecessary burdens and chaos on our loved ones as part of that legacy. Yet, without some planning on your part for your death, that is the likely result. Your family will not only suffer the grief from your death but will also have to spend untold hours of time and frustration wrapping up your affairs and trying to figure out what to do with your property.

Sara and Jack know frustration well. Their father always said he would leave his estate to both of them equally on his death. Their mother died first and he remarried. Although Sara and Jack's father had a lot of stocks and bonds when he remarried and owned the house he and his new wife occupied, he had commingled all his property with his new wife's property. Their father, moreover, was not good with paperwork. On his death, Jack and Sara found out that their father had never had a will prepared. Under the laws that applied to their father's estate, his new wife got all of his property. It was now under her control and on her death would go to the persons she designated in her will. Because the new wife had children from a prior marriage and had never liked Sara and Jack much, they had little hope that they would ever see a dime of their father's hard-earned money. They also feared that family heirlooms handed down from their grandparents would never be returned to their side of the family. Sara and Jack looked through their father's papers, such as they were, to see if they could find anything that might show that he intended they get part of the property or at least the family heirlooms. Their father's files were such a mess, however, that they couldn't find anything to prove his intentions. Moreover, he had never had a family lawyer so there were no legal records. They were simply shut out.

Maintain Complete, Clear Records of What You Own and Where It Is

Like Sara and Jack's father, most of us don't keep very organized records of our business and legal matters. We are simply too busy to spend precious time organizing our paperwork. Besides, we know what pile or drawer the papers are in. We know the background of each matter and who the key players are. What we don't think about is that upon our death, someone else is going to have to try to make sense of our affairs. If that person is a spouse, he or she may have more information about where to look and what to look for in handling these matters than would a child, other relative, or friend, but such an undertaking can still be time-consuming. The more disorganized your paperwork, the more hours that person will have to devote to figuring it out. And the less involved that person was in your business, legal, or financial affairs, the more time it will take.

Have you ever tried to sort through the business and financial affairs of a deceased relative or friend? If so, you probably know what I am talking about. You not only have to deal with the grief of losing someone you were close to, but you also lose time away from your job and family while you try to sort your way through the mass confusion of the deceased person's financial affairs. Did you agree to do this for no pay? Did you feel it would be crass to talk about money? If so, you are not alone. Unfortunately, your grief-induced devotion to this task can adversely affect your own finances and family life, and ultimately cause you to resent your deceased friend or family member and anyone else you can blame it on.

Ideally, to make things easier on the people you leave behind, you should have files containing important documents about your legal, financial, and business life all in one place. These files should include copies of real estate deeds; mortgages and deeds of trusts secured by the properties; and documents summarizing any other assets you own such as mutual funds, stocks, bonds, cars, artworks, royalty agreements, life insurance, and retirement plans. These files should also contain information about whether the assets are stored, and, if so, where or who manages the assets. For example, you should designate the brokerage house and broker that handles your stocks and bonds, the name and contact information for your mutual funds, the location of any storage space you rent and the procedure for gaining access to it, and the location of your bank accounts and safe deposit box. Your files should also contain testamentary documents, such as a will and/or trust agreement, which provide how you want your property distributed. If you keep complete, clear records of what you own and where it is, your designated executor will be able to process your estate with the least amount of confusion and in the least amount of time.

Prepare a Will or Trust

Many people, particularly young people, neglect to prepare a *will*, which is a legal document that states to whom they want to their property to be distributed on their death. They believe they have plenty of time to deal with that later. However, if a sudden, unfortunate accident occurs, or if you become ill, then, absent a will, the disposition of your property on your death will be determined by the laws of intestacy in the state in which you reside.

Each state has *intestacy laws* — laws that direct who will get your property if you die without a will. These laws are the state legislature's best guess about which relatives most people would want their estate to go to on their death. Necessarily, this must be approximated on a global scale, rather than by individual cases. These laws generally do a good job of anticipating how most people would direct their property to be distributed if they had prepared a will. For example, in California, if you die and your spouse and children survive you, your community property goes to your surviving spouse, and your separate property is divided among your surviving spouse and your children. In most cases, this distribution will closely approximate what you would have wanted. If you have recently separated from your spouse, or were planning to divorce him or her in the near future, you may not want him or her to inherit your estate. If you die unmarried and without children, your estate generally will go to your parents. If you are estranged from your parents, or if your parents have sufficient assets of their own and other people close to you would benefit more from inheriting your assets, the distribution mandated by intestacy laws may not match your wishes. No state laws of intestacy allow for friends or significant others of the deceased person to inherit part of his or her estate. If you want your property to go to someone other than the intestacy laws provide, the only way you can achieve this is through a will or trust, or by holding property in joint tenancy with your chosen recipient.

Everyone should have a will, regardless of age or financial circumstance. Even young people are not immune to deadly accidents, and even if you don't have great wealth, you likely have a few cherished possessions that you want someone in particular to have. There are three basic questions you need to answer before drawing up a will:

1. Are there specific possessions (such as a piece of art or jewelry) that you want a specified person to inherit?

2. Whom do you wish to inherit the balance of your assets (this is called the residue of your estate)?

3. Whom do you wish to designate as the person responsible for wrapping up your affairs? This person is typically referred to as your *personal representative* or *executor* (or *executrix* if the person is a woman and your will is not gender neutralized) of your estate. It is advisable to list one or more successor personal representatives or executors in case your first choice is unable to do the job.

All of this information is set out in your will. In addition, you can include instructions about how and where you wish to be buried, if you prefer to be cremated, and, if so, where you want your ashes to be disposed. If you have minor children, you should designate their guardians, in case both you and your spouse die. If you have a relative you don't like and don't want to inherit any of your property, you can state this in your will. In fact, most lawyers advise you that, if you wish to disinherit a child or other close relative, you should specifically state that you don't want that person to get any of your property. Otherwise, the disinherited person may challenge your will in court. Often, a person is excluded from inheriting property because he or she already has enough money. For example, a mother with two children, one of whom is a millionaire and one of whom is poor, might provide that all her property go to her poor child on her death rather than be divided among the two. Her will might include a clause stating that says she is excluding the rich child "not for lack of love and affection," but simply because the rich child doesn't need the money as much as the other child. Appendix E provides an example of a simple will.

If you do bequeath less to someone than you think they expect and you fear this person might try to fight in court and get part of your assets, it is advisable to include a *no-contest* clause in your will. This is a clause that provides that anyone who disputes your will will be completely disinherited. Dawn Roddenberry, the daughter of Gene Roddenberry, creator of *Star Trek*, apparently didn't understand what a no-contest clause could do. She chose to contest her father's will, even though it included one. His will granted her $500,000 and 25 percent of any proceeds from *Star Trek* merchandise, television shows, and movies, but she apparently thought this was not enough. Right before her case was to go to trial, she dropped it and then argued that the no-contest clause did not apply to her because she had not gone to trial. The Court of Appeals in California disagreed. It invoked the no-contest clause and completely stripped her of her inheritance.[96]

It is important to keep in mind that your will is not irrevocable, nor is it cast in stone. As long as you are legally competent, you can revoke it, replace it, change it, or add to it at any time. Whenever your life circumstances change, you should review your will to make sure it still fulfills your wishes. Many states require that for your will to be valid, it must be witnessed by at least two people who will not inherit anything from you. The witnesses certify, by signing their name to the will immediately after you sign it, that you, and not someone else forging your name, signed the will, and that you did so without duress. The witnessing procedure is to protect you from being coerced into signing away all your property to someone you would not otherwise give it to. A handwritten will, which is signed and dated by the author, is valid in most states. These are referred to as *holographic wills*. However, holographic wills are more frequently challenged by disgruntled heirs than are typewritten wills that are witnessed by independent witnesses. Therefore, holographic wills generally are not advisable. Each state has its own laws governing whether a will will be valid, so you need to check the laws of the state in which you live to make sure your will will be upheld.

Some very nasty court battles have revolved around will contests. One of the more recent battles that has spiked the public interest is the one between Anna Nicole Smith and the two sons of her deceased husband, oil tycoon J. Howard Marshall, whose net worth is estimated at $1.6 billion. Anna Nicole Smith, formerly Vickie Lynn Hogan, once worked as a night cook at Jim's Krispy Fried Chicken in Mexia, Texas. She later found celebrity as *Playboy*'s 1992 Playmate of the Year and as a Guess? Jeans model. She met Marshall in 1991 when she was working as a topless dancer, shortly after he lost both his wife and his mistress of twenty-two years. Marshall and Smith married in June 1994. Smith claims she gave Marshall a "reason for living," but apparently not for long — Marshall died in August 1995. Smith's 1992 will left his entire estate to his youngest son, Pierce, and the battle royals over his estate have since ensued. Smith's lawyers says Pierce, the executor of Marshall's estate, manipulated

Marshall into distrusting Smith and thus deleting gifts to her in the will. They argue that Smith is entitled to one-half of Marshall's estate under Texas community property laws, or $800 million. Marshall's older son, Howard, is also in a fight with Pierce. Howard claims that Pierce manipulated a senile Marshall into excluding Howard as well. Howard claims that, even though he and Marshall had once had a falling out, Marshall had verbally promised him that he and Pierce would be treated equally when it came to dividing up his estate. Pierce, who became Marshall's legal guardian shortly before Marshall married Smith, claims that Marshall was senile during this period and that he is only carrying out the wishes of his father as expressed in a 1992 will that provided for neither Smith nor Howard. Pierce further claims that, in their short marriage, Marshall gave Smith gifts worth $8 to $10 million, which is quite enough. Even before Marshall died, Pierce cut off funds to Smith, and utilities to a Houston condominium and New York City apartment that Marshall had given Smith were cut off for nonpayment. Everything about the case has been acrimonious. Smith and Pierce fought for ten days in court about how to dispose of Marshall's remains. Smith wanted a traditional Catholic burial, whereas Pierce said his father wished to be cremated. A judge ordered cremation but also ordered that the ashes be split between Smith and Pierce. Smith attended a memorial service she arranged after being banned from the family's memorial service. When she arrived attired in a tight white dress with plunging neckline, she said, "It's how he loved for me to dress, and I wanted to honor his memory." Five years later, Smith reportedly has not picked up her share of the ashes.[97] In 1996, Smith also filed bankruptcy in Los Angeles, in which she sought to avoid claims of her creditors and establish her right to part of Marshall's estate. Pierce filed a countersuit in bankruptcy court, in part to protect a libel lawsuit he had earlier filed against Smith and her attorneys. Since then, Smith's attorneys have paid Pierce more than $800,000 to settle his libel claims against them.

Since Marshall's death, Smith has gained and lost one hundred pounds, has guest starred on *Ally McBeal* and *Veronica's Closet*, and has a new boyfriend. Claiming she is "one of the biggest scandals of the universe and you can quote me on that," Smith has also launched a foundation known as Stars Against Scandals (SASS). (Reportedly, Smith was perplexed when a reporter asked what the extra S in SASS stands for and said she would have to find out). According to Smith, the foundation will help celebrities, politicians, and athletes involved in misbehavior and raise money for public relations, legal funds, and vacation getaways for celebrities in the midst of a scandal who "need to get away."[98] With no end in sight, this estate battle promises to entertain the public for many more years.

The tale of Doris Duke kept many a reporter and lawyer occupied. The heiress to a tobacco fortune and often described as the "richest girl in the world," Duke changed her will and the executors named in her will numerous times in the final years of her life. Her different executors included Chandi Heffner, a Hare Krishna she met at a dance class and adopted; Dr. Demopoulos, one of her doctors; her accountant, Irwin Bloom, who was accused of skimming money from her estate and later charged with tax evasion; her half-nephew, Walker Inman; and, finally, her Irish ponytailed butler, Bernard Lafferty. At the time of her death, her will named Lafferty as the sole executor and provided him with $500,000 per year and $5 million in executor fees. The balance of her estate was left to her charitable foundation to benefit art, wildlife, and other charitable causes. Estranged from her adopted daughter, Chandi, she expressly and profusely disinherited Chandi in her last will.

Following Duke's death, the fights started and the legal fees mounted to astronomical proportions.

Chandi sued for breach of contract, claiming that Duke promised to make her the sole beneficiary of her estate. Described in the court proceedings as someone who "out-Leona Helmsleyed Leona Helmsley," Chandi eventually settled for $65 million.[99] Dr. Demopoulos sued to have her final will invalidated. He claimed that Duke would not have knowingly left one of the great fortunes in the hands of the illiterate and unstable butler, Bernard Lafferty. Detractors of Dr. Demopoulos claimed that his real concern was his loss of huge executor's fees by having been removed as executor in Duke's final will. Three former Duke employees, including her chef, also filed suit. They claimed damages for $30 million for harassment and breach of promise. While Duke's lawyers dismissed these claims as ludicrous, the stakes escalated when a former Duke nurse, Tammy Payette, insisted that Duke had been murdered by an overdose of morphine through an alleged conspiracy between Lafferty and Duke's doctor. Payette's credibility suffered a substantial blow when she was subsequently arrested, convicted, and sentenced to eight years in jail for stealing jewelry and other valuable items from some of her wealthy patients, including Duke. Payette claimed that jewelry in her possession that belonged to Duke were just gifts given to her by Lafferty. The Los Angeles District Attorney's office investigated the charges of homicide and found "no credible evidence" of murder.[100]

Almost immediately upon the public announcement that Lafferty was named as Duke's executor, accusations of incompetence and worse began rolling in. The judge presiding over the probate of Duke's estate removed Lafferty and his coexecutor, the U.S. Trust Co., in 1995. The judge blasted Lafferty for commingling of estate and personal assets, waste of assets, improvidence and want of understanding, and substance abuse. She described such excesses as crashing Duke's Cadillac and then having the estate provide him with a new Cadillac along with a chauffeur. She also protested his use of estate funds to spruce up Duke's Los Angeles estate, where he still lived, including the enlargment of the area outside the bedroom facing the private garden and the installation in the private bath of a spa bathtub and marble flooring. The judge noted that even though Lafferty continued to draw an annual salary of $100,000 as Duke's executive assistant, he was nevertheless insolvent and had accumulated $89,000 in unpaid credit card bills and had borrowed $825,000 from the U.S. Trust Co. She criticized U.S. Trust Co. for failing to rein in Lafferty and making the loans of $825,000 to "appease" him. The judge appointed new executors. Lafferty and the U.S. Trust Co. appealed their removals; these removals were put on hold by an appeals court and produced the anomaly of there being two sets of executors.

Finally, in 1996, a settlement was reached. Lafferty resigned as executor in exchange for a $4.5 million executor's fee and the $500,000 yearly bequest left to him in Duke's will. Dr. Demopoulos was given a seat on the board of Duke's foundation.[101]

The lawyers may have been the real wasters of assets in this case. As many as 150 lawyers from seventeen firms got involved in the dispute before the case settled in 1996. The judge slashed their legal bills by almost $14 million of the $21 million of bills submitted. She described much of the work as "unnecessary, duplicative or excessive." Taking the biggest hit was the firm that was hired by Duke to draft her last will and that represented the estate during the labyrinthine proceedings. When the judge was finished with their bill, she had cut it from $15.3 million to $3.7 million. Some said the cost was Duke's fault for churning out so many wills late in life. Others blamed her choice of Lafferty as executor of her estate, an unusual choice under almost anyone's standards. Yet others defended it as the price of finding out the truth about Duke's intent and soundness of mind when she executed her last will.[102]

Although these cases were unusual in the amount of money involved and the length to which the potential beneficiaries of the estate would go to defend their turf, many small estates engender similar destructive fights. This is one area where preparation of legal documents carefully, thoughtfully, and with solid advice is a must. Some factors that might increase the odds of a destructive, expensive will contest are selecting of an executor who is not skilled in financial and business matters; disinheriting a child; gifting most of your estate to charity; favoring a second or third spouse over children from your first marriage; or waiting until you are very sick or feeble to prepare your will, in which your mental capacity at the time may be susceptible to challenge.[103] Expensive will contests will only serve to deplete your estate and disrupt or destroy family relationships.

Unless you have a trust, which is discussed subsequently, whether you have a will or not, your estate will be administered through probate in a local court. *Probate administration* is a court proceeding through which a judge oversees the distribution of your assets and the payment of your debts. Your will, if you had one, and a list of your financial assets and liabilities are presented to the court by your personal representative or executor if you had a will, or by the person, generally a close relative, appointed by the court to handle your estate (commonly called the *administrator*). For convenience, I will refer to both as the executor.

The executor will first petition the court for probate administration. This petition informs the court that you have died, and that the executor proposes to be responsible for handling your estate. After the court officially grants the executor authority to take charge of your estate, the executor will marshal your assets, pay off your liabilities, and distribute the remaining assets to your relatives and friends as you have designated in your will or, in the absence of a will, as provided for by the intestacy laws of your state of residency. All of these acts, however, must be approved by the judge before the executor carries them out. The judge will make sure that your assets are distributed in the manner that you intended. While the protective aspect of probate is laudable, probate administration can be time-consuming and expensive, particularly in large cities, where the courts are clogged and it can easily take more than a year to probate even the simplest estate. Most state laws allow a minimum amount of property to be distributed without full-blown probate (for example, in California, if a decedent's property is valued at $100,000 or less, probate administration is not required).

To avoid the court hassle of probate, in many states more and more people are using revocable trusts to handle the distribution of their assets after their death. These are also sometimes called family trusts, probate-avoiding trusts, and living trusts. Each state has its own laws that govern the creation of a trust and you need to check the laws of your own state before setting one up. I will discuss the general rules on trusts below. The term *trust* refers to a legal relationship in which one person — the *trustee* — holds legal title to property for the benefit of another person — the *beneficiary*. The person who sets up the trust and puts property into it is the *trustor* or *settlor*. Appendix F provides a simple revocable living trust. Under a revocable trust, the trustee is granted legal authority to deal with the trust assets as provided for in the trust agreement, and probate is not required. Because a court is not supervising the distribution of the assets, the assets can be distributed more expeditiously and at a much lower cost.

A trust agreement is a more complicated document than a will. In a typical revocable trust, you and your spouse are the initial trustees and you both contribute your assets to the trust.

The trust agreement itself will direct how you each want your assets to be dealt with, both during your lifetimes, and on your death. During your joint lifetimes, you and your spouse typically get all of the income earned by the trust and all other benefits that accrue from the trust property. You can sell the property, fix it up, and do anything else with it you wish. The trust can be revoked, amended, or replaced at any time. On the death of the first spouse, the trust typically will provide that the decedent's assets are transferred to an irrevocable trust of which the surviving spouse is the beneficiary. On the death of the second spouse, the assets of both spouses may be distributed to the children or, if they are still minors, retained in the trust and managed by a trustee for the benefit of the children until they reach a specified age, for example, age 25 or 30 (whatever the trustors decide). At this time, the balance of the trust assets is generally distributed to the children.

A trust may sound a bit scary because the trustee has a lot of power. When you and your spouse are the trustees, this of course is not a concern and is exactly what you want. But if you become incapacitated, or if your property is kept in a trust after you die for the benefit of your children, you may worry about whether the trustee will misuse the assets. Although the trustee is given a lot of power, the trustee does not have unlimited power and cannot legally use your trust assets for his or her personal benefit. The trustee is a fiduciary and is subject to strict and high legal standards imposed on fiduciaries. If a trustee misuses the assets or does not comply with the trust agreement, the beneficiary can go to court and ask the judge to remove the trustee and make him or her reimburse the trust for losses suffered by the trust.

Despite the fiduciary obligations imposed on trustees, cases do arise in which a trustee absconds with the money. Even if the beneficiaries sue the trustee and win damages, the trustee may have spent the money and may not be able to pay the amount ordered by the court. For this reason, some people designate banks or other similar institutions to be the trustee of their estate. Banks and other corporate trustees are often criticized for the fees they charge and for the slow and bureaucratic manner by which they tend to handle trust estates. However, there is a distinct advantage to a corporate trustee such as a bank: it doesn't steal the money, or at least if one of its employees does steal the money, the bank makes up the loss.

Revocable trusts avoid probate (a significant benefit in and of itself), but there are several things you need to know about what can be achieved by revocable trusts and what must be done to make them operate properly. For example, you must legally transfer your property to the trust while you are living for the trust to work and avoid probate. Your home must be transferred to the trust by legally deeding your ownership in your home to the trust, for example,the deed will transfer the property to John Smith and Linda Jones, trustees of the Jones Family Trust, created by Declaration of Trust dated January 1, 2000. Like all deeds, this deed should be recorded in the public records. Generally, a quitclaim deed is used. Your brokerage accounts and bank accounts must also be transferred to the trust. Any asset not specifically transferred to the trust won't be owned by the trust and won't be subject to the trust on your death. If even a single asset is not legally transferred to the trust, that asset will be subject to probate unless it is valued below the minimum amount that your state law allows to be distributed without full-blown probate. People often go to the trouble to pay a lawyer to set up a revocable trust for them and then fail to legally transfer their assets to it (sometimes their attorneys fail to advise them properly of this requirement). They have achieved nothing in this case, other than to waste the money they paid to have the trust agreement drafted.

A major misconception of revocable trusts is that they reduce estate taxes. They don't. There is no tax benefit from using a trust that cannot be obtained without a trust. A trust, however, can facilitate the use of several legal tax plans that do reduce estate taxes.

Most married persons leave their estate to their surviving spouse (with some variations discussed later). The federal estate tax laws and many state tax laws allow decedents to leave their estate to their surviving spouse totally free of estate tax. This is called the *unlimited marital deduction*. The federal estate tax laws as well as many state tax laws, also exempt a specified amount of property from estate tax, which is sometimes referred as the *estate tax exemption*. The estate tax exemption is $675,000 for the year 2000 and will increase to $1 million over the next few years. (Larger estate tax exemptions apply to family-owned businesses and farms.) If a husband and wife die after the estate tax exemption reaches $1 million, $2 million of their combined estates could be transferred to their children, totally free of estate tax. When the first spouse dies, usually no estate tax is due because of the unlimited marital deduction and the estate tax exemption. On the death of the second spouse, the balance of the estate owned by the second spouse less that spouse's estate tax exemption, will be subject to estate tax.

For example, assume Jim and Jill own property worth $3 million and they both die after the estate tax exemption reaches the $1 million mark. If Jim dies and Jill doesn't need all the marital assets to live on, their estate-planning documents could provide that assets owned by Jim of a value equal to $1 million could be given to their children and the balance of his assets given to Jill. In this case, no estate tax would be due on Jim's estate, after applying the estate tax exemption and the unlimited marital deduction. When Jill dies, she would also be able to transfer $1 million of her estate to their children, free of estate tax; the balance of her assets distributed to her children would be subject to estate tax. Together, Jim and Jill would have been able to transfer $2 million worth of assets to their children completely free of estate tax. The balance of their combined assets would be taxable only on Jill's death.

If Jill needed the income from all their property to live on, however, it may not be practicable for Jim to bequeath $1 million of the assets to their children on his death. If those assets were instead bequeathed to Jill, along with the balance of Jim's share of their property, the tax advantage of the estate tax exemption on Jim's death could be forever lost. A revocable trust, however, easily lets Jim and Jill take advantage of both lifetime exemptions, yet preserve Jill's right to the income from all their assets. The trust achieves this through a mechanism often called a *bypass trust*. On Jim's death, his assets would be divided among two trusts. Assets worth $1 million would be put into the bypass trust. Jill would have the right to the income from assets in this trust, and if appropriate limitations apply, she could also use part of the principal for her own benefit if she needed to. She would not, however, have the unqualified right to use the assets. On Jill's death, the assets in the bypass trust would go to their children. Because Jill did not control the final disposition of the property in the bypass trust, these assets are not counted as part of her estate for estate tax purposes. On Jill's death, her estate would be reduced by her estate tax exemption of $1 million, so Jim and Jill once again would be able to transfer $2 million worth of assets to their children, free of estate tax.

Although this tax-planning device is most easily implemented by a revocable trust, it is possible to do the same through a will by giving the surviving spouse a *life estate* in assets valued at the estate exemption amount, and the *remainder interest* in such assets to their children. This means that the surviving spouse would get all the income earned on the assets during his or her lifetime, and on the survivor's death, the assets would be distributed to the children. The estate tax exemptions highlight the need to plan for your death. Under your state law, it may not be possible to maximize the tax savings from the estate tax exemptions that both you and your husband are entitled to without a will or a trust if state intestacy law does not divide the deceased spouse's property between the surviving spouse and the children, or provides for a division that does not maximize the benefit of the estate tax exemption.

Another type of trust that has gotten more use in recent years is a so-called qualified terminable interest trust or Q-TIP. This form of trust is an outgrowth of the current higher rate of divorce and multiple marriages. It addresses the concern that if Jim leaves all his assets to Jill on his death, and Jill remarries, Jill might give all of Jim's assets to her new spouse or to children born of the second marriage. This may be particularly troublesome to Jim if he and Jill have children from their marriage and he wishes to take care of them. The Q-TIP allows Jim to give Jill all the income from his assets, yet provides that on Jill's death, his assets will be given to their children. If all the requirements are met, the trust will still qualify for the unlimited marital deduction, and Jim's estate will not owe estate taxes on the assets put into the Q-TIP.

There are many reasons for drafting a will or trust. You work all your life to build up your estate. On your death, your hard-earned property should go to the persons you love and wish to support. The best way you can make sure this happens is through a will or trust.

Beware of Estate-Planning Scams

To many people, estate taxes are the most offensive form of existing taxation. Many people spend a considerable amount of money and energy trying to reduce estate taxes. There is a deep-rooted belief by many that the government has no right to prevent people from transferring their assets to their children. After all, many people devote their whole lives to providing for their children and building up an estate to leave to them. They may believe that it is totally inconsistent with our capitalism-based economic system and *un-American* to tax inheritances. To others, however, estate taxes are harmonious with our perception of the United States as an independent, self-made, self-sufficient society where reward is commensurate with hard work and achievement and not determined by the whimsy of birth lineage. We tend to look down our hard-working, middle class noses at transfers of great family wealth. The estate tax exemption is an attempt to bridge these two competing philosophies. You can work hard, save, and transfer your assets to your children to give them a leg up on life, but you just can't do too much of it. Unfortunately, the estate tax laws have not kept up with inflation, and persons many would consider only middle class can be subject to significant estate taxes. The estate tax exemption was increased to reach $1 million to partially ameliorate this problem, but many still think $1 million is not enough, and our congressional representatives are constantly receiving proposals for different ways to make the system more fair. Proposals include the wholesale repeal of the estate tax to significantly increasing the lifetime exemption. However, they have many different views about what is fair, and it may be years before we see any significant change. Before doing your estate planning, you should check with a knowledgeable estate planner to find out what the law is at that time.

In the meantime, there are some ways to reduce estate taxes. The unlimited marital deduction and lifetime exemption I have already discussed are two ways. More sophisticated techniques also can be useful. These include transferring appreciating assets to irrevocable trusts, lifetime gifts, and charitable gifts. A detailed discussion of these techniques is beyond the scope of this book, and those techniques should be undertaken only with the advice and counsel of an experienced estate tax planner. Because of the considerable desire to reduce estate taxes, this is an area ripe for scams.

A recent vintage of trusts I would like to warn you about is often referred to as *asset protection trusts*. In these trusts, you may transfer your property to a foreign trustee. The primary purpose of these trusts is to shield your assets from creditors. However, some people believe, and some promoters assert, that these trusts also reduce your income and estate tax liability.

The people who write the tax laws back in Washington, D.C., are very smart, and they have closed almost every conceivable loophole possible in foreign trusts. Although there may be cases in which taxes might be reduced by a foreign trust, it is difficult to do so. Tax reduction through foreign trusts is most often accomplished by cheating, not by legitimate tax-planning strategies.

You also may fail to protect your assets from creditors. Most state laws prohibit fraudulent conveyances, and these laws allow creditors to petition a court to have a transfer of property set aside if the transfer was made to defraud the creditor. An asset protection trust may make it more difficult for your creditor to get your property, but the creditor may nevertheless have the legal right to do so.

Years ago, I met with a group of individuals who had been persuaded to deed their real estate to a foreign trust set up in a tax haven country to a foreign trustee they had never met. They were persuaded to do so by a promoter they did not even know. The promoter had told them that a prominent politician used this trust. The investors took him at his word (I was quite certain that the politican had done no such thing), and the investors willingly signed deeds that transferred their real estate to the unknown foreign trustee. They came to me to ask whether the tax benefits the promoter had promised were correct. The promoter had assured the investors that they would owe no tax on the income they earned on the property in this trust, and that no estate tax would be imposed on those assets on their death. After looking at their documents, I thought their tax concerns were the least of their worries. It appeared to me that they did not even own their property anymore, and that they would have little protection if the promoter and foreign trustee stole the property from them. I recall thinking that, in a perverse way, the promoter's tax plan did work. If the investors no longer owned the property, they should not be taxed on it.

Some significant brokerage houses promoted a similar scheme. They suggested that capital gains tax on your property could be eliminated if you transferred it to a charity. And this is generally correct. What they failed to highlight, however, was that to get this benefit, you actually had to give the property away to the charity. You no longer owned the property; the charity owned it.

A more recent technique, quickly shot down by the IRS and then explicitly legislated against by Congress, also involved charities — the so-called charitable split-dollar life insurance policies. Under this technique, the donor would make a "gift" to a charity and then claim an income tax deduction for the full amount of the so-called gift. The charity then would invest this amount in life insurance on the life of the donor that would give the charity only a small portion of the life insurance proceeds; the bulk of the proceeds would go to the donor's heirs. By making the gift to charity, the donor was able to convert the cost of the life insurance premium into a tax deduction. If the donor had paid the premium directly to the life insurance company, the donor would not have been able to take a tax deduction for any part of it. After a one-page article on this device appeared in the *Wall Street Journal*, the IRS moved swiftly to shut it down and began investigating the participants in this scheme. The IRS Chief of Tax-Exempt Organizations described it as "a tax shelter on steroids." Under legislation enacted in the fall of 1999, Congress gave the IRS clear authority to deny tax deductions for these "gifts." The donors who participated in these schemes are now faced with their money and insurance policies being controlled by the charity even though they don't get the benefit of the desired tax deduction. In a catch-22, the donors are faced with the dilemma of leaving their money with charity or admitting that the whole scheme was fraudulent in the first place. The IRS is also investigating whether the charities should have their tax exemption revoked for violating the rule that a charity has to be operated for the benefit of the public, and not private individuals.[104] Most tax practitioners are not at all surprised that these schemes have been shut down. They are only surprised that so many people thought they would work in the first place.

As these stories illustrate, estate tax planning is an area fraught with many scams and few legitimate tax-planning techniques. Some tax lawyers have recently begun to ask their clients to sign confidentiality agreements after creating some form of trust or other tax-planning device for the client. Many of these lawyers assert that their plans are legal, and that they ask for the confidentiality agreement only because their plan is so creative and unique that they don't want other lawyers to find out about it. Typically, when a lawyer asks you to sign a confidentiality agreement, this should serve as a red flag that he or she may be putting you into some plan that is illegal or at least highly dubious. It certainly should raise questions, and you should be very careful before going along with it. Do not buy into the "I'm so creative and must protect myself against competition" diatribe. There are many creative lawyers, and the more professional and respected ones would never ask for a confidentiality agreement. It is doubtful that professionals who ask for confidentiality agreements have really thought of techniques that comply with the law that are not already generally known among sophisticated estate tax planners. It is, of course, possible that the lawyer promotes confidentiality agreements as a marketing tool — to induce the client into believing that he or she is getting something so special and unique that it is worth paying top dollar to get it. In this case, you may have been overcharged by an aggressive lawyer, but the plan may not run afoul of the tax laws.

Estate planning can be an emotional experience. Taxpayers have a high resistance to the perceived unfair estate tax, which many believe is nothing short of confiscation of the hard-earned property that they just want to leave to their children. The perception of unfairness is exacerbated by the common belief that wealthy taxpayers somehow avoid paying estate taxes. This can lead people to forsake caution and enter into tax-planning schemes that are too good to be true. Don't be one of them. If your tax plan gets set aside, your estate will owe the estate taxes, and interest. It may also have to pay penalties. In addition, you may lose the opportunity to engage in proper planning techniques that would reduce estate taxes payable on your estate.

Plan for the Needs of Your Business after Your Death.

If you have your own business, it is important to make sure one or more employees has sufficient knowledge of your business so that the operation can immediately be taken over on a short-term basis. Otherwise, your customers may quickly desert your business, and its value may plummet. If your business has outstanding debts, it is possible that your family could be left with a business with no discernible value, but saddled with substantial debts.

If you are a professional, such as a doctor or lawyer, it is imperative that in the event of your death, you have another professional available to step in to review your files immediately, in order to make sure your clients and patients get the care they need. If you are a doctor, one of your patients may require constant monitoring for a very serious condition. A lawyer may have a client's case scheduled for trial within the next few days. An immediate and careful review of the outstanding files of the deceased professional could well prevent a malpractice action against your estate and serious harm to a client or patient. You cannot count on the goodwill of others to ensure that your clients won't be harmed in case of your death.

Several years ago, two acquaintances of mine died in a small airplane crash, both of whom were lawyers. One of them, Monica, had a case scheduled for trial the week after her death. Her colleagues called opposing counsel and explained that Monica had died and that she was the only lawyer in the office familiar with the case. Her colleagues asked the opposing counsel to agree to delay the trial. To their great surprise, the opposing counsel refused, and one of Monica's colleagues had to go to court on the morning of her funeral to get a court order to delay the trial. Needless to say, it became a cause célèbre among her colleagues to make the opposing counsel's life as difficult as possible after that experience.

Think about the needs of your business on your death. Make contingency arrangements with an employee, a professional colleague, or some other person to come in and make sure your customers are taken care of in the short run. In the long run, your family may wish to sell your business. If you are a professional, your clients or patients should be transferred to other qualified professionals.

Durable Power of Attorney for Health Care and Related Documents

It is not enough to plan for death. We should also plan for serious injury or illness. Most estate-planning attorneys advise their clients to execute durable powers of attorney for health care and for the handling of their property, in addition to wills and trusts. The legalities of these types of documents vary from one state to the next, so you should consult with a qualified professional in your state to make sure they are done right.

A *power of attorney* is a written document in which one person, the principal, gives another person, the agent or the *attorney-in-fact*, legal authority to take certain actions and do particular things on behalf of the principal. A power of attorney may be special, under which the agent's authority is limited to certain specified acts, or general, under which the agent is granted authority to transact all business for the principal. Third parties, such as someone buying property owned by the principal, can rely on the power of attorney and the legal authority granted to the attorney-in-fact. As Doris Day found out, granting an unlimited power of attorney is fraught with peril. However, a principal generally is entitled to revoke the power of attorney at any time, and Doris could have revoked Marty's power of attorney, but instead chose to "trust" him when he demanded that she do so. In some cases, which I will talk about subsequently, a power of attorney is helpful and should be considered.

Most state laws historically provided that a power of attorney automatically would be revoked if the principal became incapacitated and not mentally competent to take care of his or her affairs. The power to revoke a power of attorney was viewed as a fundamental right of the principal, and if the principal became incompetent and was not able to exercise his or her right to revoke, old law fixed the problem through automatic revocation of the power. This created a number of problems. A person most critically needs an attorney-in-fact when he or she is not able to make decisions for himself or herself — when he or she has become incompetent. Yet, under the old law, a power of attorney was automatically revoked on incompetency. The revoked power of attorney could not be replaced with a new one, because the law does not allow an incompetent person to enter into a legally binding power of attorney. This problem has been resolved by a new creature of the law, which is recognized in most states: the durable power of attorney. A durable power of attorney continues in effect for the period of time specified in the power of attorney, even if the principal becomes incompetent. A durable power of attorney, like a nondurable power of attorney, terminates on the principal's death.

Under a durable power of attorney for health care, if you become incapacitated, the person you designate in your power of attorney, your attorney-in-fact, is legally empowered to make your medical decisions for you, subject to any restrictions you insert in the power of attorney. Under a durable power of attorney for property, your attorney-in-fact is legally empowered to transact your business and property affairs for you, subject to any restrictions you insert in the power of attorney. Different people can be designated for different tasks. Successor attorneys-in-fact are typically named so that if the first person you designate cannot serve as your attorney-in-fact, the second person designated may be able to do so. It is advisable to have powers of attorney for health care as well as for property, even if you are married, and even if you designate your spouse as your attorney-in-fact (who would be granted many of the same powers under state law). You and your spouse could be injured simultaneously and both incapacitated. If you don't trust your next of kin to make medical decisions for you, or to run your business or handle your property, it is imperative that you execute a power of attorney in which you designate the person whom you wish to make those decisions.

In a durable power of attorney for health care, the laws of most states allow you to specify how you want other matters involving your medical care and death handled. For example, if you want your organs donated, you can state that in your power of attorney for health care, and you can specify the medical facility your organs should go to. If you wish to be cremated, generally you can include that in your power of attorney. These matters can also be covered in your testamentary will, but it is useful to insert them in your durable power of attorney for health care as well, because this document is the one that will most likely be given to your doctor.

Most states allow living wills, a document in which a person can direct his or her doctor to withdraw artificial life support systems in the event he or she becomes comatose. Many states allow you to include a living will in a durable power of attorney for health care, or, if you prefer, execute a separate living will. Many of us, if we enter a vegetative state following a serious injury or illness, don't wish to be maintained on life support systems, because this would only prolong our family's suffering and drain their financial resources. A living will must strictly adhere to the legal requirements imposed under the applicable state law, it must be filled out properly, and it must be properly executed by the patient and properly witnessed. If the legal requirements are not adhered to, your doctor won't to be able to rely on the patient's directive to withdraw life support systems, and your doctor may refuse to do so.

A number of reports suggest that even if you have a living will, some doctors won't comply with it. Doctors fear that the patient's family will sue the them if they fail to undertake all efforts to prolong the patient's life or, even worse, that they will be charged with a crime. Some doctors won't follow the living will even when it is completed properly and all the legal requirements are rigorously observed. Given that, there is little chance that a doctor will follow a patient's directive in a living will if the living will is incomplete, ambiguous, and fails to strictly conform to legal requirements. In that case your family may spend years tending to you while you remain in a comatose state. You won't be taken off artificial life support unless your family is able to get a court order authorizing the withdrawal of artificial life support. To most families, however, the step of asking for a court order is emotionally traumatic. Often, family members feel guilt when another family member suffers a tragic injury or illness, and they will try to prove their love for the patient and assuage their guilt by opposing any attempt to remove life support. Consequently, other family members may retreat from seeking a court order. However, if you have a living will that directs the withdrawal of life support, your family may feel more comfortable seeking court authorization if needed, because they will know that this is what you want. Appendix G provides a sample of a durable power of attorney for health care and Appendix H a sample of a durable power of attorney for property. If you don't wish to be kept on artificial life support systems, or you don't wish to break the family bank, having a living will is one thing you can do to help your family.

Final Note

Gloria Steinem says "Power can be taken, but not given. The process of the taking is empowerment in itself." It takes a lot of work and courage to take care of your legal affairs, particularly in the face of female socialization to be accommodating, trusting, and deferential. It is possible to do so, however, and I hope this book will provide you with the tools and knowledge necessary to start the journey to your legal empowerment. I wrote this book because I have known too many women who suffered debilitating financial losses and months and even years of anguish, shame, humiliation, and fear because they did not take care of their legal business. It is my desire and hope to help other women avoid similar chaos and financial and emotional despair in their lives. As I stated in the Introduction, this book may be frightening to you because it highlights legal dangers you may not know even exist that can ruin you financially. Your greatest protection from legal and financial harm is awareness of your legal risks and your legal responsibilities, and your willingness to take responsibility for your legal affairs. With awareness and responsibility, you can protect yourself, your family, and your assets. With *awareness* and *responsibility*, you are legally empowered.

APPENDIX A
QUITCLAIM DEED

Order No._____
Escrow No._____
Loan No. _____

WHEN RECORDED MAIL TO:

_____
_____
_____

QUITCLAIM DEED

FOR A VALUABLE CONSIDERATION, receipt of which is hereby acknowledged,

John Smith and Ann Jones, husband and wife,

do(es) hereby REMISE, RELEASE AND FOREVER QUITCLAIM to John Smith and Ann Jones, Trustees of

The John Smith and Ann Jones Family Living Trust dated January 1, 2000

the real property in the City of Los Angeles, County of Los Angeles, State of California, commonly known as 100 Main Street, Los Angeles, California 90000, and described as

Lot 100 of the Rosewood Avenue Tract, as per map recorded in Book 10, page 100 of Maps, in the office of the County Recorder, County of Los Angeles

Dated January 1, 2000

STATE OF CALIFORNIA }
COUNTY OF LOS ANGELES_____ }ss

_____
John Smith

_____
Ann Jones

On January 1, 2000, before me, Notary Ann Black, personally appeared John Smith and Ann Jones, personally known to me (or proved to me on the basis of satisfactory evidence) to be the person(s) whose name(s) is/are subscribed to the within instrument and acknowledged to me that he/she/they executed the same in his/her/their authorized capacity(ies), and that by his/her/their signature(s) on the instrument the person(s) or the entity upon behalf of which the person(s) acted, executed the instrument. WITNESS my hand and official seal.

Signature_____

Ann Black

(This area for official notarial seal)

MAIL TAX STATEMENTS TO:
John Smith and Ann Jones
100 Main Street
Los Angeles, California

222

Order No._____
Escrow No._____
Loan No. _____

WHEN RECORDED MAIL TO:
_____
_____
_____

SPACE ABOVE THIS LINE FOR RECORDER'S USE

DEED OF TRUST WITH ASSIGNMENT OF RENTS
(LONG FORM)

This DEED OF TRUST, made as of January 1, 2000, between Linda Jones and John Smith, husband and wife, herein called TRUSTOR, whose address is 100 Main Street, Los Angeles, California 90000

and REPUTABLE TITLE INSURANCE COMPANY, a California corporation, herein called TRUSTEE, and LENDING BANK, herein called BENEFICIARY,

WITNESSETH: That Trustor grants to Trustee in trust, with power of sale, that property in the Los Angeles, County of Los Angeles, State of California, described as:

Lot 100 of the Rosewood Avenue Tract, as per map recorded in Book 10, page 100 of Maps, in the office of the County Recorder, County of Los Angeles

together with the rents, issues and profits thereof, subject, however, to the right, power and authority hereinafter given to and conferred upon Beneficiary to collect and apply such rents, issues and profits for the purpose of securing (1) payment of the sum of $50,000, with interest thereon according to the terms of a promissory note or notes of even date herewith made by Trustor, payable to order of Beneficiary, and extensions or renewals thereof, (2) the performance of each agreement of Trustor incorporated by reference or contained herein and (3) payment of additional sums and interest thereon which may hereafter be loaned to Trustor, or his successors or assigns, when evidenced by a promissory note or notes reciting that they are secured by this Deed of Trust.

A. To protect the security of this Deed of Trust, Trustor agrees:

1) To keep said property in good condition and repair, not to remove or demolish any building thereon; to complete or restore promptly and in good and workmanlike manner any building which may be constructed, damaged or destroyed thereon and to pay when due all claims for labor performed and materials furnished therefor, to comply with all laws affecting said property or requiring any alterations or improvements to be made thereon, not to commit or permit waste thereof; not to commit, suffer or permit any act upon said property in violation of law; to cultivate, irrigate, fertilize, fumigate, prune and do all other acts which from the character or use of said property may be reasonably necessary, the specific enumerations herein not excluding the general.

2) To provide, maintain and deliver to Beneficiary Fire Insurance satisfactory to and with loss payable to Beneficiary. The amount collected under any fire or other insurance policy may be applied by Beneficiary upon any indebtedness secured hereby and in such order as Beneficiary may determine, or at option of Beneficiary the entire amount so collected or any part thereof may be released to Trustor. Such application or release shall not cure or waive any default or notice of default hereunder or invalidate any act done pursuant to such notice.

3) To appear in and defend any action or proceeding purporting to affect the security hereof or the rights or powers of Beneficiary or Trustee; and to pay all costs and expenses, including cost of evidence of title and attorney's fees in a reasonable sum, in any such action or proceeding in which Beneficiary or Trustee may appear, and in any suit brought by Beneficiary to foreclose this Deed.

4) To pay at least ten days before delinquency all taxes and assessments affecting said property, including assessments on appurtenant water stock; when due, all encumbrances, charges and liens, with interest, on said property or any part thereof, which appear to be prior or superior hereto; all costs, fees and expenses of this Trust.

Should Trustor fail to make any payment or to do any act as herein provided, then Beneficiary or Trustee, but without obligation to do so and without notice to or demand upon Trustor and without releasing Trustor from any obligation hereof, may; make or do the same in such manner and to such extent as either may deem necessary to protect the security hereof, Beneficiary or Trustee being authorized to enter upon said property for such purposes; appear in and defend any action or proceeding purporting to affect the security hereof or the rights or powers of Beneficiary or Trustee; pay, purchase, contest or compromise any encumbrance, charge or lien which in the judgment of either appears to be prior or superior hereto; and, in exercising any such powers, pay necessary expenses, employ counsel and pay his reasonable fees.

5) To pay immediately and without demand all sums so expended by Beneficiary or Trustee, with interest from date of expenditure at the amount allowed by law in effect at the date hereof, and to pay for any statement provided for by law in ef fect at the date hereof regarding the obligation secured hereby any amount demanded by the Beneficiary not to exceed the maximum allowed by law at the time when said statement is demanded.

B. It is mutually agreed:

1) That any award of damages in connection with any condemnation for public use of or injury to said property or any part thereof is hereby assigned and shall be paid to Beneficiary who may apply or release such moneys received by him in the same manner and with the same effect as above provided for disposition of proceeds of fire or other insurance.

2) That by accepting payment of any sum secured hereby after its due date, Beneficiary does not waive his right either to require prompt payment when due of all other sums so secured or to declare default for failure so to pay.

3) That at any time or from time to time, without liability therefor and without notice, upon written request of Beneficiary and presentation of this Deed and said note for endorsement, and without affecting the personal liability of any person for payment of the indebtedness secured hereby, Trustee may: reconvey any part of said property; consent to the making of any map or plat thereof; join in granting any easement thereon, or join in any extension agreement or any agreement subordinating the lien or charge hereof.

4) That upon written request of Beneficiary stating that all sums secured hereby have been paid, and upon surrender of this Deed and said note to Trustee for cancellation and retention or other disposition as Trustee in its sole discretion may choose and upon payment of its fees, Trustee shall reconvey, without warranty, the property then held hereunder. The recitals in such reconveyance of any matters or facts shall be conclusive proof of the truthfulness thereof. The Grantee in such reconveyance may be described as "the person or persons legally entitled thereto."

5) That as additional security, Trustor hereby gives to and confers upon Beneficiary the right, power and authority, during the continuance of these Trusts, to collect the rents, issues and profits of said property, reserving unto Trustor the right, prior to any default by Trustor in payment of any indebtedness secured hereby or in performance of any agreement hereunder, to collect and retain such rents, issues and profits as they become due and payable. Upon any such default, Beneficiary may at any time without notice, either in person, by agent, or by a receiver to be appointed by a court, and without regard to the adequacy of any security for the indebtedness hereby secured, enter upon and take possession of said property or any part thereof, in his own name sue for or otherwise collect such rents, issues, and profits, including those past due and unpaid, and apply the same, less costs and expenses of operation and collection, including reasonable attorney's fees, upon any indebtedness secured hereby, and in such order as Beneficiary may determine. The entering upon and taking possession of said property, the collection of such rents, issues and profits and the application thereof as aforesaid, shall not cure or waive any default or notice of default hereunder or invalidate any act done pursuant to such notice.

6) That upon default by Trustor in payment of any indebtedness secured hereby or in performance of any agreement hereunder, Beneficiary may declare all sums secured hereby immediately due and payable by delivery to Trustee of written declaration of default and demand for sale and of written notice of default and of election to cause to be sold said property, which notice Trustee shall cause to be filed for record. Beneficiary also shall deposit with Trustee this Deed, said note and all documents evidencing expenditures secured hereby.

After the lapse of such time as may then be required by law following the recordation of said notice of default, and notice of sale having been given as then required by law, Trustee, without demand on Trustor, shall sell said property at the time and place fixed by it in said notice of sale, either as a whole or in separate parcels, and in such order as it may determine, at public auction to the highest bidder for cash in lawful money of the United States, payable at time of sale. Trustee may postpone sale of all or any portion of said property by public announcement at such time and place of sale, and from time to time thereafter may postpone such sale by public announcement at the time fixed by the preceding postponement. Trustee shall deliver to such purchaser its deed conveying the property so sold, but without any covenant or warranty, express or implied. The recitals in such deed of any matters or facts shall be conclusive proof of the truthfulness thereof. Any person, including Trustor, Trustee or Beneficiary as hereinafter defined, may purchase at such sale.

After deducting all costs, fees and expenses of Trustee and of this Trust, including cost of evidence of title in connection with sale, Trustee shall apply to proceeds of sale to payment of: all sums expended under the terms hereof, not then repaid, with accrued interest at the amount allowed by law in effect at the date hereof; all other sums then secured hereby; and the remainder, if any, to the person or persons legally entitled thereto.

7) Beneficiary, or any successor in ownership of any indebtedness secured hereby, may from time to time, by instrument in writing, substitute a successor or successors to any Trustee named herein or acting hereunder, which instrument, executed by the Beneficiary and duly acknowledged and recorded in the office of the recorder of the county or counties where said property is situated shall be conclusive proof of proper substitution of such successor Trustee or Trustees, who shall, without conveyance from the Trustee predecessor, succeed to all its title, estate, rights, powers and duties. Said instrument must contain the name of the original Trustor, Trustee and Beneficiary hereunder, the book and page where this Deed is recorded and the name and address of the new Trustee.

8) That this Deed applies to, inures to the benefit of, and binds all parties hereto, their heirs, legatees, devisees, administrators, executors, successors and assigns. The term Beneficiary shall mean the owner and holder, including pledgees, of the note secured hereby, whether or not named as Beneficiary herein. In this Deed, whenever the context so requires, the masculine gender includes the feminine and/or neuter, and the singular number includes the plural.

9) That Trustee accepts this Trust when this Deed, duly executed and acknowledged, is made a public record as provided by law. Trustee is not obligated to notify any party hereto of pending sale under any other Deed of Trust or of any action or proceeding in which Trustor, Beneficiary or Trustee shall be a party unless brought by Trustee.

The undersigned Trustor requests that a copy of any notice of default and of any notice of sale hereunder be mailed to him at his address hereinbefore set forth.

Signature of Trustor   Signature of Trustor

_____   _____

John Smith   Linda Jones

STATE OF CALIFORNIA   }
                             }ss
COUNTY OF Los Angeles_____}

On January 1, 2000, before me, Notary Ann Black, personally appeared John Smith and Linda Jones personally known to me (or proved to me on the basis of satisfactory evidence) to be the person(s) whose name(s) is/are subscribed to the within instrument and acknowledged to me that he/she/they executed the same in his/her/their authorized capacity(ies), and that by his/her/their signature(s) on the instrument the person(s) or the entity upon behalf of which the person(s) acted, executed the instrument.

WITNESS my hand and official seal.

Signature _____
          Ann Black

(This area for official notarial seal)

<u>DO NOT RECORD</u>   **REQUEST FOR FULL RECONVEYANCE**

TO REPUTABLE TITLE INSURANCE COMPANY, TRUSTEE:

The undersigned is the legal owner and holder of the note or notes, and of all other indebtedness secured by the foregoing Deed of Trust. Said note or notes, together with all other indebtedness secured by said Deed of Trust, have been fully paid and satisfied; and you are hereby requested and directed, on payment to you of any sums owing to you under the terms of said Deed of Trust, to cancel said note or notes above mentioned, and all other evidences of indebtedness secured by said Deed of Trust delivered to you herewith, together with the said Deed of Trust, and to reconvey, without warranty, to the parties designated by the terms of said Deed of Trust, all the estate now held by you under the same.

Dated _____   _____

                                      _____

Please mail Deed of Trust,
Note and Reconveyance to

_____

_____

Do Not lose or destroy this Deed of Trust OR THE NOTE which it secures. Both must be delivered to the Trustee for cancellation before reconveyance will be made.

Order No._____
Escrow No._____
Loan No. _____

WHEN RECORDED MAIL TO:

_____
_____
_____

SPACE ABOVE THIS LINE FOR RECORDER'S USE

PRENUPTIAL AGREEMENT

This Agreement is entered into in the City of Los Angeles, County of Los Angeles, State of California, between John Smith (referred to as John) and Linda Jones (referred to as Linda) with reference to the following facts:

1. John and Linda are contemplating marriage.

2. John and Linda are currently unmarried and have not previously been married.

3. John has substantially disclosed to Linda the nature, extent, and value of his property interests, including, without limitation, his various present and potential business and investment interests and his present and potential income from various sources, including, without limitation, his business and investment interests.

4. Linda has substantially disclosed to John the nature, extent, and value of her property interests, including, without limitation, her various present and potential business and investment interests and her present and potential income from various sources, including, without limitation, her business and investment interests.

5. John has had separate and independent counsel to advise him of his rights under this Agreement. Counsel has been fully advised and informed of previous and existing financial and marital facts of both parties and has apprised John of his rights under this Agreement with full knowledge of those facts.

6. Linda has had separate and independent counsel to advise her of her rights under this Agreement. Counsel has been fully advised and informed of previous and existing financial and marital facts of both parties and has apprised Linda of her rights under this Agreement with full knowledge of those facts.

7. For good and valuable consideration, including, without limitation, the contemplated marriage between the parties and the mutual promises contained in this Agreement, the parties define here the respective rights of each in the property, income, assets, and liabilities that each may have or may acquire, and the parties agree that, except as may be expressly set forth here, all property, real and personal, owned by either of them at the time of the contemplated marriage, from whatever source, shall remain the respective separate property of the person acquiring the property, and neither shall acquire any interest or right to any of the property of the other.

8. John and Linda acknowledge to each other that each does not now have, possess, or claim any right or interest in the present or future income, property, or assets of the other.

In consideration of the foregoing, the parties agree to the following.

I.   REQUIREMENT OF MARRIAGE

If John and Linda shall be married, their rights with respect to the property owned by either of them at the time of the contemplated marriage or acquired after marriage to each other shall be subject to the terms of this Agreement, provided that if for any reason and irrespective of fault, the parties do not marry, then this Agreement shall be void.

II.   DISCLOSURE OF PROPERTY

A.   At the time this Agreement is executed, John discloses that he has listed in Exhibit A, attached to this Agreement and incorporated in it by reference, all real and personal property in which he has an interest and the extent of that interest and all obligations for which he is liable.

B.   At the time this Agreement is executed, Linda discloses that she has listed in Exhibit B, attached to this Agreement and incorporated in it by reference, all real and personal property in which she has an interest and the extent of that interest all obligations for which she is liable.

III.   REPRESENTATION BY INDEPENDENT COUNSEL

John acknowledges here that he has been represented by independent counsel and Linda acknowledges here that she has been represented by independent counsel in negotiation of this Agreement; that counsel representing each party was of his or her own choosing; and that this Agreement has been read by the parties and that its meaning and legal consequences have been explained fully to them by their counsel and are understood.

IV.   PROPERTIES OF EACH SPOUSE THAT ARE TO REMAIN SEPARATE

A.   John and Linda agree that, except as provided for in paragraphs IV(C) and IV(D) below, all property, including the property set forth in Exhibit A belonging to John at the commencement of the marriage, shall remain his separate property. John shall have sole management and control over the property, and the property shall be subject to his disposition as his separate property in the same manner as if no marriage had been entered into.

B.   John and Linda agree that all property, including the property set forth in Exhibit B belonging to Linda at the beginning of the marriage, shall remain her separate property. Linda shall have sole management and control over the property, and the property shall be subject to her disposition as her separate property in the same manner as if no marriage had been entered into.

C.   John and Linda agree that the residence located at 100 Main Street, Los Angeles, California, and described in Exhibit A, belonging to Linda at the beginning of the marriage, shall remain her separate property. Linda shall have sole management and control of the residence. Until such time as the parties may live separate and apart, each shall have an equal right to the use and occupancy of the residence.

D.   The parties further agree that their respective earnings shall remain their separate property. For purposes of this paragraph, the term "earnings" means compensation for labor or services, in any form whatsoever for labor or services performed that is paid to the spouse earning it.

V.   MUTUAL WAIVER OF MARITAL RIGHTS IN SEPARATE PROPERTY

A.   John and Linda agree that each party relinquishes all right, claim, or interest, whether actual, inchoate, or contingent, in law and equity, that he or she may acquire in the separate property of the other by reason of the proposed marriage, including, without limitation:

1. Community property rights;

2. The right to a family allowance;

3. The right to a probate homestead;

4. The rights or claims of dower, curtesy, or any statutory substitutes provided by the statutes of the State of California or any other state in which the parties may die domiciled or in which they may own real property;

5. The right of election to take against the Will of the other;

6. The right to distributive share in the estate of the other should he or she die intestate;

7. The right to declare a homestead in the separate property of the other; and

8. The right to act as administrator of the estate of the other.

B. Any pre-existing Will or Testament, or any other instrument which disposes of the estate of the other on death, shall remain in full force and shall not be revoked in whole or part by the occurrence of the marriage. Each party specifically waives the benefits of all probate or other similar statutes that might be in existence with respect to revocation of Wills on marriage, including, without limitation, California Probate Code 147 and similar statutes in other jurisdictions.

C. Nothing contained here shall constitute a waiver by either party of any bequest or devise that the other party may choose to make to him or her by Will or Codicil. However, the parties acknowledge that no promises of any kind have been made either of them about any such bequest or devise.

D. The parties agree that all rents, issues, profits, increase, appreciation, and income from the separate property of John shall remain his separate property. The parties agree that a change in the form of John's separate property shall not constitute a change of characterization, and the separate property shall remain John's separate property regardless of any change in form. For example, if John sold his business and deposited the proceeds from the sale in a bank account, that bank account would remain John's separate property; if John used the payments that he received to invest in a business, that business, together with all of its assets, tangible and intangible, would remain John's separate property.

E. The parties agree that all rents, issues, profits, increase, appreciation, and income from the separate property of Linda shall remain her separate property. The parties agree that a change in the form of Linda's separate property shall not constitute a change of characterization, and the separate property shall remain Linda's separate property regardless of any change in form. For example, if Linda sells her personal residence and deposited the proceeds from the sale in a bank account, that bank account would remain Linda's separate property. If she used the proceeds to purchase another personal residence, the new personal residence would be her separate property.

F. The parties agree that John may devote considerable time, skill, and effort to the investment and management of his separate property and the income from it. The parties agree that, notwithstanding that the expenditure of John's time, skill, and effort might constitute a community interest or asset in the absence of this Agreement, neither party shall acquire any community interest from the expenditure of John's time, skill, and effort, and any rents, issues, profits, increase, appreciation, and income from the separate property of John shall remain the separate property of John.

G. The parties agree that Linda may devote considerable time, skill, and effort to the investment and management of her separate property and the income from it. The parties agree that, notwithstanding that the expenditure of Linda's time, skill, and effort might constitute a community interest or asset in the absence of this Agreement, neither party shall acquire any community interest from the expenditure of Linda's time, skill, and effort, and any rents, issues, profits, increase, appreciation, and income from the separate property of Linda shall remain the separate property of Linda.

H. The occurrence of commingling or otherwise failing to segregate the separate property or separate income of either party shall not change or constitute a change of character of that property, nor shall it constitute a transmutation of the separate property or income into community, quasi-community, joint marital, or similar type of property.

I. The election, if any, of the parties after their marriage to file federal or state income tax returns on a joint, rather than on a separate, return shall not constitute a creation of any community property or of any other rights or interests in contravention of this Agreement.

VI. SEPARATE AND COMMUNITY OBLIGATIONS

A. All obligations secured by, or incurred for the purchase of, real property set forth in Exhibits A or B (referred to here as real property obligations) shall remain the separate obligations of John and Linda, respectively. Linda shall not be liable for obligations relating to real estate owned by John, and John shall indemnify Linda from such obligations. John shall not be liable for obligations relating to real estate owned by Linda, and Linda shall indemnify John from such obligations.

B. Except as provided for in paragraph VI(D) below, Linda's real property obligations, and all unsecured obligations, taxes, insurance premiums, and maintenance costs on Linda's separate property, shall be paid from the income derived from her separate property, or from her separate property funds, at her election. If there is inadequate separate property income or separate property funds to pay all of Linda's real property obligations, and all taxes, insurance premiums, and maintenance costs on Linda's separate property, the balance may be paid from community income or from community property funds, at Linda's election. In the event that community income or community property funds are used, the community shall acquire no interest in Linda's separate property, and the community shall be entitled only to reimbursement of the funds used on the sale of such separate property.

C. John's real property obligations, and all unsecured obligations, taxes, insurance premiums, and maintenance costs on John's separate property, shall be paid from the income derived from his separate property, or from his separate property funds, at his election. If there is inadequate separate property income or separate property funds to pay all of John's real property obligations, and all taxes, insurance premiums, and maintenance costs on John's separate property, the balance may be paid from community income or from community property funds, at John's election. In the event that community income or community property funds are used, the community shall acquire no interest in John's separate property, and the community shall be entitled only to reimbursement of the funds used on the sale of such separate property.

D. Trust deed payments, taxes, insurance premiums, and maintenance of the real property commonly known as 100 Main Street, Los Angeles, California, shall be paid from Linda's separate income or separate funds, from community income or from community property funds, at Linda's election. To the extent that community income or community property funds are used to make the payments, the community shall acquire no interest in the real property and no right of reimbursement because the benefit to the community of the use of the property is equal to the amount of community income or community property funds expended.

E. Except as provided for in paragraphs VI(A) - VI(D), all obligations incurred during marriage shall be the community obligations of the parties, and the parties shall be equally liable for them.

F. Community obligations and joint living expenses shall be paid from community income or from community property funds, which shall be maintained in a joint checking account. John and Linda agree that they will determine from time to time the amount each must contribute from their separate property into the joint checking account for payment of community obligations and joint living expenses. If there is inadequate community income or community property funds to pay all community obligations, the balance may be paid from the separate income or separate property funds of either spouse, and the paying spouse shall be entitled to a right of reimbursement to the extent that separate income or separate property funds are used.

G. The term "joint living expenses," as used in this paragraph, includes: food; household supplies; utilities; telephone; laundry; cleaning; clothing; medical and dental expenses; medical, life, accident, and auto insurance; gasoline, oil, and auto repairs; automobile purchase and lease payments; entertainment; child care, schooling and support of any minor children that are the issue of the marriage; and joint gifts.

VII. COMMUNITY INCOME AND COMMUNITY PROPERTY

Except as otherwise expressly provided in this Agreement, the parties agree that the sole source of community property shall be the contribution of either spouse to the joint checking account. For purposes of this paragraph, the term "earnings" is defined as compensation for labor or services performed that is paid to the spouse earning it.

VIII. EXECUTION OF OTHER INSTRUMENTS

A. Each party agrees that he or she shall, on the request of the other, take all steps, and execute, acknowledge, and deliver to the other party all further instruments necessary or expedient to effectuate the purposes of this Agreement.

B.   Specifically, Linda agrees to execute, acknowledge, and deliver to John quitclaim deeds to the real property set forth in Exhibit A. John agrees to execute, acknowledge, and deliver to Linda quitclaim deeds to the real property set forth in Exhibit B.

IX. PARTIES BOUND

This Agreement shall bind and inure to the benefit of the parties to it, and of their respective heirs, executors, administrators, personal representatives, successors, and assigns.

X. ENTIRE AGREEMENT: MODIFICATION

A.   This Agreement contains the entire understanding and agreement of the parties, and there have been no promises, representations, agreements, warranties, or undertakings by either party to the other, either oral or written, of any character or nature, except as set forth here. This Agreement may be altered, amended, or modified only by an instrument in writing, executed and acknowledged by the parties to the Agreement and by no other means. Each party waives the future right to claim, contend, or assert that this Agreement was modified, cancelled, superseded, or changed by an oral agreement, course of conduct, or estoppel.

B.   The parties agree that they occasionally may use such expressions as "our property," "our house," or "our bank account," when referring to property that is by the terms of this Agreement separate property. The parties further agree that they sometimes may commingle separate and community property, or may make statements or take actions that are or appear to be inconsistent with the terms of this Agreement. Notwithstanding any of the above, the parties agree that this Agreement may be altered, amended, or modified only as set forth in Paragraph X(A).

C.   The parties agree that no gift may be made between them with a value in excess of $5,000, unless the gift is conveyed by an instrument in writing, executed an acknowledged by both parties, and by no other means. Each party waives the future right to claim, contend, or assert that any such gift was made by an oral agreement, course of conduct, presumed intent, or estoppel.

XI. APPLICABLE LAW

This Agreement is executed in the State of California and shall be subject to and interpreted under the laws of the State of California. Although this Agreement is executed in the State of California, and makes reference to separate, community, and quasi-community property, the parties agree that it is their intent that this Agreement cover all rights in property, whether the property is situated within or without the State of California, or within or without the United States of America.

XII. SEVERABILITY

If any term, provision, covenant, or condition of this Agreement is held by a court of competent jurisdiction to be invalid, void, or unenforceable, the remainder of the provisions shall remain in full force and shall in no way be affected, impaired, or invalidated.

XIII. CAPTIONS

The captions of the various paragraphs in this Agreement are for convenience only, and none of them is intended to be any part of the text of this Agreement, nor intended to be referred to in construing any of the provisions of it.

XIV. EXECUTION OF COUNTERPARTS

This Agreement may be executed in counterparts, any of which shall be deemed to be an original.

Dated: _____   _____

                                                        John Smith

APPENDIX C

Dated: _____

_____
Linda Jones

XV. CERTIFICATION OF ATTORNEYS

I, _____, certify that I am a duly licensed attorney, admitted to practice law in the State of California; that I have consulted with John Smith, a party of this Agreement, and have fully advised him of his property rights and the legal significance of the Agreement; and that John Smith has acknowledged his complete understanding of the legal consequences of the Agreement, and has voluntarily executed the Agreement in my presence.

Dated:

_____
Attorney for John Smith

I, _____, certify that I am a duly licensed attorney, admitted to practice law in the State of California; that I have consulted with Linda Jones, a party to this Agreement, and have fully advised her of her property rights and the legal significance of the Agreement; and that Linda Jones has acknowledged her complete understanding of the legal consequences of the Agreement, and has voluntarily executed the Agreement in my presence.

Dated:

_____
Attorney for Linda Jones

STATE OF CALIFORNIA
COUNTY OF LOS ANGELES

)
) ss.
)

On _____ , 2000, before the undersigned, a notary public in and for said county and state, personally appeared John Smith and Linda Jones, known to me to be the persons whose name are subscribed to the within instrument and acknowledged that he/she executed the same.

WITNESS my hand and official seal.

_____
Notary Public

Order No._____
Escrow No._____
Loan No. _____

WHEN RECORDED MAIL TO:

_____
_____
_____

SPACE ABOVE THIS LINE FOR RECORDER'S USE

ARTICLES OF INCORPORATION
OF
NEW COMPANY, INC.

Article I

The name of this Corporation is NEW COMPANY, INC.

Article II

The purpose of this Corporation is to engage in any lawful act or activity for which a corporation may be organized under the General Corporation Law of California other than the banking business, the trust company business or the practice of a profession permitted to be incorporated by the California Corporations Code.

Article III

The name and address in the State of California of this Corporation's initial agent for service of process is:

Linda Jones
100 Main Street
Los Angeles, California 90000

Article IV

The liability of the directors of the Corporation for monetary damages shall be eliminated to the fullest extent permissible under California law.

Article V

The Corporation is authorized to provide indemnification of agents (as defined in Section 317 of the Corporations Code) for breach of duty to the Corporation and its stockholders through bylaw provisions or through agreements with the agents, or both, in excess of the indemnification otherwise permitted by Section 317 of the Corporations Code, subject to the limits of such excess in indemnification set forth in Section 204 of the Corporations Code.

Article VI

This Corporation is authorized to issue one class of shares of stock, and the total number of shares which this Corporation is authorized to issue is 10,000.

Dated: _____   _____
                                                                    Linda Jones, Incorporator

233

LAST WILL AND TESTAMENT OF LINDA JONES

I, LINDA JONES, a resident of the County of Los Angeles, State of California, declare this to be my Will and do hereby expressly revoke any and all wills and codicils previously made by me.

ARTICLE I
DECLARATIONS

Section 1.01 <u>Family</u>. I am married to JOHN SMITH and all references in this Will to "my spouse" are to him. I have three children, all adults, whose names are DONALD SMITH, MARY SMITH, AND SAM SMITH. All references in this Will to "my children" are to them. I have no other children, living or deceased.

Section 1.02 <u>Property</u>. I confirm to my spouse my spouse's one-half community property interest in all our community assets. I intend that this Will dispose of all property subject to my testamentary power.

ARTICLE II
EXPENSES AND TAXES

Section 2.01 <u>Payment of Expenses</u>. I direct the Executor to pay all my expenses of last illness and funeral expenses as soon as convenient after my death.

Section <u>2.02 Payment of Taxes</u>. All estate, inheritance, succession, or other death taxes, duties, charges, or assessments, imposed upon or in relation to any of my property by reason of my death, whether passing under this Will or otherwise, shall be paid by the Executor out of my estate without proration of any charge therefor against any person who received such property under the terms of this Will or otherwise.

ARTICLE III
GIFTS

Section 3.01 <u>Gifts of Personal Property</u>. I give all my jewelry to my daughter MARY, my car to my son DONALD, and my camera equipment to my son SAM. I give my clothing, household furniture and furnishings, personal automobiles, and other tangible articles of a personal nature, or my interest in any such property, not otherwise specifically disposed of by this Will or in any other manner, together with any insurance on the property, to my spouse if my spouse survives me. If my spouse does not survive me, I give all such property in equal shares on the basis of valuation to my children who survive me. The provisions at the immediately preceding two sentences notwithstanding, I may provide the Executor with a list of some or all of such items that I want to be distributed to specific individuals. However, such list, if any, shall be only a guide and not compelling, and such list shall not be deemed a part of or an amendment or codicil to this Will. The Executor shall, nonetheless, be entitled to make distribution based upon such list and shall have no liability to any person upon such distribution.

Section 3.02 <u>Gift of Residue</u>. I give the residue of my estate to my spouse, JOHN SMITH, if he survives me. If my spouse, JOHN SMITH, does not survive me, I give the residue of my estate to my three children in equal shares, if they survive me. If any of my children do not survive me, I direct that the share of my deceased child be given to his or her children, if any. If my deceased child has no children then living, I direct that the share of my deceased child be divided between my surviving children. If none of my children survive me, and if none of their children survive me, I direct that each of my children's shares be given to their heirs at law.

If, at the time of my death, or at any later time before full distribution of the estate, all of my issue are deceased and no other disposition of the estate is directed by this Will, the remaining estate shall be distributed to those persons who would then be my heirs, their identities and respective shares to be determined as if my death had then occurred and in accordance with the laws of the State of California then in effect.

ARTICLE IV
OFFICE OF EXECUTOR

Section 4.01 <u>Nominations</u>. I nominate as Executor and as successor Executor of this Will those named below. Each successor Executor shall serve in the order designated if the prior designated Executor fails to qualify or ceases to act. The term "Executor" shall include any personal representative of the estate.

First:	My spouse JOHN
Second:	My child MARY
Third:	My child DONALD
Fourth:	My child SAM

Section 4.02 <u>Bond — Waiver</u>. I request that the court not require bond of any Executor nominated in this Will.

Section 4.03 <u>Independent Administration — Permitted</u>. The Executor may administer my estate under the California Independent Administration of Estates Act.

Section 4.04 <u>Sell Assets</u>. The Executor shall have the power to sell, with or without notice, at either public or private sale, for cash or terms, subject to court order, any property of my estate as the Executor, in the Executor's reasonable discretion, considers necessary for the proper administration and distribution of my estate.

Section 4.05 <u>Lease Property</u>. The Executor shall have the power to lease all or any property of my estate on such terms that the Executor considers proper.

ARTICLE V
NO CONTEST, DISINHERITANCE, DEFINITIONS

Section 5.01 <u>No Contest — Contestant Disinherited</u>. If any beneficiary under this Will in any manner, directly or indirectly, contests or attacks this Will or any of its provisions, any share or interest in my estate given to that contesting beneficiary under this Will is revoked and shall be disposed of in the same manner provided herein as if that contesting beneficiary had predeceased me without issue.

Section 5.02 <u>Disinheritance — General</u>. Except as otherwise provided in this Will, I have intentionally omitted to provide herein for any of my heirs, or persons claiming to be my heirs, living at the date of my death, whether or not known to me.

Section 5.03 <u>Survivorship Requirement</u>. For all gifts under this Will, I require that the beneficiary survive me for thirty (30) days before entitlement to such gift.

Section 5.04 <u>Interpretation</u>.

(1) The masculine, feminine, or neuter gender and the singular or plural number shall each include the others whenever the context indicates.

(2) Clause headings are for reading convenience and shall be disregarded when construing this Will.

Signature Clause. I subscribe my name to this Will at Los Angeles, California, on _____, 2000.

TESTATOR   LINDA JONES

Attestation Clause. The testator declared to us, the undersigned, that this instrument consisting of the number of pages indicated below, including the page signed by us as witnesses, was the testator's Will and requested us to act as witnesses to it. The testator thereupon signed this Will in our presence, all of us being present at the same time. We now, at the testator's request, in the testator's presence, and in the presence of each other, subscribe our names as witnesses.

        Pages: Three
        Date: _____, 2000
        Place: Los Angeles, California

      It is our belief that the testator is of sound mind and memory and is under no constraint or undue influence whatsoever.

      We declare under penalty of perjury under the laws of the State of California that the foregoing is true and correct.

                                Print name and address:

_____

Signature of Witness

_____

Signature of Witness

_____

Signature of Witness

Order No._____
Escrow No._____
Loan No. _____

WHEN RECORDED MAIL TO:

_____
_____
_____

SPACE ABOVE THIS LINE FOR RECORDER'S USE

DECLARATION OF TRUST

THE JOHN SMITH AND LINDA JONES FAMILY TRUST

John Smith and Linda Jones, Husband and Wife, of Los Angeles County, California, declare that:

ARTICLE 1. DECLARATIONS

Conveyance to Trustee

Section 1.01. They have conveyed and transferred, without consideration, to the Trustee named in this Declaration the property described in an inventory hereto attached marked Exhibit A.

Insurance Policies

Section 1.02. They have designated or have agreed to designate the Trustee named in this Declaration, or the successor of such Trustee, as:

(a) Beneficiary on certain policies of insurance listed on an inventory hereto attached marked Exhibit B insuring the life of Husband; and

(b) Beneficiary on certain policies of insurance listed on an inventory hereto attached and marked Exhibit C insuring the life of Wife.

Identity of Trust Estate

Section 1.03. All property described in the inventory hereto attached marked Exhibit A, the proceeds of all insurance policies described in the inventories hereto attached marked Exhibit B and Exhibit C, and any other property that may hereafter be transferred or conveyed to and received by the Trustee to be held pursuant to the terms of this instrument is herein called the "Trust Estate" and shall be held, administered, and distributed by the Trustee as provided in this Declaration of Trust.

Identity of Husband, Wife, and Trustors

Section 1.04. As used in this Declaration of Trust:

(a) The term "Husband" shall mean John Smith;
(b) The term "Wife" shall mean Linda Jones; and
(c) The term "Trustors" shall refer collectively to Husband and Wife.

Designation of Trustee

Section 1.05. Husband and Wife are hereby designated as Co-Trustees of all trusts created by or to be created pursuant to this Declaration of Trust. Should either Husband or Wife, because of death, incompetency, or other cause, become unable to serve as Co-Trustee, or should either resign as Co-Trustee, before the natural termination of all trusts provided for in this Declaration, the remaining Co-Trustee, Husband or Wife, shall thereafter serve as sole Trustee of all trusts provided for in this Declaration. The term "Trustee" as used in this Declaration shall refer collectively to Husband and Wife so long as they shall serve as such Co-Trustees and thereafter to such of them as may serve as sole Trustee.

Additions to Trust

Section 1.06. The Trustors, or either of them, may from time to time add other property acceptable to the Trustee to the Trust Estate by conveyance, assignment, transfer, or Will. Such property when received and accepted by the Trustee shall become part of the Trust Estate and be subject to all the terms and provisions of this Declaration of Trust.

Community Property to Remain Community Property

Section 1.07. All property now or hereafter conveyed or transferred to the Trustee to be held by the Trustee pursuant to this Declaration which was community property, quasi-community property, or separate property at the time of such conveyance or transfer, shall remain, respectively, community property, quasi-community property, or separate property of the Trustor transferring such property of the Trustee.

Revocation of Trust

Section 1.08. At any time and from time to time during the joint lives of the Trustors, the Trustors jointly as to community property and either Trustor as to his or her separate property may, by serving written notice on the Trustee, revoke the trust created by this Declaration in whole or in part. Any property withdrawn from the Trust Estate by reason of any such revocation shall be delivered by the Trustee to the Trustor or Trustors revoking the trust.

Modification of Trust

Section 1.09. At any time and from time to time during the joint lives of the Trustors, the Trustors jointly as to community property and either Trustor as to his or her separate property may, by serving written notice on the Trustee, alter, modify, or amend the trusts created by this Declaration in any respect.

Trusts Irrevocable on Death of First Trustor

Section 1.10. Except as otherwise expressly provided in this Declaration, on the death of either Trustor the trusts created by this Declaration shall become irrevocable and not subject to amendment or modification.

ARTICLE 2. DISTRIBUTIONS DURING JOINT LIVES OF TRUSTORS

Net Income to Trustors

Section 2.01. During the joint lives of the Trustors, the Trustee shall at least annually, unless otherwise directed by both Trustors in writing, pay to or apply for the benefit of Husband and Wife all of the net income from the Trust Estate in the same proportion as each of the respective interests in the Trust Estate.

Incompetency of Husband or Wife

Section 2.02. During the joint lives of the Trustors, should either Trustor be adjudged by a court of competent jurisdiction under the provisions of the California Probate Code relating to the appointment of conservators unable to manage his or her own affairs, the Trustee may, in the Trustee's discretion:

(a) Pay the entire net income of the Trust Estate in monthly or other convenient installments to the remaining competent Trustor; or

(b) Apply such portion of the net income, up to the whole thereof, of the Trust Estate as the Trustee may deem in his discretion reasonable and proper for the benefit of the Trustor so adjudged to be incompetent or unable to manage his or her own affairs.

Invasion of Corpus

Section 2.03. During the joint lives of the Trustors, should the net income of the Trust Estate be insufficient to provide for the care, maintenance, or support of the Trustors as herein defined, the Trustee may, in the Trustee's absolute discretion, pay to or apply for the benefit of the Trustors, or either of them, or any of their dependents, such amounts from the principal of the Trust Estate as the Trustee may, in the Trustee's discretion, from time to time deem necessary or advisable for the care, maintenance, or support of the Trustors. As used in this section, the term "care, maintenance, or support of the Trustors" shall mean:

(a) The providing of proper care, maintenance, and support for the Trustors, or either of them, during any period of illness, or other want or necessity;

(b) The maintenance of the Trustors and each of them in the manner of living to which they, and each of them, are accustomed on the date of this Declaration;

(c) The support and maintenance in the manner in which they are accustomed on the date of this Declaration of any person, whether adult or minor, dependent on the Trustors, or either of them, for support and maintenance; and

(d) The education in the manner desired by the Trustors of any person, whether adult or minor, dependent on the Trustors, or either of them, for such education.

ARTICLE 3, DISTRIBUTIONS AFTER DEATH OF FIRST TRUSTOR TO DIE

Creation of Two Trusts

Section 3.01. On the death of either Trustor leaving the other Trustor surviving, the Trustee shall collect all insurance proceeds payable to the Trustee by reason of such death, all bequests and devises distributable to the Trust Estate under the terms of the last Will of the deceased Trustor, and shall divide the entire Trust Estate into two separate trusts to be known and herein designated as "Trust A" and "Trust B."

Principal of Trust A

Section 3.02. The principal or Trust Estate of Trust A shall consist of:

(a) The Surviving Trustor's interest in all property in the Trust Estate; and

(b) Other assets selected by the Trustee from assets in the Trust Estate which qualify for the federal estate tax marital deduction, equal in value to an amount which, when added to the final estate tax value of all other property included in the gross estate of the first Trustor to die which passes to the Surviving Trustor and which qualifies for the federal estate tax marital deduction, will entitle the estate of the first Trustor to die to the minimum federal estate tax marital deduction necessary to reduce the taxable estate of the first Trustor to die to an amount on which no federal estate tax is due and the federal unified credit available to the estate of the first Trustor to die is fully utilized, provided that the allocation to Trust A shall be satisfied with assets valued as of the date of allocation or distribution.

Principal of Trust B

Section 3.03. The principal or Trust Estate of Trust B shall consist of all of the interests in each and every asset held by the Trustee pursuant to this Declaration, including any assets received by the Trustee to be held pursuant to this Declaration on or by reason of the death of the Deceased Trustor, not allocated to the principal or Trust Estate of Trust A pursuant to Section 3.02 of this Declaration.

Payment of Funeral Expenses and Death Taxes

Section 3.04. On the death of the first of the Trustors to die, the Trustee shall pay either from the income or principal of Trust B or partly from the principal and partly from the income of Trust B, as the Trustee in the Trustee's discretion may determine, the expenses of the Deceased Trustor's last illness, funeral, and burial, and any federal estate tax and state death taxes that may be due by reason of the Deceased Trustor's death, unless the Trustee in his or her discretion determines that other adequate provisions have been made for the payment of expenses and taxes.

All Income to Surviving Trustor

Section 3.05. After the death of the first of the Trustors to die, the Trustee shall pay to or apply for the benefit of the Surviving Trustor, monthly or at more frequent intervals, all of the net income from the principal of both Trust A and Trust B.

Power to Make Withdrawals from Trust A

Section 3.06. After the death of the first of the Trustors to die, the Surviving Trustor may at any time and from time to time withdraw such amounts, up to the whole thereof, from the principal or Trust Estate of Trust A as such Surviving Trustor may, at the time of any such withdrawal, designate in a written notice served on the Trustee.

ARTICLE 4. DISTRIBUTIONS ON DEATH OF SURVIVING TRUSTOR

Survivor's Power to Appoint Trust A

Section 4.01. On the death of the last Trustor to die, herein called "Surviving Trustor," the principal of Trust A and any accrued or undistributed net income from the principal of Trust A shall be distributed by the Trustee in such manner and to such persons, including the estate, the creditors, or the creditors of the estate of the Surviving Trustor as the Surviving Trustor shall appoint and direct by specific reference to this power of appointment in his or her last Will admitted to probate by a court of competent jurisdiction.

Failure to Exercise Power of Appointment

Section 4.02. Should the Surviving Trustor fail to exercise effectually, in whole or in part, the power of appointment described in Section 4.01 of this Declaration, the unappointed portion of the principal of Trust A and the unappointed portion of any accrued or undistributed net income from the principal of Trust A shall be added to the principal of Trust B, and shall be held, administered, and distributed by the Trustee in the same manner as if they had been, pursuant to the provisions of this Declaration, originally included in the principal of Trust B.

Payment of Survivor's Funeral Expenses and Death Taxes

Section 4.03. On the death of the Surviving Trustor, the Trustee shall pay either from the income or principal of Trust A or partly from the income, and partly from the principal of Trust A, as the Trustee in the Trustee's discretion may determine, the expenses of the Surviving Trustor's last illness, funeral, and burial, and any federal estate tax and state death taxes that may be due by reason of the inclusion of any portion of the Trust Estate in the Surviving Trustor's estate for the purposes of any such tax, unless the Trustee in the Trustee's discretion determines that other adequate provisions have been made for the payment of expenses and taxes.

Distribution of Trust B to Trustors' Children

Section 4.04. On the death of the Surviving Trustor, Trust B shall terminate and all the Trust Estate of Trust B then in the possession of the Trustee shall be distributed in fee by the Trustee to the children of the Trustors, share and share alike as a class gift and not as named individuals, the issue of any child who does not survive termination of the Trust taking his or her parent's share.

ARTICLE 5. POWERS OF TRUSTEE

Retain Investments of Trustors

Section 5.01. The Trustee is authorized to retain in the trusts provided for in this Declaration, for as long as the Trustee may deem advisable and in the best interests of these trusts, any property received by the Trustee from the Trustors, or either of them, whether or not such property is of the character permitted by law for investment of trust funds. After the death of the first Trustor to die, the Trustee may retain such property in the trusts as long as the Trustee deems advisable, provided, however, if the surviving Trustor shall by written instrument delivered to the Trustee direct the Trustee to convert any non-income producing property into income-producing property, the Trustee within a reasonable time after its receipt shall comply with such direction.

Management of Trust Property

Section 5.02. The Trustee shall with respect to any and all property which may at any time be held by the Trustee in trust pursuant to this Declaration, whether such property constitutes principal or accumulated income of any trust provided for in this Declaration, have power, exercisable in the Trustee's discretion at any time and from time to time on such terms and in such manner as the Trustee may deem advisable, to:

(a) Sell, convey, exchange, convert, improve, repair, partition, divide, allot, subdivide, create restrictions, easements, or other servitudes thereon, manage, operate, and control;

(b) Lease for terms within or beyond the term of any trust provided for in this Declaration and for any purpose, including exploration for and removal of gas, oil, and other minerals; and enter into any covenants and agreements relating to the property so leased or any improvements which may then or thereafter be erected on such property;

(c) Encumber or hypothecate for any trust purpose by mortgage, deed of trust, pledge, or otherwise;

(d) Carry insurance of such kinds and in such amounts at the expense of the trusts provided for in this Declaration as the Trustee may deem advisable;

(e) Commence or defend at the expense of any trust provided for in this Declaration such litigation with respect to any such trust or any property of the Trust Estate as the Trustee may deem advisable, and employ, for reasonable compensation payable by any such trust, such counsel as the Trustee shall deem advisable for that purpose;

(f) Invest and reinvest the trust funds in such property as the Trustee, in the exercise of reasonable business judgment, may deem advisable, whether or not such property is of the character specifically permitted by law for the investment of trust funds; provided, however, that after the death of the first Trustor to die, the Trustee shall convert non-income-producing property to income-producing property if so directed by the Surviving Trustor by a written instrument delivered to the Trustee;

(g) Vote, by proxy or otherwise, in such manner as the Trustee may determine to be in the best interests of the trusts provided for in this Declaration, any securities having voting rights held by the Trustee pursuant to this Declaration;

(h) Pay any assessments or other charges levied on any stock or other security held by the Trustee in trust pursuant to this Declaration;

(i) Exercise or not exercise as the Trustee may deem best any subscription, conversion, or other rights or options which may at any time attach, belong, or be given to the holders of any stocks, bonds, securities, or other instruments held by it in trust pursuant to this Declaration;

(j) Participate in any plans or proceedings for the foreclosure, reorganization, consolidation, merger, or liquidation of any corporation or organization that has issued securities held by the Trustee in trust pursuant to this Declaration, and incident to such participation, to deposit securities with and transfer title or securities on such terms as the Trustee may deem in the best interest of the trusts to any protective or other committee established to further or defeat any such plan or proceedings;

(k) Enforce any mortgage or deed of trust or pledge held by the Trustee in trust pursuant to this Declaration and at any sale under any such mortgage, deed of trust, or pledge to bid and purchase at the expense of any trust, provided for in this Declaration any property subject to such security instrument;

(l) Compromise, submit to arbitration, release with or without consideration, and otherwise adjust any claims in favor of or against any trust provided for in this Declaration; and

(m) Subject to any limitations expressly set forth in this Declaration and faithful performance of the Trustee's fiduciary obligations, to do all such acts, take all such proceedings, and exercise all such rights and privileges as could be done, taken, or exercised by an absolute owner of the trust property.

Power to Borrow Money

Section 5.03. The Trustee shall have the power to borrow money for any trust purpose on such terms and conditions as the Trustee may deem proper from any person, firm, or corporation, including the power to borrow money on behalf of one trust from any other trust provided for in this Declaration, and to obligate the trusts, or any of them, provided for in this Declaration to repay such borrowed money.

Power to Loan Money to Trusts

Section 5.04. The Trustee is authorized to loan or advance Trustee's own funds to any trust provided for in this Declaration for any trust purpose and to charge for such loan or advance the rate of interest that the Trustee, at the time such loan or advance is made, would have charged had such loan or advance been made to a person not connected with such trust having a net worth equal to the value of the principal of such trust. Any such loan or advance, together with the interest accruing on such loan or advance, shall be a first lien against the principal of the trust to which such loan or advance is made and shall be repaid from the income or principal of such trust as in the discretion of the Trustee appears for the best interests of such trust and its beneficiaries.

Dealings with Estates of Trustors

Section 5.05. The Trustee is authorized to purchase securities or other property from and to make loans and advances from the Trust Estate with or without security to the executor or other representative of the estate of either Trustor.

Manner of Holding Trust Securities

Section 5.06. The Trustee may hold securities or other property held by Trustee in trust pursuant to this Declaration in Trustee's name as Trustee under this Declaration, in Trustee's own name without a designation showing it to be Trustee under this Declaration, in the name of Trustee's nominee, or the Trustee may hold such securities unregistered in such condition that ownership will pass by delivery.

Allocation of Principal and Income

Section 5.07. Except as otherwise specifically provided in this Declaration, the Trustee shall allocate all receipts and expenditures received or incurred by Trustee in administering the trusts provided for in this Declaration to the income or principal of each such trust in the manner provided by the Revised Uniform Principal and Income Act in effect on the date of this Declaration in the State of California.

ARTICLE 6. ADMINISTRATIVE PROVISIONS

Accrued Income on Termination of Beneficial Interest

Section 6.01. Whenever the right of any beneficiary to payments from the net income or principal of any trust provided for in this Declaration shall terminate, either by reason of death or other cause, any accrued net income from such trust undistributed by the Trustee on the date of such termination shall be held, administered, and distributed by the Trustee in the same manner as if such income had accrued and been received by the Trustee after the date such beneficiary's right to receive payments from such trust terminated.

Periodic Accountings

Section 6.02. The trustee shall periodically, at least annually, prepare and deliver to each Trustor and beneficiary mentioned in this Declaration an accounting in writing of the Trustee's administration of the trusts provided for in this Declaration. Written approval of any such accounting signed by any Trustor or beneficiary shall constitute an absolute release of the Trustee from any and all liability for any matters stated in such accounting. Such approval and release shall be binding not only on the Trustor or beneficiary who signed it, but also on the administrators, executors, successors, and assigns of such Trustor or beneficiary.

Spendthrift Provision

Section 6.03. Except as otherwise expressly provided in this Declaration, no beneficiary of Trust B provided for in this Declaration shall have any right, power, or authority to alienate, encumber, or hypothecate his or her interest in the principal or income of such trust in any manner, nor shall such interest of any beneficiary be subject to claims of his or her creditors or liable to attachment, execution, or other process of law.

Division or Distribution in Kind or in Cash

Section 6.04. On any division of the assets of the Trust Estate into shares or partial shares and on any final or partial distribution of the assets of the Trust Estate or any trust provided for in this Declaration, the Trustee, in its discretion, may divide and distribute such assets in kind, may divide or distribute undivided interests in such assets, or may sell all or any part of such assets and make division or distribution in cash, in kind, or partly in cash and partly in kind. The decision of the Trustee, either prior to or on any division or distribution of such assets, as to what constitutes a proper division of such assets of the Trust Estate or any trust provided for in this Declaration shall be binding on all persons in any manner having an interest in any trust provided for in this Declaration.

Definition of "Children"

Section 6.05. The terms "child" and "children" as used in this Declaration mean the lawful issue of the Trustors or either of them and includes children legally adopted by the Trustors or either of them.

Law for Construction of Trusts

Section 6.06. This Declaration of Trust and the validity of, construction of, and all rights under the trusts provided for in this Declaration shall be governed by the laws of the State of California.

Invalidity of Any Provision

Section 6.07. Should any provision of this Declaration be or become invalid or unenforceable, the remaining provisions of this Declaration shall be and continue to be fully effective.

Successor Trustee of Last Trustor

Section 6.08. On the death of the last Trustor to die, or should such Trustor, after the death or incapacity of the other Trustor, resign or become unable, for any reason, to serve as Trustee of the trusts provided for in this Declaration, Big Bank shall forthwith become Trustee of the trusts provided for in this Declaration, shall succeed to title of the Trustee to the Trust Estate, and shall have all the powers, rights, discretions, and obligations conferred on such Trustee by this Declaration.

Certification of Husband and Wife

We, and each of us, certify that:

1. We, and each of us, have read the foregoing Declaration of Trust;

2. The foregoing Declaration of Trust correctly states the terms and conditions under which the Trust Estate is to be held, managed, administered, and disposed of by the Trustee;

3. We, and each of us, approve such Declaration of Trust in all particulars; and

4. As the Trustee named in such Declaration of Trust we, and each of us, approve and accept the trusts provided for in such Declaration.

EXECUTED on _____, at Los Angeles County, California.

                                                  _____[*signature*]
                                                  John Smith

                                                  _____[*signature*]
                                                  Linda Jones

Approved:

_____[*signature*]
Attorney for Trustors

Acknowledgment

State of California
County of Los Angeles

On _____, before me, [*name and title of officer taking acknowledgment*], personally appeared John Smith and Linda Jones [*name(s) of person(s) signing instrument*], _____[personally known to me or proved to me on the basis of satisfactory evidence] to be the person[s] whose name[s] [is *or* are] subscribed to the within instrument and acknowledged to me that [he *or* she *or* they] executed the same in [his *or* her *or* their] authorized [capacity *or* capacities], and that by [his *or* her *or* their] signatures[s] on the instrument the person[s], or the entity upon behalf of which the person[s] acted, executed the instrument.

              WITNESS my hand and seal.

Signature_____   [*Seal*]

NOTE: This form of Trust Agreement does not include a bypass trust as described on page 209.

STATUTORY FORM DURABLE POWER OF ATTORNEY FOR HEALTH CARE

Order No._____
Escrow No._____
Loan No. _____

WHEN RECORDED MAIL TO:

_____
_____
_____

SPACE ABOVE THIS LINE FOR RECORDER'S USE

STATUTORY FORM DURABLE POWER OF ATTORNEY FOR HEALTH CARE
(California Civil Code Section 2500)

WARNING TO PERSON EXECUTING THIS DOCUMENT

THIS IS AN IMPORTANT LEGAL DOCUMENT WHICH IS AUTHORIZED BY THE KEENE HEALTH CARE AGENT ACT. BEFORE EXECUTING THIS DOCUMENT, YOU SHOULD KNOW THESE IMPORTANT FACTS:

THIS DOCUMENT GIVES THE PERSON YOU DESIGNATE AS YOUR AGENT (THE ATTORNEY IN FACT) THE POWER TO MAKE HEALTH CARE DECISIONS FOR YOU. YOUR AGENT MUST ACT CONSISTENTLY WITH YOUR DESIRES AS STATED IN THIS DOCUMENT OR OTHERWISE MADE KNOWN.

EXCEPT AS YOU OTHERWISE SPECIFY IN THIS DOCUMENT, THIS DOCUMENT GIVES YOUR AGENT THE POWER TO CONSENT TO YOUR DOCTOR NOT GIVING TREATMENT OR STOPPING TREATMENT NECESSARY TO KEEP YOU ALIVE.

NOTWITHSTANDING THIS DOCUMENT, YOU HAVE THE RIGHT TO MAKE MEDICAL AND OTHER HEALTH CARE DECISIONS FOR YOURSELF SO LONG AS YOU CAN GIVE INFORMED CONSENT WITH RESPECT TO THE PARTICULAR DECISION. IN ADDITION, NO TREATMENT MAY BE GIVEN TO YOU OVER YOUR OBJECTION AT THE TIME, AND HEALTH CARE NECESSARY TO KEEP YOU ALIVE MAY NOT BE STOPPED OR WITHHELD IF YOU OBJECT AT THE TIME.

THIS DOCUMENT GIVES YOUR AGENT AUTHORITY TO CONSENT, TO REFUSE TO CONSENT, OR TO WITHDRAW CONSENT TO ANY CARE, TREATMENT, SERVICE, OR PROCEDURE TO MAINTAIN, DIAGNOSE, OR TREAT A PHYSICAL OR MENTAL CONDITION. THE POWER IS SUBJECT TO ANY STATEMENT OF YOUR DESIRES AND ANY LIMITATIONS THAT YOU INCLUDE IN THIS DOCUMENT. YOU MAY STATE IN THIS DOCUMENT ANY TYPES OF TREATMENT THAT YOU DO NOT DESIRE. IN ADDITION, A COURT CAN TAKE AWAY THE POWER OF YOUR AGENT TO MAKE HEALTH CARE DECISIONS FOR YOU IF YOUR AGENT (1) AUTHORIZES ANYTHING THAT IS ILLEGAL, (2) ACTS CONTRARY TO YOUR KNOWN DESIRES, OR (3) WHERE YOUR DESIRES ARE NOT KNOWN, DOES ANYTHING THAT IS CLEARLY CONTRARY TO YOUR BEST INTERESTS.

THE POWERS GIVEN BY THIS DOCUMENT WILL EXIST FOR AN INDEFINITE PERIOD OF TIME UNLESS YOU LIMIT THEIR DURATION IN THE DOCUMENT.

YOU HAVE THE RIGHT TO REVOKE THE AUTHORITY OF YOUR AGENT BY NOTIFYING YOUR AGENT OR YOUR TREATING DOCTOR, HOSPITAL, OR OTHER HEALTH CARE PROVIDER ORALLY OR IN WRITING OF THE REVOCATION.

YOUR AGENT HAS THE RIGHT TO EXAMINE YOUR MEDICAL RECORDS AND TO CONSENT TO THEIR DISCLOSURE UNLESS YOU LIMIT THIS RIGHT IN THIS DOCUMENT.

UNLESS YOU OTHERWISE SPECIFY IN THIS DOCUMENT, THIS DOCUMENT GIVES YOUR AGENT TO THE POWER TO (1) AUTHORIZE AN AUTOPSY, (2) DONATE YOUR BODY OR PARTS THEREOF FOR TRANSPLANT OR THERAPEUTIC OR EDUCATIONAL OR SCIENTIFIC PURPOSES, AND (3) DIRECT THE DISPOSITION OF YOUR REMAINS.

APPENDIX G

THIS DOCUMENT REVOKES ANY PRIOR DURABLE POWER OF ATTORNEY FOR HEALTH CARE.

YOU SHOULD CAREFULLY READ AND FOLLOW THE WITNESSING PROCEDURE DESCRIBED AT THE END OF THIS FORM. THE DOCUMENT WILL NOT BE VALID UNLESS YOU COMPLY WITH THE WITNESSING PROCEDURE.

IF THERE IS ANYTHING IN THIS DOCUMENT THAT YOU DO NOT UNDERSTAND, YOU SHOULD ASK A LAWYER TO EXPLAIN IT TO YOU.

YOUR AGENT MAY NEED THIS DOCUMENT IMMEDIATELY IN CASE OF ANY EMERGENCY THAT REQUIRES A DECISION CONCERNING YOUR HEALTH CARE. EITHER KEEP THIS DOCUMENT WHERE IT IS IMMEDIATELY AVAILABLE TO YOUR AGENT AND ALTERNATE AGENTS OR GIVE EACH OF THEM AN EXECUTED COPY OF THIS DOCUMENT. YOU MAY ALSO WANT TO GIVE YOUR DOCTOR AN EXECUTED COPY OF THIS DOCUMENT.

DO NOT USE THIS FORM IF YOU ARE A CONSERVATEE UNDER THE LANTERMAN-PETRIS-SHORT ACT AND YOU WANT TO APPOINT YOUR CONSERVATOR AS YOUR AGENT. YOU CAN DO THAT ONLY IF THE APPOINTMENT DOCUMENT INCLUDES A CERTIFICATE OF YOUR ATTORNEY.

1. DESIGNATION OF HEALTH CARE AGENT.

I, Linda Jones, residing at 100 Main Street, Los Angeles, California, do hereby designate and appoint my spouse John Smith, residing at 100 Main Street, Los Angeles, California, Tel. No. 213-555-0000

(insert name, address and telephone number of one individual only as your agent to make health care decisions for you. None of the following may be designated as your agent: (1) your treating health care provider, (2) a nonrelative employee of your treating health care provider, (3) an operator of a community care facility, (4) a nonrelative employee of an operator of a community care facility, (5) an operator of a residential care facility for the elderly, or (6) a nonrelative employee of an operator of a residential care facility for the elderly)

as my attorney in fact (agent) to make health care decisions for me as authorized in this document. For the purposes of this document, "health care decision" means consent, refusal of consent, or withdrawal of consent to any care, treatment, service, or procedure to maintain, diagnose, or treat an individual's physical or mental condition.

2. CREATION OF DURABLE POWER OF ATTORNEY FOR HEALTH CARE.

By this document, I intend to create a durable power of attorney for health care under Sections 2430 and 2445, inclusive, of the California Civil Code. This power of attorney is authorized by the Keene Health Care Agent Act and shall be construed in accordance with the provisions of Sections 2500 to 2506, inclusive, of the California Civil Code. The power of attorney shall not be affected by my subsequent incapacity.

3. GENERAL STATEMENT OF AUTHORITY GRANTED.

Subject to any limitations in this document, I hereby grant to my agent full power and authority to make health care decisions for me to the same extent that I could make such decisions for myself if I had capacity to do so. In exercising this authority, my agent shall make health care decisions that are consistent with my desires as stated in this document or otherwise made known to my agent, including but not limited to, my desires concerning obtaining or refusing or withdrawing life-prolonging care, treatment, services, and procedures.

(If you want to limit the authority of your agent to make health care decisions for you, you can state the limitations in paragraph 4 ("Statement of Desires, Special Provisions, and Limitations"), below. You can indicate your desires by including a statement of your desires in the same paragraph.)

4. STATEMENT OF DESIRES, SPECIAL PROVISIONS, AND LIMITATIONS.

(Your agent must make health care decisions that are consistent with your known desires. You can, but are not required to, state your desires in the space provided below. You should consider whether you want to include a statement of your desires concerning life-prolonging care, treatment, services, and procedures. You can also include a statement of you desires concerning other matters relating to your health care. You can also make your desires known to your agent by discussing your desires with your agent by some other means. If there are any types of treatment that you do not want to be used, you should state them in the space below. If you want to limit in any other way the authority given your agent by this document, you should state the limits in the space below. If you do not state any limits, your agent will have broad powers to make health care decisions for you, except to the extent that there are limits provided by law.)

In exercising the authority under this durable power of attorney for health care, my agent shall act consistently with my desires as stated below and is subject to the special provisions and limitations stated below:

(a) Statement of desires concerning life-prolonging care, treatment, services, and procedures:

If I should have an incurable and irreversible condition that has been diagnosed by two physicians and that will result in my death within a relatively short time without the administration of life-sustaining treatment or has produced an irreversible coma or persistent vegetative state, and I am no longer able to make decisions regarding my medical treatment, I direct my attending physician to withhold or withdraw treatment, including artificially administered nutrition and hydration, that only prolongs the process of dying or the irreversible coma or persistent vegetative state and is not necessary for my comfort or to alleviate pain.

(b) Additional statement of desires, special provisions, and limitations: I wish to be cremated.

(You may attach additional pages if you need more space to complete your statement. If you attach additional pages, you must date and sign EACH of the additional pages at the same time you date and sign this document.)

5. INSPECTION AND DISCLOSURE OF INFORMATION RELATING TO MY PHYSICAL OR MENTAL HEALTH.

Subject to any limitations in this document, my agent has the power and authority to do all of the following:

(a) Request, review, and receive any information, verbal or written, regarding my physical or mental health, including, but not limited to, medical and hospital records.

(b) Execute on my behalf any releases or other documents that may be required in order to obtain this information.

(c) Consent to the disclosure of this information.

(If you want to limit the authority of your agent to receive and disclose information relating to your health, you must state the limitations in paragraph 4 ("Statement of Desires, Special Provisions, and Limitations") above.)

6. SIGNING DOCUMENTS, WAIVER, AND RELEASES.

Where necessary to implement the health care decisions that my agent is authorized by this document to make, my agent has the power and authority to execute on my behalf all of the following:

(a) Documents titled or purporting to be a "Refusal to Permit Treatment" and "Leaving Hospital Against Medical Advice."

(b) Any necessary waiver or release from liability required by a hospital or physician.

7. AUTOPSY; ANATOMICAL GIFTS; DISPOSITION OF REMAINS.

Subject to any limitations in this document, my agent has the power and authority to do all of the following:

(a) Authorize an autopsy under Section 7113 of the Health and Safety Code.

(b) Make a disposition of a part or parts of my body under the Uniform Anatomical Gift Act (Chapter 3.5 (commencing with Section 7150) of Part 1 of Division 7 of the Health and Safety Code).

(c) Direct the disposition of my remains under Section 7100 of the Health and Safety Code. (If you want to limit the authority of your agent to consent to an autopsy, make an anatomical gift, or direct the disposition of your remains, you must state the limitations in paragraph 4 ("Statement of Desires, Special Provisions, and Limitations") above.)

8. DURATION.

(Unless you specify otherwise in the space below, this power of attorney will exist for an indefinite period of time.)

This durable power of attorney for health care expires on _____

_____

(Fill in this space ONLY if you want to limit the duration of this power of attorney.)

9. DESIGNATION OF ALTERNATE AGENTS.

(You are not required to designate any alternate agents but you may do so. Any alternate agent you designate will be able to make the same health care decisions for you as the agent you designated in paragraph 1, above, in the event that agent is unable or ineligible to act as your agent. If the agent you designated is your spouse, he or she becomes ineligible to act as your agent if your marriage is dissolved.)

If the person designated as my agent in paragraph 1 is not available or become ineligible to act as my agent to make a health care decision for me, or if I revoke that person's appointment or authority to act as my agent to make health care decisions for me, then I designate and appoint the following persons to serve as my agent to make health care decisions for me as authorized in this document, such persons to serve in the order listed below:

A. First Alternate Agent: Mary Smith, residing at 100 Hill Street, Los Angeles, California; Tel. No. 213-444-0000_____

_____

(Name, address, and telephone number of first alternate agent)

B. Second Alternate Agent _____

_____

(Name, address, and telephone number of second alternate agent)

10. NOMINATION OF CONSERVATOR OF PERSON.

(A conservator of the person may be appointed for you if a court decides that one should be appointed. The conservator is responsible for your physical care, which under some circumstances includes making health care decisions for you. You are not required to nominate a conservator but you may do so. The court will appoint the person you nominate unless that would be contrary to your best interests. You may, but are not required to, nominate as your conservator the same person you named in paragraph 1 as your health care agent. You can nominate an individual as your conservator by completing the space below.)

If a conservator of the person is to be appointed for me, I nominate the following individual to serve as conservator of the person: Dr. John Smith; first alternate — _____

_____

_____

(Name and address of person nominated as conservator of the person.)

11. PRIOR DESIGNATIONS REVOKED.

I revoke any prior durable power of attorney for health care.

DATE AND SIGNATURE OF PRINCIPAL

(YOU MUST DATE AND SIGN THIS POWER OF ATTORNEY)

I sign my name to this Statutory Form Durable Power of Attorney for Health Care on _____ at _____.

(City, State)

Linda Jones

_____

(Signature)

(THIS POWER OF ATTORNEY WILL NOT BE VALID UNLESS IT IS SIGNED BY TWO QUALIFIED WITNESSES WHO ARE PRESENT WHEN YOU SIGN OR ACKNOWLEDGE YOUR SIGNATURE. IF YOU HAVE ATTACHED ANY ADDITIONAL PAGES TO THIS FORM, YOU MUST DATE AND SIGN EACH OF THE ADDITIONAL PAGES AT THE SAME TIME YOU DATE AND SIGN THIS POWER OF ATTORNEY.)

STATEMENT OF WITNESSES

(This document must be witnessed by two qualified adult witnesses. None of the following may be used as a witness: (1) a person you designate as your agent or alternate agent, (2) your health care provider, (3) an employee of your health care provider, (4) an operator of a community care facility, (5) an employee of an operator of a community care facility, (6) an operator of a residential care facility for the elderly, or (7) an employee of an operator of a residential care facility for the elderly. At least one of the witnesses must make the additional declaration set out following the place where the witnesses sign.)

(READ CAREFULLY BEFORE SIGNING. You can sign as a witness only if you personally know the principal or the identity of the principal is proved to you by convincing evidence.)

(To have convincing evidence of the identity of the principal, you must be presented with and reasonably rely on any or more of the following:

(1) An identification card or driver's license issued by the California Department of Motor Vehicles that is current or has been issued within five years.

(2) A passport issued by the Department of State of the United States that is current or has been issued within five years.

(3) Any of the following documents if the document is current or has been issued within five years and contains a photograph and description of the person named on it, is signed by the person, and bears a serial or other identifying number:

(a) A passport issued by a foreign government that has been stamped by the United States Immigration and Naturalization Service.

(b) A driver's license issued by a state other than California or by a Canadian or Mexican public agency authorized to issue drivers' licenses.

(c) An identification card issued by a state other than California.

(d) An identification card issued by any branch of the armed forces of the United States.

(4) If the principal is a patient in a skilled nursing facility, a witness who is a patient advocate or ombudsman may rely upon the representations of the administrator or staff of the skilled nursing facility, or of family members, as convincing evidence of the identity of the principal if the patient advocate or ombudsman believes that the representations provide a reasonable basis for determining the identity of the principal.)

(Other kinds of proof of identity are not allowed.)

I declare under penalty of perjury under the laws of California that the person who signed or acknowledged this document is personally known to me (or proved to me on the basis of convincing evidence) to be the principal, that the principal signed or acknowledged this durable power of attorney in my presence, that the principal appears to be of sound mind and under no duress, fraud, or undue influence, that I am not the person appointed as attorney in fact by this document, and that I am not the principal's health care provider, an employee of the principal's health care provider, the operator of a community care facility, an employee of an operator of a community care facility, the operator of a residential care facility for the elderly, or an employee of an operator of a residential care facility for the elderly.

Signature:_____
Print Name:_____
Date:_____
Residence Address: _____
_____

Signature:_____
Print Name:_____
Date:_____
Residence Address: _____
_____

(AT LEAST ONE OF THE ABOVE WITNESSES MUST ALSO SIGN THE FOLLOWING DECLARATION.)

I further declare under penalty of perjury under the laws of California that I am not related to the principal by blood, marriage, or adoption, and, to the best of my knowledge, I am not entitled to any part of the estate of the principal upon the death of the principal under a will now existing or by operation of law.

Signature:_____

Signature:_____

STATEMENT OF PATIENT ADVOCATE OR OMBUDSMAN
(If you are a patient in a skilled nursing facility, one of the witnesses must be a patient advocate or ombudsman. The patient advocate or ombudsman must sign both parts of the "Statement of Witnesses" above AND must also sign the following statement.)

I further declare under penalty of perjury under the laws of California that I am a patient advocate or ombudsman as designated by the State Department of Aging and that I am serving as a witness as required by subdivision (f) of Section 2432 of the Civil Code.

Signature: _____

CERTIFICATE OF PRINCIPAL'S LAWYER

I am a lawyer authorized to practice law in the state where this power of attorney was executed, and the principal was my client at the time this power of attorney was executed. I have advised my client of his or her rights in connection with this power of attorney and the applicable law and the consequences of signing or not signing this power of attorney, and my client, after being so advised, has executed this power of attorney.

_____
Attorney

Order No._____
Escrow No._____
Loan No. _____

WHEN RECORDED MAIL TO:

_____
_____
_____

SPACE ABOVE THIS LINE FOR RECORDER'S USE

UNIFORM STATUTORY FORM POWER OF ATTORNEY
(California Civil Code § 2475)

NOTICE: THE POWERS GRANTED BY THIS DOCUMENT ARE BROAD AND SWEEPING. THEY ARE EXPLAINED IN THE UNIFORM STATUTORY FORM POWER OF ATTORNEY ACT (CALIFORNIA CIVIL CODE SECTIONS 2475-2499.5, INCLUSIVE). IF YOU HAVE ANY QUESTIONS ABOUT THESE POWERS, OBTAIN COMPETENT LEGAL ADVICE. THIS DOCUMENT DOES NOT AUTHORIZE ANYONE TO MAKE MEDICAL AND OTHER HEALTH-CARE DECISIONS FOR YOU. YOU MAY REVOKE THIS POWER OF ATTORNEY IF YOU LATER WISH TO DO SO.

I, Linda Jones, residing at 100 Main Street, Los Angeles, California, appoint my daughter, Mary Smith, residing at 100 Hill Street, Los Angeles, California; Tel. No. 213-444-0000

(Name and address of person appointed, or of each person appointed if you wish to designate more than one)

as my agent (attorney-in-fact) to act for me in any lawful way with respect to the following initialed subjects:

TO GRANT ALL OF THE FOLLOWING POWERS, INITIAL THE LINE IN FRONT OF (N) AND IGNORE THE LINES IN FRONT OF THE OTHER POWERS.

TO GRANT ONE OR MORE, BUT FEWER THAN ALL, OF THE FOLLOWING POWERS, INITIAL THE LINE IN FRONT OF EACH POWER YOU ARE GRANTING.

TO WITHHOLD A POWER, DO NOT INITIAL THE LINE IN FRONT OF IT. YOU MAY, BUT NEED NOT, CROSS OUT EACH POWER WITHHELD.

INITIAL   POWER

_____   (A)   Real property transactions.
_____   (B)   Tangible personal property transactions.
_____   (C)   Stock and bond transactions.
_____   (D)   Commodity and option transactions.
_____   (E)   Banking and other financial institution transactions.
_____   (F)   Business operating transactions.
_____   (G)   Insurance and annuity transactions.
_____   (H)   Estate, trust, and other beneficiary transactions.
_____   (I)   Claims and litigations.
_____   (J)   Personal and family maintenance.
_____   (K)   Benefits from social security, medicare, medicaid, or other governmental programs, or civil or military service.
_____   (L)   Retirement plan transactions.
_____   (M)   Tax matters.
_____   (N)   ALL OF THE POWERS LISTED ABOVE.

YOU NEED NOT INITIAL ANY OTHER LINES IF YOU INITIAL LINE (N).

SPECIAL INSTRUCTIONS:
ON THE FOLLOWING LINES YOU MAY GIVE SPECIAL INSTRUCTIONS
LIMITING OR EXTENDING THE POWERS GRANTED TO YOUR AGENT.

_____

_____
_____
_____
_____

UNLESS YOU DIRECT OTHERWISE ABOVE, THIS POWER OF ATTORNEY
IS EFFECTIVE IMMEDIATELY AND WILL CONTINUE UNTIL IT IS
REVOKED.

This power of attorney will continue to be in effect even though I become incapacitated.

STRIKE THE PRECEDING SENTENCE IF YOU DO NOT WANT THIS
POWER OF ATTORNEY TO CONTINUE IF YOU BECOME INCAPACITATED.

**EXERCISE OF POWER OF ATTORNEY WHERE
MORE THAN ONE AGENT IS DESIGNATED**

If I have designated more than one agent, the agents are to act _____

IF YOU APPOINT MORE THAN ONE AGENT AND YOU WANT EACH
AGENT TO BE ABLE TO ACT ALONE WITHOUT THE OTHER AGENT
JOINING, WRITE THE WORD "SEPARATELY" IN THE BLANK SPACE
ABOVE. IF YOU DO NOT INSERT ANY WORD IN THE BLANK SPACE, OR IF
YOU INSERT THE WORD "JOINTLY," THEN ALL OF YOUR AGENTS MUST
ACT OR SIGN TOGETHER.

I agree that any third party who receives a copy of this document may act under it. Revocation
of the power of attorney is not effective as to a third party until the third party has actual knowledge of
the revocation. I agree to indemnify the third party for any claims that arise against the third party
because of reliance on this power of attorney.

Signed this day of_____ , 1999

_____
Linda Jones
Soc. Sec. No. 000-00-0000

State of California
County of Los Angeles

**CERTIFICATE OF ACKNOWLEDGMENT OF
NOTARY PUBLIC**

State of California   )
County of Los Angeles   )

Before me _____, personally appeared _____

_____

_____ , per-
sonally known to me (or proved to me on the basis of satisfactory evidence) to be the person(s) whose
name(s) is/are subscribed to the within instrument and acknowledged to me that he/she/they executed
the same in his/her/their authorized capacity(ies), and that by his/her/their signature(s) on the instrument the person(s), or the entity upon behalf of which the person(s) acted, executed the instrument.

WITNESS my hand and official seal.

Endnotes

1. Witkin, *Summary of California Law*, 9th ed. (1990), Vol. 11, p. 374 et seq.

2. Id.; Property Division — Equitable Distribution, www.divorcesource.com /NY/ARTICLES/donovan2.html; *What Is Equitable Distribution*, www.uspn.com/ironbound/legal/divorces/equitable_distribution.htm.

3. Norton and Miller, *Marriage, Divorce and Remarriage in the 1990's*, U.S. Dept. of Commerce (1992).

4. I. Glink, "Nuptial Saga:'48 Hours' of Marriage, 'For Better, For Worse,'" *Chicago Tribune* (May 19, 1991).

5. C. Amende, *Hollywood Confidential*, Plume (1997), 216.

6. Ibid, 244.

7. "Newsmakers, Eavesdropping," *Chicago Tribune* (January 5, 1995).

8. J. Moses, "Boesky Gets $20 Million in Divorce Pact," *The Wall Street Journal* (June 10, 1993).

9. E. Helmore, "Real Lives: Signed and Sealed, I'm Yours, It's A Deal . . . " *The Guardian* (May 21, 1998).

10. A. Attwood, "Trump's New Book: Money, Marriage and Caviar for the Poor," *The Age* (October 21, 1997).

11. Ibid.

12. T. Welsh and J. Connelly, "Divorce: Getting the Best Deal," *Fortune* (May 17, 1993)

13. Attwood, "Trump's New Book."

14. T. Welsh and J. Connelly, "Divorce."

15. "Why Are They Famous?: Marla Maples," *The Independent* — London (October 12, 1997).

16. D. M. Walker, "Post Marital Bliss," *The Age* (August 9, 1999).

17. A. Hicks, "Maples Wouldn't Have Married Trump if She'd Read Prenuptial Agreement," *Cincinnati Enquirer* (October 23, 1997).

18. M. Sheldon, "President Trump? I Will Not Be Silent," *The Daily Telegraph* (October 18, 1999); S. Minahan, "Sign Here, My Dear," *Sun Herald* (April 2, 2000).

19. M. Shear, "Marlene Cooke Stakes Claim on Estate; Lawsuit Challenges Prenuptial Agreement with Late Husband, *The Washington Post* (June 7, 1997).

20. P. Finn and M. Shear, "Cooke Estate, Widow Settles Lawsuit; Wife of Late Redskins Owner to Get $20 Million, Sources Say," *The Washington Post* (April 14, 1998); M. Kilian, "Cooke Settlement Puts Skins in Son's Hands, *The Chicago Tribune* (April 14, 1998); P. Finn, "Cooke Lawyers Rebut Widow's Claim of Duress," *The Washington Post* (March 29, 1998); M. Shear, "Cooke's Fourth Wife Appears Ready to Fight for His Money," *The Washington Post* (May 10, 1997).

21. Amende, *Hollywood Confidential*, 214.

22. Walker, "Post Marital Bliss."

23. A. Marston, "Planning for Love: The Politics of Prenuptial Agreements," 49 Stanford L. Rev. 887 (1997).

24. Shear, "Marlene Cooke Stakes Claim on Estate."

25. Minahan, "Sign Here, My Dear."

26. D. Day, *Doris Day: Her Own Story*, William Morrow and Company (1975).

27. C. Champlin, "Doris Day: Singing and Looking for Pet Projects," *Los Angeles Times* (March 13, 1988).

28. R. Ryon, "Hot Property: Doris Day Investments Subject of Suit," *Los Angeles Times* (June 14, 1987).

29. D. Moran, "High Court Rejects Judgment Appeal: Doris Day Wins 17-Year Battle with Ex-Attorney," *Los Angeles Times* (October 17, 1985).

30. P. Hager, "Doris Day's Former Lawyer Disbarred," *Los Angeles Times* (July 14, 1987).

31. D. Brookoff, et. al, "Characteristics of Participants in Domestic Violence: Assessment at the Scene of Domestic Assault," *Journal of the American Medical Association*. (1997): 1369.

32. J. Berlinger, "Why Don't You Just Leave Him," *Nursing* (April 1998). Used with permission from *Nursing* 9828(4): 34-39, © Springhouse Corporation, www.Springnet.com.

33. B. Carlson, "A Stress and Coping Approach to Intervention with Abused Women," *Family Relations* (July 1997).

34. Ibid.

35. Berlinger, "Why Don't You Just Leave Him."

36. T. Savage, "Women Need to Plan Now to Avoid Poverty Later," *Denver Post* (June 27, 1999), quoting the National Center for Women and Retirement Research at Long Island University. The drop in income postdivorce has been estimated to be as high as 50 percent. S. McLanahan and G. Sandefur, *Growing Up with a Single Parent: What Hurts, What Helps*, Harvard University Press (1994).

37. B. Willats, "Breaking Up Is Easy to Do," *Michigan Family Forum*, in which he quoted sources estimating the rate of poverty experienced by divorced women and their children. One source he cited was the Statistical Abstract of the United States (1993), .385, which estimated that "[f]our times as many divorced women with children fell under the poverty line than married women with children." He also cited D. Eggebeen and D.T. Lichter, "Race, Family Structure, and Changing Poverty among American Children," *American Sociological Review*, 56, no.5: 808, as estimating that "[c]hildren from female-headed homes are five times as likely to be poor as children in two-parent families and nine times as likely to be in deep poverty." A report by the Heritage Foundation estimated that almost one-half of households with a divorced parent and children end up in poverty. C. Wetzstein, "Marriage Called Key to Fighting Poverty; Study Cites Links to Divorce, Low Income," *Washington Times* (June 11, 1999).

38. G. Jensen, "Q: Is Court-Ordered Child Support Doing More Harm Than Good? No: Child Support Fights Poverty for Millions of Kids and Helps Families Get Off Welfare," *Insight Magazine* (August 2, 1999).

39. M. Magnet, "The American Family, 1992," *Fortune* (August 10, 1992). The Census Bureau estimated that the rate of divorce could drop to 40 percent to 50 percent in the 1990s, a slight drop from the 1980s. Welsh and Connelly, "Divorce:

Getting the Best Deal."

40. B. Morris, and L. Urresta, "It's Her Job Too: Lorna Wendt's $20 Million Divorce Case Is the Shot Heard around the Water Cooler," *Fortune* (February 2, 1998).

41. Ibid.

42. "Order to Split $86M, 50-50," *New York Daily News* (April 23, 1998).

43. L. Pulliam and J. Raebel, "A Tough Lesson in the Economics of Divorce: A Pasadena School Administrator Lost Ground Monetarily When She Ended Her Marriage, But She Still Has Time to Rebuild Her Life," *Los Angeles Times* (March 23, 1999).

44. Welsh and Connelly, "Divorce: Getting the Best Deal."

45. B. Jackson, "Storm Center: John Fedders of SEC Is Pummeled by Legal and Personal Problems," *Wall Street Journal* (February 25, 1985).

46. A. Mackey, "Why Women Lose Out in Divorce," *Los Angeles Times* (September 5, 1989).

47. K. McDonald, "Personal Fortune/Planning: Getting Yours, What Women Need to Know When a Split-Up Requires Splitting a Company's Assets," *Fortune* (March 3, 1997).

48. Welsh and Connelly, "Divorce: Getting The Best Deal."

49. R. Roberts, "The Other Big A Word; It's Alimony and It May Mean More or Less Than You Think," *Washington Post* (July 11, 1995).

50. Ibid.

51. S. Khashoggi, "Are You Sure He Was Worth It, Mrs. Douglas?" *Sunday Times — London* (October 24, 1999).

52. *1999 Facts On Women-Owned Businesses: Trends in the U.S. and the 50 States*, National Foundation for Women Business Owners (1999); J. Norman, "Number of Women-Owned Businesses Doubles Since 1987, Study Says," *Knight-Rider Tribune Business News* (May 11, 1999); S. Armour, "Women Leap Off Corporate Ladder: Many Turn to Start-Ups for Freedom," *USA Today* (June 8, 1998).

53. P. Thomas, "Closing the Gender Gap: In the 1990s, the Number of Women-Owned Businesses Exploded — And So Did the Stereotype of Women Entrepreneurs," *Wall Street Journal* (May 24, 1999); C. Kleinman, "Women at Work: Being Boss Can Be a Great Escape," *Chicago Tribune* (August 18, 1998).

54. 1999 Facts on Women-Owned Businesses: Trends in the U.S. and The 50 States. "Women in Business," Office of Advocacy, U.S. Small Business Administration (October 1998), also offers valuable information.

55. "What It Takes: Some People Are Natural Entrepreneurs; Others Shouldn't Even Think about It; We Asked the Experts to Explain," *Wall Street Journal* (March 30, 1998).

56. M. Dickerson, "Women Are Geared for Growth; Female Entrepreneurs Are Agile, Tech-Savvy, Work Well at Home," *Los Angeles Times* (October 7, 1998).

57. Fact Sheet, National Foundation for Women Business Owners (2000); *Access to Credit Continues to Improve for Women Business Owners*, National Foundation for Women Business Owners (November 17, 1998).

58. Dickerson, "Women Are Geared for Growth."

59. P. Howard, *The Death of Common Sense*, Random House (1994).

60. Sections 31.3401(c)-1 (income tax withholding), 31.3121(d)-1 (FICA), and 31.3306(i)-1 (FUTA) of Income Tax Regulations issued by the U.S. Department of Treasury.

61. M. Barrett, "Tax Issues Concerning Independent Contractors and Loan-Out Corporations," *Tax Management Compensation Planning Journal,* (2 parts) September 3, 1993, and October 1, 1993.

62. *The State of Small Business: A Report of the President*, 1996 edition, U.S. Government Printing Office.

63. T. Coelho, "The Disabled Go to Work — And the Law Supports Them," *Business Week* (November 30, 1998).

64. J. Cole, "The Sexual-Harassment Waters Have Just Gotten Murkier," *FSB/Managing* (May 30, 2000).

65. D. Wagner, "Burns vs. Burns: Financial Secrets Unveiled in High-Stakes, Jet-Set Divorce," *Arizona Republic* (January 1, 1998).

66. J. Granelli and G. Edes, "Kareem's Financial Crisis: Balboa Inn Goes from a Landmark to a Major Liability," *Los Angeles Times* (April 8, 1997): T. Bonk and S. McManis, "Whose Last Season? Kareem on Verge of Signing Again," *Los Angeles Times* (October 1, 1986); K. Murphy," $55-Million Action Alleges Financial Mismanagement, Abdul-Jabbar Sues Former Manager," *Los Angeles Times* (July 19, 1986).

67. "Wondering Where the Money Went," *USA Today* (June 22, 1987).

68. A. Belser, "Inheritance Divides Family: Two Sisters, Born into Wealth, Sue Brother for Clues to 'Lost Estate,'" *Pittsburgh Post-Gazette* (May 30, 1995).

69. D. R. White, *White's Law Dictionary,* (Warner Books, 1985), 58.

70. S. Paltrow, "Hotel 'Queen' Helmsley Convicted of Tax Fraud," *Los Angeles Times* (August 31, 1989).

71. S. Hubler, "Fleiss Sentenced To 37 Months For Tax Evasion," *Los Angeles Times* (January 8, 1997).

72. Eleanor Norton Holmes's Web page at www.house.gov/norton/dctax.

73. Internal Revenue Code of 1986, as amended, §6015(b).

74. "The New Innocent Spouse Relief: More Popular Than Anyone Thought," *Tax Analysts*, 2000 TNT 99-2 (May 19, 2000).

75. See, for example, *Grossman vs. Commissioner*, 83 AFTR 2nd ¶99-976 (1999); *Wiksell vs. Commissioner*, 85 AFTR 2nd ¶ 2000-564 (March 28, 2000); *Butler vs. Commissioner*, 114 T.C. No. 19 (April 28, 2000). But see, *Charlton vs. Commissioner*, 114 T.C. No. 22 (May 16, 2000), holding that the husband was not liable for unreported self-employment tax under a separate return election. In a study based on years before the law was changed, the Government Accounting Office found that most innocent spouse claims presented to the IRS are denied and that the Tax Court denied relief in more than one third of all innocent spouse cases filed with the Court. In many cases in which the Tax Court did grant innocent spouse relief, it granted only partial relief, and the spouse claiming innocence remained liable for a portion of the taxes, although not the full amount claimed by the IRS.

76. Internal Revenue Code of 1986, as amended, §6015(c).

77. IRS Chief Counsel Notice (January 11, 2000), 2000 TNT 14-37.

78. *Corson vs. Commissioner*, 114 T.C. No. 24 (May 18, 2000).

79. Internal Revenue Code of 1986, as amended, §6015(e) and (g).

80. Internal Revenue Code of 1986, as amended, §6015(f).

81. Letter from Congresswoman Nancy Pelosi to Robert Rubin, Secretary of the U.S. Department of Treasury, February 22, 1999, 1999 TNT 52-47.

82. Letter From Donald C. Lubick, Assistant Secretary (Tax Policy), U.S. Department of Treasury, to Congresswoman Nancy Pelosi, May 18, 1999, 1999 TNT 102-19.

83. Section 61 of the Internal Revenue Code of 1986, as amended.

84. G. Nemeti, "Many Have Learned Their Lesson: It Doesn't Pay to Mess with the IRS," *Seattle Times* (April 14, 1998).

85. Ibid.

86. Ibid.

87. R. Draper, "Poor Willie," *Texas Monthly Magazine* (May 1991).

88. *Summary of Abusive Trust Schemes*, Criminal Investigation Division, Internal Revenue Service (issued April 2000).

89. O. Ullmann, "IRS Hunts Corporate Schemes," *USA Today* (April 17, 2000).

90. "Casino Builders Settling with NJ in Property Title Dispute," *Dow Jones News Service* (June 20, 1979); D. Janson, *New York Times Abstracts* (June 5, 1981); D. Janson, *New York Times Abstracts* (November 8, 1981); D. Janson, *New York Times Abstracts* (May 28, 1982).

91. D. Williams, "Assemblies of God, Local Church in Dispute," *Atlanta Journal* (February 11, 1988); D. Williams, "Render unto the Church: Assemblies of God Relinquish Claims against Congregation," *Atlanta Journal and Constitution* (July 28, 1988).

92. Witkin, Summary of California Law, 9th ed. (1990); Vol. 4, p. 185 et seq.

93. Ibid.

94. Ibid.

95. "Opening a Joint Account with No Strings Attached Could Leave You Empty-Handed," *St. Louis Post-Dispatch* (May 4, 2000).

96. "Daughter of *Star Trek* Creator Disinherited," *Los Angeles Times* (June 28, 1996).

97. G. Garcia, "One Blonde, Two Brothers and $1.6 Billion," *USA Today* (March 27, 2000).

98. J. E. Bourgoyne, "Model Has a New Waistline, New Man, and Work," *New Orleans Times-Picayune* (October 13, 1999); A. Vigoda, "Smith Battles Scandal with SASS," *USA Today* (August 13, 1998).

99. P. Brennan, "Doris Duke: the Curse of Money," *Washington Post* (February 21, 1999); S. Mansfield, "Billionaire's Heir out of Place; Alimony Suit Filed against Doris Duke," *Washington Post* (April 7, 1993).

100. P. Lieberman, "Inquiry Rejects Claim Doris Duke Was Murdered," *Los Angeles Times* (July 25, 1996); P. Lieberman, "Doris Duke Nurse Gets 8 Years in Prison for Theft," *Los Angeles Times* (February 29, 1996).

101. J. Goldman and P. Lieberman, "Judge to Approve Settlement in $1.2-Billion Duke Estate Battle; Courts: in End to 2.5 Year Fight, Tobacco Heiress' Butler Agrees to Play No Role in New Foundation, Which Will Be One of Nation's Largest," *Los Angeles Times* (May 15, 1996); J. Goldman and P. Lieberman, "Heiress Duke's Ex-Butler Ousted as Estate's Executor Probate: Judge Cites His Substance Abuse and Waste of Assets from the $1.2-Billion Fund. Bank Is Also Replaced," *Los Angeles Times* (May 23, 1995).

102. "Judge Slashes Fees 14M in Heiress Estate Fight," *New York Daily News* (May 2, 2000); P. Lieberman and J. Goldman, "Doris Duke's Will Evolves into Ultimate Probate Fight; Law: 2 Years After Heiress' Death, Millions in Legal Fees Have Been Rung Up. Conduct of Case Prompts Questions," *Los Angeles Times* (January 1, 1996).

103. W. Stovall, "Left out: Disinheriting Someone Can Leave Deep Scars on a Family: Inheritance When Wealth Divides a Family," *Dallas Morning News* (November 23, 1998); R. Duff, "How to Make Headlines the Hard Way, Part II," *Journal of Financial Planning* (August 1, 1997).

104. M. Langley, "Out in the Cold: A Popular Tax Shelter Sounded Too Good to Be True, It Was; After Congress Ends Plan, Everyone from Charities to Heirs Is Left Reeling; Why Mr. Hancock Signed On," *Wall Street Journal* (December 20, 1999).

Index

INDEX